THE THIRD GOSPEL FOR THE THIRD WORLD

The Third Gospel *for the* Third World

VOLUME THREE–C
TRAVEL NARRATIVE – III
(Luke 17:11–19:44)

Herman Hendrickx, cicm

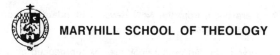

MARYHILL SCHOOL OF THEOLOGY

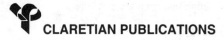

CLARETIAN PUBLICATIONS

THE THIRD GOSPEL FOR THE THIRD WORLD Vol. III-C

Copyright © 2001 by **Claretian Publications**
A division of **Claretian Communications, Inc.**
U.P. P.O. Box 4, Diliman 1101 Quezon City, Philippines
TE: 921-3984 • FAX: 921-7429
E-mail: claret@info.com.ph/claret@cnl.net
Website: www.bible.claret.org

Claretian Publications is a pastoral endeavor of the Claretian Missionaries in the Philippines. It aims to promote a renewed spirituality rooted in the process of total liberation and solidarity in response to the needs, challenges and pastoral demands of the Church today.

Cover design by Maria d.c. Zamora

Biblical texts are taken from the New Revised Standard Version (NRSV) unless otherwise indicated.

ISBN 971-501-892-0

TABLE OF CONTENTS

FOREWORD

This book is the third part of the third volume of a commentary on the Gospel of Luke under the general title The Third Gospel for the Third World, which will eventually consist of four or five volumes. The first volume, covering Luke's Preface (Lk 1:1-4) and the Infancy Narrative (Lk 1:5–2:52), was published in September 1996. The second volume was supposed to cover the ministry of Jesus in Galilee (Lk 3:1–9:50). For practical reasons the author decided to divide the said volume into two parts, namely A (Lk 3:1–6:49) and B (Lk 7:1–9:50) published in 1997 and 1998 respectively. For the same reasons the third volume, covering the Travel Narrative (Lk 9:51–19:44) is divided into three parts: A (Lk 9:51–13:21), B (Lk 13:22–17:10), and C (Lk 17:11–19:44). Volume III-A was published in April 2000 and III-B in November 2000.

Like the previous volumes, the present book intends to pay special, though not exclusive attention to whatever may be of particular interest to third world or two-thirds world readers. Again we try to deal with questions raised by the sociological approach to the Gospels, as well as anthropological and cultural features, like matters of family, clan and tribe, matters of honor and shame, the conditions of rural and urban life, etc. We also try to take into account some findings of recent literary criticism, without however neglecting the basic tenets of the historico-critical method.

The commentary will especially try to make available to a wider-reading public what the author considers to have pastoral implications first and foremost in a third world setting. But it goes almost without saying that many of these features are also of importance to committed first world Christians.

Since this commentary tries to bring together findings of various fields of research, several of which are rather new, it is obvious that we are very much indebted to scholars in these various disciplines. We trust that the text notes and the bibliography will sufficiently account for the extent of this indebtedness. We tried to make available the insights of present-day scholarship to people who have no access to the books and periodical articles in which these insights are found and/or cannot afford to buy them.

Like the previous volumes, this book is no easy reading, although the author tried to avoid becoming too technical. But the disciplines mentioned above are not exactly easy. So the reader will again have to invest time and effort in order to discover and assimilate the riches of the Third Gospel presented in this commentary. We wish that you may have the courage and stamina to bring this to a fruitful end.

III. The Third Phase of the Journey to Jerusalem
(Lk 17:11–19:44)

In the episode of Jesus' healing of ten lepers, the reader comes to the beginning of the third part of the Lukan Travel Narrative (Stein, 1992: 432). The third mention of Jerusalem as Jesus' destination is met in verse 11a. Though the latter part of the verse creates a classic *crux interpretum*, with its geographical references to Samaria and Galilee, it alerts the reader once again to the Lukan geographical perspective (Fitzmyer, 1981: 164–171), to the evangelist's theological concern to move Jesus to the city of destiny, where salvation is to be definitively achieved for human beings. The third part of the Lukan Travel stretches according to some scholars, to Lk 18:14, the end of the specifically Lukan account, or, according to most commentators, to Lk 19:27, its end in the Gospel as a whole, the last part of the narrative (Lk 18:15–19:27) being that wherein Luke incorporates material from "Mark" about the journey (Fitzmyer, 1985: 1149), or to Lk 19:44 (Ellis, 1966: 146; Denaux, 1993: 364–366; Bock, 1996: 957–959; see Hendrickx, 2000: 2–3). The present author follows the last opinion (Hendrickx, 2000: 1–4).

THE HEALING OF THE TEN LEPERS
(LK 17:11-19)

The story of the cleansing of the ten lepers is found only in Luke. The introductory verse 11 and the final verse 19 are clearly of Lukan composition, both containing several of his favorite constructions. The rest of the pericope (verses 12-18) may be derived from a pre-Lukan source (e.g., "L" [see Fitzmyer, 1981: 84]), but the Lukan redaction of the material is very pronounced (Tiede, 1988: 296; Nolland, 1993: 844), almost as heavy in these verses as in verses 11, 19. This has led a few commentators to argue that Luke is the author of the whole narrative (Bruners, 1977: 297–306; Busse, 1977: 319–322). Many other commentators, however, are not so certain, and prefer to reckon with a pre-Lukan form of the story, which in the earlier tradition may have been affected by the account of the cleansing of a leper in Mk 1:40-45 [cf. Lk 5:12-16] or even by the Old Testament story of Naaman (2 Kgs 5:1-15). Many scholars ascribe the origin of the story to a pre-Lukan source (Betz, 1971: 317–321; Schneider, 1977: 350; Ernst, 1977: 482; Pesch, 1970: 114–123; Glöckner, 1083: 128–131). The line between Lukan composition and Lukan redaction is uncertain (Fitzmyer, 1985: 1149; Nolland, 1993: 844).

Though the episode begins as a miracle-story (verses 12-14), recounting a healing performed by Jesus, it contains an injunction from him which might at first seem to be a pronouncement, "Go and show yourselves to the priests." Yet that injunction really serves as an expression of Jesus' powerful word, such as one would expect in a miracle-story. The miracle-story has been made subservient to something more (verses 15-18), to a pronouncement which contrasts gratitude with ingratitude, Jews with a Samaritan, and the sight of faith with the miracle itself. The emphasis is on Jesus' pronouncement about the reaction of the Samaritan who was a "stranger." Hence we have here a pronouncement-story (Betz, 1971: 322–323). It is not a pronouncement-story, which has grown from a simple saying (as is sometimes the case [see Lk 17:20-21]). Rather, it is a miracle-story that has become a pronouncement-story either under Luke's pen or—more likely—in the pre-Lukan tradition. In adding verse 19, Luke has further related Jesus' pronouncement to faith and salvation—in effect, added a further pronouncement. The Lukan story at this point in the Travel Narrative depicts Jesus as making use of his "power" (recall Lk 4:14, 36; 5:17) once again to aid unfortunate human beings afflicted with an evil which ostracized them from normal society; he liberates these outcasts from their evil condition (Fitzmyer, 1985: 1150).

A number of socio-cultural boundaries are contained within the perimeters of the story. The first of these is leprosy, a disorder with social and spiritual ramifications that outstrip the difficulties of its physical presentation. The boundary established by leprosy is marked in this pericope by the phrase "keeping their distance" (verse 12). The second is the identification of one of the lepers as a Samaritan, a foreigner, employing language that draws a well-defined boundary between this person, on the one hand, and Jesus and his (implied) entourage, on the other. The first of these two barriers has been surmounted before, with the consequence that Luke's readers may well have already begun to place "lepers" in the category of "the poor" to whom good news is preached (Lk 4:18-19, 27; 5:12-14; 7:22). The second boundary is presented late in the narrative, as a surprise, where it will have the greatest effect (Sheely, 1992: 105–106; Tannehill, 1986: 118–119). First, Luke's readers are given a positive impression of this one leper who returns to Jesus in gratitude; he behaves appropriately, his response is prototypical. Only then does Luke report that he is an outsider. Impressed by his behavior, Luke's audience may have walked into the trap. Indeed, Luke has narrated this episode in a way that seems deliberately to challenge notions of the privileged position of the Jewish people within the redemptive economy of God.

People who discern God at work through Jesus worship God at his feet (Hamm, 1994: 273-287). In restoring to wholeness a Samaritan leper, Jesus has countered not only notions of acceptance based on ritual purity but also, and more importantly for this episode, conceptions of election grounded in nationality and genealogy. As the one in whom God's purpose is manifest and through whom God's salvific prerogative is available, Jesus is the instrument of healing in the midst of these long-standing and deeply rooted rifts (Green, 1997: 619–620, 621).

Verse 11:   On the way to Jerusalem
             Jesus was going through the region
             between Samaria and Galilee.

The expression *kai egeneto*, "and it happened," usually not translated into English, indicates the beginning of an altogether new act. The whole expression, literally, "and it happened in the going," is a favorite Lukan formula which shows the influence of the Septuagint. The phrase "he was going. . ." is also dependent on the Septuagint. The verb *poreuesthai*, "to go," "to travel," is characteristic of Luke (about fifty-one times in the Gospel and thirty-seven times in Acts). Used in connection with Jerusalem, it has a special meaning for Luke (Lk 9:51, 53; Acts 19:21). Even when Jerusalem is not explicitly mentioned *poreuesthai* is a reminder of Jesus' journey to Jerusalem (Lk 9:57; 10:38; 13:33; 19:28; Hendrickx, 1987: 228).

For Luke, Jerusalem is a "theological" place (Conzelmann, 1960: 65). But it is not only the place of Jesus' suffering. Also in Jerusalem, the risen Christ meets the disciples (Lk 24:34, 36ff.); by his word they must stay there "until you have been clothed with the power from on high" (Lk 24:49; compare Acts 1:4). In Jerusalem too the mission begins (compare Acts 2:1ff.), and from there it expands (Lk 24:47; Acts 1:8). Not only the solemn Old Testament style, but also the notice that Jesus was on his way to *Jerusalem* gives weight to this introductory verse of a pericope which by its mention of Jerusalem forms the beginning of a larger section of several literary units beyond Lk 17:11-19.

The verb *dierchesthai*, "to pass through," "to pass along," is often used by Luke after the example of the Septuagint (ten times in the Gospel; twenty-one times in Acts, against twice in Mark and once in Matthew). He uses it to say that Jesus "went about doing good and healing all who were oppressed. . ." (Acts 10:38), as well as to describe the journeys of early Christian missionaries (Acts 8:4, 40; 9:32, 38; 11:19; 13:6, 14, etc.; Geiger, 1999: 665). The clearest verbal parallel to Lk 17:11c is Lk 4:30, "But he passed through the midst of them and went on his way," the conclusion of the programmatic scene at the beginning of Jesus' "Galilean" ministry (Lk 4:16-30).

Since Galilee lies north of Samaria, one would think that Jesus would have been going in a north-south direction, but "along between" suggests an east-west direction. Some scholars have suggested that Luke revealed here a great ignorance of Palestinian geography (Conzelmann, 1960: 68–70; see Fitzmyer, 1985: 1152–1153). But we learned early in the journey to Jerusalem that references to places cannot be lined up on a route from Galilee to Judea. Geography is sometimes literary, sometimes theological, and sometimes physical. Here the border between Galilee and Samaria is a fitting location for a story involving both Jews and a Samaritan (Craddock, 1990: 202; Schweizer, 1984: 267; Nolland, 1993: 846). Although one might expect the reverse, Samaria is mentioned first because of the importance the Samaritan leper plays in the story (Stein, 1992: 433).

Except for Lk 17:11, Samaria is mentioned in the New Testament only in Acts (seven times) and John (three times). Luke's repeated mention of a positive attitude toward Samaria is characteristic of the evangelist. Jesus' prohibition, "enter no town of the Samaritans" (Mt 10:5), is not found in Luke. In the Acts of the Apostles Samaria is mission country and constitutes the next stage of the mission after Jerusalem and Judea (Acts 1:8). Luke's three Samaritan pericopes (Lk 9:51-56; 10:30-37; 17:11-19) show a special interest in the Samaritans. Jesus' contact with them, as is clear from Lk

9:51-56 and 17:11-19, originates apparently from Luke's intention to anchor the Samaritan mission in Jesus' life and mission.

Unlike Samaria, Galilee is often mentioned in the New Testament (sixty-one times). Compared with Mark, Luke has a very personal way of using Galilee. Only in Lk 4:14 does he take over the term from Mk 1:14, while he introduces it in five texts where it is not found in Mark (Lk 4:31; 5:17; 8:26; 23:49, 55). Galilee is not just a region of Palestine, but rather the place that marks the beginning of Jesus' ministry, "teaching throughout all Judea, from Galilee where he began even to this place" (Lk 23:5; compare Acts 10:37). Luke also specially mentions those who have followed Jesus from Galilee to Jerusalem (Lk 23:49, 55).

The association of Samaria and Galilee is also found in Acts 9:31 (together with Judea). In both cases the order "Samaria and Galilee" is the same, and it is therefore probably from Luke's hand. As to the topographical reference which underlies Lk 17:11, many opinions have been expressed. Most interpreters understand it to mean "in between Samaria and Galilee," i.e., along the border of Samaria and Galilee, but often disagree on the direction from which Jesus approached this border. It is especially intriguing that Samaria is mentioned before Galilee. Most probably, Samaria is mentioned first simply because of the important part played by the Samaritan in the account, and no deep explanation is called for. The geographical statement is totally obscure. But, as suggested above, Luke's only purpose is to account for the presence of a Samaritan among the Jews (Schweizer, 1984: 267; Green, 1997: 619). The whole expression is definitely Lukan and reveals a typically Lukan topographical reference in which this indication does not contradict the previous indication "on the way to Jerusalem" (Bruners, 1977: 124–163).

When in his solemn Old Testament style Luke begins an account by saying that Jesus went up to Jerusalem, this is not just an indication of the goal of his journey. Jerusalem is the place of Jesus' death and resurrection, of his appearances to his disciples, and his ascension. In Jerusalem the disciples receive the Spirit and the mission begins. It is the place where Jesus experiences acceptance and rejection; faith and unbelief is also the reaction there to the preaching of the disciples (Acts 2:13, 37ff.). Jerusalem is the place of the beginning of the mission which from there reaches out beyond Judea and Samaria to the end of the earth (Acts 1:8; 9:13), and in the mission of Samaria (Acts 8:5ff.) goes beyond the circle of the Jews and includes for the first time "foreigners." Among them the message is accepted with a faith that was not found among the Jews. The Samaritan and the nine in Lk 17:11-19 represent the two poles of this tension. Also in Galilee (Lk 4:15, 28-30) and in Samaria (Lk 9:52; 10:1, 17) Jesus and his disciples experience acceptance and rejection. In the context of Luke-Acts, then, and alongside Jerusalem, "Samaria and Galilee" suggest the basic tension of the account: faith and unbelief (Bruners, 1977: 383–386; Hendrickx, 1987: 228–230; Green, 1997: 621–622).

Verses 12-13: (12) As he entered a village,
                    ten lepers approached him.
                    Keeping their distance,
               (13) they called out, saying,
                    "Jesus, Master, have mercy on us!"

In verse 12a we have a third indication of the situation: "As he entered a village" (after "on the way to Jerusalem" and "through the region between Samaria and Galilee" in verse 11). The verb *eiserchesthai*, "to enter," is used about fifty times in Luke and thirty-two times in Acts and is often redactional. Apart from Lk 17:12, it is used in combination with *eis kōmēn*, "into a village," in Lk 9:52 and 10:38. The vague indication "a village" is typical of Luke, and it has been maintained that Luke's geographical and topographical material is a purely literary device employed to heighten the effect of this account, not because they actually meant anything concrete to him (McCown, 1941: 15–17). Luke several times fails to mention the names of villages (Lk 5:12; 9:52, 56; 11:1; 13:10; 14:1, etc.; Van der Loos, 1965: 496). All attempts to locate the village should therefore be considered futile (Hendrickx, 1987: 230).

The real action begins in verse 12b, "ten lepers approached him." Apart from Lk 17:12 the verb *apantaō*, "to approach," "to meet," is found in the New Testament only in Mk 14:13 (different in Luke), but it is used more often in the Septuagint. The number "ten" is used nine times in Luke against once in Mark and three times in Matthew. Since Luke has the tendency to omit numbers mentioned in Mark (e.g., Lk 5:18 compared with Mk 2:3), the use of "ten" here may be considered the result of a deliberate choice. This is confirmed by the further use of the numbers "nine" and "one." The contrast between these numbers belongs to the essence of the account. Unlike the New Testament where outside Luke and the Book of Revelation the number "ten" does not play an important part, in the Old Testament it is found in important contexts (Ex 34:28; Deut 4:13; 10:4) and is there the symbol of a rounded-off whole; ten representatives can legitimately represent the whole community (Ruth 4:2). It is, however, difficult to establish whether Luke would have been aware of this background.

The adjective *lepros*, "leprous," is found only here in the New Testament, but often occurs in the Septuagint (Lev 13:44; 2 Sam 3:29; 2 Kgs 7:3, etc.). The word *anēr*, "man," is a favorite word of Luke's (twenty-seven times in Luke; a hundred times in Acts; four times in Mark; eight times in Matthew). The expression *deka andres*, "ten men," is found only here in the New Testament, but seven times in the Septuagint. Only in 2 Kgs 7:3, which is not too far from the story of Naaman (2 Kgs 5), do we find another text dealing with several (four) lepers. The question exactly which kind of leprosy the story talks about must be left open. From the medical, historical and palaeopathological evidence it is clear that biblical "leprosy" (*lepra*) is not modern leprosy (Hansen disease). In the Greco-Roman world, modern leprosy was called *elephas* and was described just as moderns know it by Celsus, Pliny the Elder, and Galen (Pilch, 1981: 108 quoting E.V. Hulse). More important is that any kind of leprosy made the leper cultically unclean and thus excluded him from the community. Leprosy was considered a severe punishment from heaven (Num 12:10-15; 2 Chron 26:19).

The lepers stood "at a distance," in Greek *porrōthen*, which occurs only here and in Heb 11:13 in the New Testament, but sixteen times in the Septuagint. The phrase is based on Num 5:2-3; Lev 13:46. The author of verse 12, who may be Luke, as several indications suggest, continues to use the vocabulary of the Septuagint (Bruners, 1977: 164–180). According to many commentators, because the lepers were not allowed to enter the village, they met Jesus at the gate, yet maintaining the distance prescribed by the law of Moses (Lev 13:46; Danker, 1988: 290). But no trace of the prohibition is found in the other cleansing of a leper (Mk 1:40-45 parallel Lk 5:12-16), and besides, Luke's special material contains several references to "far" and "at a distance" (Lk 15:13, 20; 16:23, followed in Lk 16:24 by "Father Abraham, have mercy on me"; 18:13). In the same context Acts 2:39 should be mentioned: "For the promise is for you, for your children, and for all who are far away, everyone whom the Lord our God calls to him." The text may refer to the Gentile mission by which God calls to himself those who were far (Isa 57:19; Eph 2:13, 17). Thus "keeping their distance" in Lk 17:12 may also have a deeper, theological meaning. This is supported by the observation that many Psalms speak in similar terms about being far from God: "Why, O Lord, do you stand far off?" (Ps 10:1); "Why are you so far from helping me, from the words of my groaning?" (Ps 22:1b); "But you, O Lord, do not be far away! O my help, come quickly to my aid!" (Ps 22:19). Guilt, suffering and persecution cause

not only religious isolation, but also cultic uncleanness. A
sick person is not to perform worship. He calls on God "from
afar" and waits for the saving word (Ps 130:5). His condition also causes social isolation: "My friends and companions stand aloof from my affliction, and my neighbors stand
far off" (Ps 38:11). Unlike in Lk 17:12, in the Psalms it is
always the sufferer who looks towards God; it is God who is
"far off," while in Lk 17:12 the narrator stands with Jesus,
and the lepers stood at a distance (kept their distance). But
despite this difference, the same experience is expressed in
both instances; their existence is characterized by "being at
a distance"—from Jesus, or from their fellow human beings
(Glöckner, 1983: 141–142).

On his way to the city in which he will experience acceptance and rejection, while travelling through the regions
in which he encounters faith and unbelief, Jesus is met by
ten lepers. Unlike the leper of Lk 5:12-16, they remain at a
distance, which in Luke's account has less to do with exist-
ing regulations than with the fundamental distance between
Jesus and the ten which—at least for nine of them—even
the miracle of their cleansing does not bridge (Bruners, 1977:
386–388).

In verse 13, the expression *ēran phōnēn*, "they called out
(they lifted up their voices)," continues the biblical style of
the previous verses. In the New Testament the expression is
found only here and in Acts 4:24, where it introduces a
solemn prayer of the early Christian community: "When they
heard it, they raised their voices together to God and said,
'Sovereign Lord. . .'" In the Old Testament the expression
"to lift up one's voice" is almost always combined with the
verb "to weep" (Judg 2:4; 21:2f.; 1 Sam 24:16; 30:4, etc.), the
utterance of a shaken soul. While the expression "to lift up
one's voice" is not found in the Psalms (but see Ps 93:3, "the
floods have lifted up their voice"), they contain several expressions in which people, in a way similar to Lk 17:13,
address themselves to God with a loud voice (Ps 28:1-2,

etc.). When in Lk 17:13 the lepers "called out, saying," the formulation shows a close relationship with the vocabulary and the motifs of Old Testament prayer language. It expresses their situation of special distance as well as their cultic-social isolation and the anguish of soul at being far from God (Glöckner, 1983: 142–144). The clause is again patterned in imitation of the Septuagint (e.g., Judg 2:4; 9:7; 21:2).

The address "Jesus" does not often occur in the New Testament (five times in Luke; once in Acts; three times in Mark; none in Matthew). Apart from Lk 23:42, it is never found alone but always combined with a title or another designation; "Jesus of Nazareth" (Lk 4:34), "Jesus, Son of the Most High God" (Lk 8:28), "Jesus, Son of David" (Lk 18:38), and here in Lk 17:13, "Jesus, Master."

The word *epistatēs*, "master," occurs in the New Testament only in Luke (seven times), and twelve times in the Septuagint. Luke uses it four times where his source has *didaskale*, "teacher." Apart from Lk 17:13, *epistatēs* always serves as an address by people who belong to the circle of disciples, usually when they are in some consternation (Lk 5:5; 8:24, 25; 9:33, 49; Tiede, 1988: 297; Fitzmyer, 1985: 1154), whereas *didaskale*, "teacher," is attributed to people who are not disciples, or opponents (Stein, 1992: 433). We also find *kurie*, "lord," as an address by disciples and people in need. In Lk 17:13 *kurie* would be expected rather than *epistata*. So, in this verse Luke may have found *epistata* in his source.

The use of "master" seems to suggest that the lepers were already on friendly terms with Jesus. It has been pointed out that in all instances where people use *epistata*, "master," they misunderstand Jesus' *exousia*, "authority/power," and their faith can be considered only preliminary. This interpretation also seems to fit Lk 17:13. Nine of the lepers who address Jesus as "master" have only a "preliminary" faith. They ask Jesus for mercy, obey his order, but do not understand the real meaning of their cleansing.

In Luke, the formula "have mercy on us" occurs only four times (Lk 16:24; 17:13; 18:38, 39). In the tradition it had its fixed place in the healings of the blind (Mk 10:47, 48 parallel Lk 18:38, 39). Luke may have introduced the expression in Lk 17:13 from Lk 18:38, 39. In fact, the present verse is reminiscent of Lk 18:38f.: "Then he shouted, 'Jesus, Son of David, have mercy on me!' Those who were in front sternly ordered him to be quiet; but he shouted even more loudly, 'Son of David, have mercy on me!'"

The ten lepers turn to Jesus in the same way as the afflicted of the Old Testament turn to God.

Verse 14:   When he saw them, he said to them,
             "Go and show yourselves to the priests."
             And as they went, they were made clean.

The beginning of verse 14, literally, "and seeing he said to them," should not be understood as if Jesus first *saw* the lepers and then *spoke* to them (should one not rather expect *heard* in that case?), but as an example of biblical style where *idōn*, "seeing," is often used pleonastically (e.g., Gen 18:2; 38:15; 49:15). There is a definite connection between "seeing" and "saving" in the Old Testament as well as in the Gospel of Luke (e.g., Lk 13:12). The situation described in Lk 17:13-14 corresponds closely to that presented in Lk 15:20. Just as "when he was still far off, his father saw him," his father ran to him to bring about reconciliation, so Jesus "saw" the lepers who called out to him for mercy "from a distance," and healed them (Glöckner, 1983: 108, 115–117, 144).

Instead of speaking a word of healing (as in Lk 5:13), Jesus tells the ten lepers to show themselves to the priests (see Lk 5:14). That is like saying, "Get another physical examination from your local physician." Jesus didn't say, "Kneel down here, for I'm going to lay my hands on your head." There was nothing spectacular or dramatic about it (Bailey, 1977: 89–90). As "health care consultants," priests functioned as "purity inspectors" to exclude persons or restore them to their social roles; they were not themselves active in any therapeutic process. The point is important for the understanding of the sequence for the lepers are not yet healed. But when they do find themselves healed, will they attribute their good fortune to Jesus or go on their way without one word of recognition? The text does not specify the precise moment when the lepers were healed. But it was while they were on their "journey" (*poreuthentes*, "as they went"; Danker, 1988: 290). That Jesus anticipated that the Samaritan would go to a Samaritan priest is speculative. Luke was not concerned with this detail (Stein, 1992: 433).

Jesus' order, "go and show," should again be understood in a pleonastic way. The expression may have been influenced by Lk 5:14, "go and show," and 2 Kgs 5:10, "go and wash." The beginning of verse 14b (*kai egeneto en tōi hupagein*) constitutes a clear parallel with the beginning of verse 11 (*kai egeneto en tōi poreuesthai*) which forms a syntactic framework around verses 11-14. Luke uses different verbs for the lepers going (*hupagein*) and for Jesus' going to Jerusalem (*poreuesthai*—but see Lk 17:19, *poreuou*, "go on your way") which has for him a highly theological meaning.

The verb "to cleanse" is often used in the Septuagint to refer to the cure of a leper (Lev 13:6, 7, 13, 17, 28, etc.). Luke uses it seven times in his Gospel and three times in Acts. The passive "were cleansed" presents the healing as a divine act (2 Kgs 5:10; compare 5:14). The description of the action is here clearly more influenced by 2 Kgs 5:8-19 than by Lk 5:12-16 (as can also be shown by a comparison of the structure of the different accounts).

The healing of the lepers happened while they were on their way to the priests. Indeed the account leaves no doubt that all ten lepers were healed. That Jesus does not heal them right away, as in Lk 5:12-16, but sends them off unhealed is, in comparison with 2 Kgs 5:10-12, interpreted by a number of scholars as a test of faith. But this seems to remain in the background (Schweizer, 1984: 267–268). The account stresses not that the nine did not pass the faith test, but that after their cleansing they did not praise God and thank Jesus. The feature of the sending creates the necessary distance between Jesus and the lepers which makes it possible for one of them to *return* (Betz, 1971: 317–318). For Luke faith appears only in the return to Jesus after the cleansing. He therefore avoids speaking of faith in the first part of the account. The feature of the sending and the return may be dependent on the Naaman story. Elisha sent Naaman to the Jordan; surpassing the Naaman story, the ten are cleansed along the way. Their obedience results in a healing at a distance (compare Lk 7:7-10; Hendrickx, 1987: 235).

Without doubt, verse 14 concludes the miracle story proper, which is framed by the expression *kai egeneto*, "and it happened" (not translated in English) in verses 11-14. The account reached a first peak in the request for Jesus' mercy (verse 13). However, with "they were made clean" the deliverance from leprosy is established. Here the first scene reaches its climax: the fulfillment of the request, the removal of the distress. As such, nothing indicates a continuation of the account. However, with "then one of them" a second scene begins which likewise reaches its climax in a "healing," which with the words "has made you well (has saved)" takes on a more comprehensive meaning than "they were made clean" (Bruners, 1977: 194–214).

Verses 15-16: (15) Then one of them,
            when he saw that he was healed,
            turned back,
            praising God with a loud voice.
        (16) He prostrated himself at Jesus' feet
            and thanked him.
            And he was a Samaritan.

The beginning of verse 15 constitutes a clear break with the previous. Not only does the subject change, but with "one," which is emphasized with "then," (*de* could be translated "but") and placed at the beginning of the clause, a totally new subject appears, which is further specified by the partitive genitive "of them," thus assuring the logical connection with the previous subject. The phrases "praising God" and "thanked him [giving thanks]" (verse 16b) are parallel. The former seems to be the more important phrase since it is referred to once more in verse 18, "to return and give praise to God," while the actions of verse 16 are not mentioned a second time (Hendrickx, 1987: 235).

The comment (verse 15) has a built-in ambiguity that obfuscates the lines separating Jesus from God. The use of pronouns instead of nouns in the last phrase leaves the grammatical antecedent, God, to temper the audience's commonsense inference that the leper knelt at Jesus' feet. In the eyes of the narrator, Jesus and God are almost indistinguishable, and both are worshiped. But in the same account of the Samaritan leper Jesus attempts to direct attention away from himself and toward God (Lk 17:18). And actually, this is a general concern of the Lukan Jesus. He plays down attempts of the community to worship him and emphasizes the message that he is delivering from God (see Lk 11:27-28). In line with the prophetic tradition of the Old Testament, Jesus focuses attention on what God is doing (Dawsey, 1986: 143-144).

As introduction to a sentence, the expression "[then] one of them" is found only here in the New Testament. Since Luke has the tendency to omit numbers, it is almost certain that here where it is placed at the beginning of a sentence, "one" receives a special emphasis, and may be read as "only one!" This one leper becomes a leading actor while the others become secondary actors (Theissen, 1983: 44).

The expression *idōn hoti*, "seeing that," occurs in Luke only here and in Lk 8:47, but several times in Acts, and may be attributed to Luke. The phrase *iathē*, "he was healed," is found eleven times in Luke and four times in Acts, against once in Mark, four times in Matthew, and four in John. In the New Testament cures of lepers, however, what is found is usually not "healed" but "cleansed." In the Septuagint "to heal" is used of lepers in Lev 14:3, 48; Num 12:13. It seems that the use of "he was healed" should here be attributed to Luke. It is possible that he used it for stylistic purposes, i.e., to avoid the repetition of "cleansed" (verses 14 and 17), but it is remarkable that the latter word is used twice for the "ten," while the "one" who returns is "healed." Luke may be using this "neutral" term here as a transition from the technical term "they were cleansed" to the highly significant "has made well" (saved!; verse 19).

That Jesus uttered his promise of healing "when he saw (*idōn*) them" corresponds to the present note that "one of them, when he saw (*idōn*) that he was healed, turned back." To Jesus' merciful, saving "seeing" there corresponds the insightful "seeing" of the Samaritan. The correspondence between the two is not accidental and plays a part in the structure of the account (Nolland, 1993: 846). A similar agreement is found in Lk 5:1-11. The calling of the first disciples begins with the note that Jesus "saw two boats there at the shore of the lake" (Lk 5:2), and selected Peter's boat, which led on to the miraculous catch of fish. Peter's conversion and following is introduced by the words, "But when Simon Peter saw it, he fell down at Jesus' knees. . ." The Samaritan who returned "saw that he was healed." The nine others must also have noticed that they were cured, but this one man's seeing was different, meaning that he had understood what happened to him. For this Samaritan the very concept of healing received a deeper meaning: the realization "that he was healed" became the realization that he was "saved" (*sesōken*; NRSV: "has made [you] well"; Betz, 1971: 325).

In Luke-Acts the connection between the experience of salvation in "seeing" and the faithful, praising response of the person concerned has special importance. In Lk 2:15, 17, after the appearance of the angels, the shepherds go to Bethlehem to "see this thing that has taken place." Afterwards "the shepherds returned, glorifying and praising God for all they had heard and seen, as it had been told them" (Lk 2:20). Simeon was promised that "he would not see death before he had seen the Lord's Messiah" (Lk 2:26). At the presentation of Jesus in the temple Simeon "praised God. . . for my eyes have seen your salvation" (Lk 2:28, 30). Acts 9:32-35, the healing of Aeneas by Peter, ends with the remark: "And all the residents of Lydda and Sharon saw him and turned to the Lord." In the healing of the paralytic we are told: "All the people saw him walking and praising God" (Acts 3:9). At the end of the healing of Bartimaeus, Lk 18:43 considerably reformulates Mk 10:52. While Mark says only that the blind man saw and followed Jesus, Luke adds the motif of "praising God" and again, "and all the people, when they saw it, praised God." Lk 18:43 particularly indicates that the connection between "seeing" and "praising" betrays to some extent a literary preference of the evangelist's, but since most of the instances are found in Luke's special material and in Acts it is difficult to determine exactly to what extent Luke has edited his sources (Glöckner, 1983: 145–146).

The verb *hupostrephein*, "to return," is used twenty-one times in Luke and twelve times in Acts, while it does not occur in the other gospels. It may be said, therefore, that Luke has a special predilection for the motif of "return." Just as after his cleansing Naaman returned to Elisha, so one of the ten cleansed men returned to Jesus. That one out of ten returned is emphasized so strongly as to recall the one sheep out of a hundred (Lk 15:3-7) or the one drachma out of ten (Lk 15:8-10). Since these parables deal among other things with conversion, *metanoia*, return, it is not excluded that Lk 17:11-19 also alludes to it (Hendrickx, 1987: 237).

At issue is not whether the Samaritan in Luke's story had access to appropriate members of the priestly establishment to certify his healing, or whether he returned to Jesus because he would not be welcomed by Jewish priests. Instead, the point is that the Samaritan recognized that God could be praised—and that God's holy and saving power could be addressed—in Jesus' presence as well as in God's recognized "homes" in the temples of Jerusalem or (for Samaritans) Mount Gerizim (Ringe, 1995: 220).

The participle-construction "praising God" is found only in Luke in the New Testament (Lk 2:20; 5:25; 17:15; 18:43). The object of praise in Luke-Acts is most of the time God, twice Jesus (Lk 4:15; Acts 3:13), and once "the word of the Lord" (Acts 13:48). "Praise of God" in Luke is always the reaction of people who receive or are witnesses of a marvelous event. In three instances Jesus' deeds are the occasion for praising God (Lk 7:16; 8:39; 23:47; cf. Lk 17:18). The phrase "with a loud voice" recalls "they called out (= lifted up their voices)" of verse 13. This may suggest that the "praise of God" of the one is "louder" than the request of the ten (Bruners, 1977: 215–228).

The Samaritan praises God with a loud voice. This reminds us of the multitude of disciples who at the descent of the Mount of Olives "began to rejoice and praise God with a loud voice for all the mighty works that they had seen" (Lk 19:37; in particular, the last part of the verse constitutes an interesting parallel with Lk 17:15). Elsewhere in the Gospel too, the powerful deeds of Jesus draw praise to God from the people (Lk 7:16: Jesus himself is referred to as a prophet; Lk 23:47: Jesus himself is called "innocent" or "just" [*dikaios*]). In parallel with 2 Kgs 5:15 the praise of God precedes the thanks given to Jesus, which, moreover, is not repeated in verse 18. But Jesus is not dissociated from the praise given to God (Hendrickx, 1987: 237).

While the expression "to prostrate oneself at somebody's feet," or "to fall on one's face" (Mk 5:22; 7:25) are both found in the tradition, the combination of the two occurs only in Lk 17:16. The expression "to fall on one's face" occurs in Luke only here and in Lk 5:12 (different Mk 1:40; Mt 8:2), in both cases most probably influenced by the Septuagint, where it occurs forty-four times (e.g., Gen 17:3, 17; Lev 9:24). In more than half the Septuagint passages the expression refers to God or to the messenger of God, but it is also applied to other persons (Ruth 2:10; 2 Sam 9:6, etc.). In the New Testament people fall on their faces before Jesus and God. In contrast to other New Testament writings, Luke uses it only with regard to Jesus. It may here be attributed to Luke (Hendrickx, 1987: 237).

Whereas Mark and Matthew use the verb *eucharistein*, "to thank," only in a eucharistic or quasi-eucharistic sense, in Lk 18:11 we find it used in the sense of "to thank" (see also Acts 27:35; 28:15). In these instances the thanks are addressed to God, except in Lk 17:16 where "him" clearly refers to Jesus. This is in fact the only place in the New Testament where thanks are explicitly expressed in a healing story, presumably under the influence of the Naaman story (2 Kgs 5:15). Only here in the New Testament are thanks directed to Jesus rather than God (Stein, 1992: 434).

It has been noted that verses 15-16 are arranged in a chiastic structure:

then one of them
    praising *God* with a loud voice
        turned back;
        and he fell
    on his face at *Jesus'* feet, giving him thanks;
now he was a Samaritan.

The phrases "praising God" and "fell (falling) on his face at Jesus' feet" are clearly parallel. In this way Luke places Jesus in parallel with God and in God's immediate vicinity. Whereas Luke, unlike Mark and Matthew, avoids the use of *proskunein*, "to prostrate," in reference to Jesus until after the resurrection (Lk 24:52), he does refer to worship of Jesus during his ministry, though in a veiled way and in close relation to God's activity through Jesus. From now on the only place where one can properly give thanks to God is at Jesus' feet (Hendrickx, 1987: 238).

One of the centers of gravity of Lk 17:11-19 is situated in the affirmation that the right place for praising God is Jesus himself. As God's representative, Jesus is the locus where God is to be praised (Pesch, 1970: 133). This is already presupposed in the return of the Samaritan. Exactly what place Jesus occupies in this connection is expressed in the conduct of the returned man: "He prostrated himself at Jesus' feet and thanked him." Luke has given the whole scene a "liturgical" character. Even though before the ascension the evangelist does not use the verb *proskunein*, "to prostrate," there cannot be any doubt about the place which Jesus occupies. In the light of 2 Kgs 5:15 where Naaman "returned to the man of God. . . and came and stood before him," it becomes clear that Jesus' dignity far exceeds that of the prophet Elisha, who would not have allowed Naaman to fall down before him, and who actually refused the thanks of the Syrian. But see also 2 Kgs 4:37, "She came and fell at his feet, bowing to the ground. . ."

"One of them" is now emphatically (*kai autos*; compare Lk 1:22; 3:23; 6:20; 22:41; 24:25, 31) identified as a Samaritan. Apart from Lk 17:16, a Samaritan is mentioned only in Lk 10:33 (both in Luke's special material). If it is true that this indicates a particular interest of Luke's special source(s), Acts 1:8; 8:1, 5, 9, 14, 25; 9:31; 15:3 show that Luke's interest goes beyond that of his source(s). The clause "and he was a Samaritan" is probably redactional (Bruners, 1977: 229–245). Mention of this has been delayed in the story to dramatize this fact (Stein, 1992: 434). It may be worth noticing that when all ten were lepers, the nine and the one Samaritan were together sharing the same predicament. But now that they are cured the old cultural and religious boundaries are back and they go again their own way.

Like Naaman the Syrian, the returnee of Lk 17:11-19 is not a Jew; he is a Samaritan, and therefore in the eyes of the Jews a pagan (for a short history of the Samaritans, see e.g., Heutger, 1977: 276–280). In his return and subsequent behavior this non-Jew acts as the Jews should have acted. The Samaritan represents the pagan nations who turn to the Lord, whereby Luke expresses that the time of salvation has come. The contrast between the Samaritan and the nine others may be compared to that between the Samaritan and the priest and the Levite in Lk 10:30-37. But by his return to Jesus and his praising God in Jesus' presence the Samaritan of Lk 17:11-19 surpasses the Samaritan of the parable. He recognizes that in Jesus he receives much more than the cleansing from leprosy. The miracle has for him the character of a sign that refers to Jesus. Therefore, within the journey towards Jerusalem, the Samaritan of Lk 17:11-19 occupies a place comparable to that of the centurion of Capernaum during Jesus' travels in Galilee (Lk 7:1-10). Both are contrasted with Israel, for they show the only attitude which truly responds to Jesus: faith (Bruners, 1977: 395–397).

Up to this point, the narrative has followed the familiar pattern of a healing miracle. With the additional information that the one ex-leper who returns to Jesus is a Samaritan, the narrative changes from a story of miraculous healing to one of miraculous salvation. Whereas the reader was quite content to watch the ten lepers go through the motions required to allow them back into society, she or he is now amazed at the turn taken by the story. The identification of the leper who has modeled the correct response to Jesus as a Samaritan shocks the reader into reflection on the nature of the gospel. This reflection is reinforced by the questions posed by Jesus, as they point out the painful difference between the responses of the nine and that of the foreigner. In Lk 17:17-18 the reader shares Jesus' amazement, not only that the one who returned was a Samaritan, but that he was the only one who responded properly to Jesus' deed. The aside found in Lk 17:16 is essential to the impact of the passage, and the information it contains has been withheld by the narrator until the moment in which it will have the most effect. The presence of the Samaritan in worship at the feet of Jesus forces the reader to reconsider his or her own response to Jesus (Sheeley, 1992: 105–106).

Verses 17-18: (17) Then Jesus asked,
                    "Were not ten made clean?
                    But the other nine, where are they?
            (18) Was none of them found to return
                    and give praise to God except this foreigner?"

The phrase "then Jesus asked," literally "then answering/taking the floor Jesus said," which constitutes another caesura or break in the account, introduces three rhetorical questions. A literal parallel to this introduction is found in Lk 22:51: "Then Jesus said. . ." (and Mt 20:22). The name "Jesus" occurs about ninety times in Luke and sixty-eight times in Acts. In Luke almost half the occurrences are found in connection with a verb of speaking.

One may wonder whether the three questions constituted an original unity. Some scholars believe that the first two questions formed a double question expressing Jesus' astonishment that the nine others did not come back. It has also been pointed out that this double question is formally parallel to that found in Lk 13:15-16: "Does not each of you on the sabbath untie his ox or his donkey from the manger and lead it away to give it water? And ought not this woman, a daughter of Abraham whom Satan bound for eighteen long years be set free from this bondage on the sabbath day?" The third question was probably added at a later stage, together with the secondary development in verse 16, "and he was a Samaritan" (Busse, 1977: 321–322; Betz, 1971: 320–321).

As is quite often the case in the Septuagint (e.g., Gen 18:9, 27; 24:50), it is not mentioned to whom the statements/questions are addressed. They do not immediately concern the Samaritan, but rather the disciples (Lk 17:5) and the Pharisees (Lk 17:20). They constitute a reflection which ultimately aims at the (real) addressees: Luke's community (Hendrickx, 1987: 239–240).

The subject of the first question, "ten," refers back to the "ten lepers" of verse 12. "Were made clean" is a traditional term which Luke last used in verse 14. The second question has as subject "the nine," an entity logically implied by the expression "one of them" in verse 15.

The subject of the third question is not explicitly mentioned, but it is clear that the "nine" are meant who are the subject of the previous clause. Luke often uses the verb *heuriskein*, "to find" (forty-five times in Luke and thirty-five times in Acts, against eleven times in Mark, and twenty-seven times in Matthew). But apart from Lk 17:18, the passive "to be found" occurs in Luke-Acts only in Lk 9:36; 15:24, 32; Acts 5:39; 8:40. As already mentioned under verse 15, *hupostrephein*, "to return," is a favorite Lukan verb. Together with "ten" and "were made clean," "return" is repeated and constitutes a solid link with the earlier part of the story. The motif of the "return" gives a parenetic character to the account.

The expression "to give praise (*doxa*, 'glory') to God" is obviously biblical. Apart from Lk 4:6 (different in Mt 4:9), the New Testament always says that glory is given to God. Luke speaks of Jesus' glory only in connection with the resurrection and exaltation (Lk 9:26; 21:27; 24:26; Acts 22:11: "brightness" [NRSV]). Since there are hardly any abstract nouns in the account, one may suspect that the only two that are found in it—*doxa*, "praise, glory" (verse 18) and *pistis*, "faith" (verse 19)—have a special importance. Moreover, "praise" is emphasized since it constitutes a resumption of "praising God" in verse 15. In both cases it is God who is praised (Hendrickx, 1987: 240). The "nine," therefore, are not criticized for failing to give thanks to Jesus but for failing to return and give God the glory, that is, the credit for disclosing the divine identity in and through Jesus, their Messiah. This is faith—to recognize the point at which God's glory is revealed, namely to Jesus who welcomes the lowly, the poor, the leper. This Jesus invites all to shed their legal self-confidence and their self-aggrandisement that is maintained at the expense of others (Danker, 1988: 290–291).

"This foreigner," that is, part of the group excluded from the inner barrier of the temple (Dawsey, 1986: 146–147), stands in contrast with "the nine" (adversative *ei mē*, rather than exceptive) and refers to the "Samaritan" of verse 16. Strictly speaking, the Samaritans were viewed as half-foreign, Israelites of doubtful descent (Nolland, 1993: 847). This part of the verse is apparently influenced by Lk 4:27, "none of them was cleansed except Naaman the Syrian." The word *allogenēs*, "foreigner," occurs only here in the New Testament, but is found quite often in the Septuagint (e.g., Ex 12:43; 29:33; 30:33; Lev 22:10, 12, 13, 25). By calling the Samaritan a "foreigner," Luke makes him a representative of all aliens (*pace* Jervell, 1972: 117–123), who were excluded from the temple worship and therefore could not give glory to God where, according to the Jews, it should be done. But here a foreigner is said to give glory to God without having to break through the barriers of the temple. He has found a new locus of worship (cf. Jn 4:21). The Samaritan returns to give thanks vis-à-vis the new temple, namely Jesus. This pericope, therefore, shows some affinity to John 4 (Ford, 1983: 93). For Luke, the Samaritan is one of the true worshipers mentioned in Jn 4:23. If Lk 17:11-19 is to be considered a transformation of Mk 1:40-45 (parallel Lk 5:12-16), the detailed reshaping of the story is due to the switch to a mission to the Gentiles and inner dissociation from the temple. If one wishes to thank God, one no longer uses the mediation of the temple, but the mediation of Jesus (Theissen, 1983: 187). According to some interpreters, Lk 17:11-19 presupposes the definite breach between Judaism and Christianity and the success of the Christian mission to the Samaritans (Betz, 1971: 321).

The three questions were developed from the story it-self. Of course, Jesus "knows" that all ten were cleansed. The question "where are the nine?" can be answered only by "with the priests." That too Jesus must know since he sent them there himself. What is unusual is the behavior not of the nine, but of the one who does not stick to Jesus' instructions. The third question is likewise rhetorical, since the fact that none but this foreigner has returned to give praise to God is obvious. No answer is expected to any of these rhetorical questions (Tiede, 1988: 297). Moreover, who should give the answers? The Samaritan? This is definitely ruled out by the third question. Or the disciples mentioned in Lk 17:5? The account clearly leaves the question of the addressees open. The questions thereby acquire a meaning which goes beyond the immediate setting. The readers are drawn into the account and have to take a stand.

By these questions Luke intends to clarify what the ac-count is all about. They are superfluous for the course of the action and add no new elements. Verse 19 could easily fol-low right after verse 16 and the introduction to Jesus' reply, "and answering Jesus said" [NRSV: "Then Jesus asked"] (verse 17a). Verses 17-18 are a commentary which Luke places on the lips of Jesus. By way of key words he repeats once more the whole account: "the ten"—"were cleansed"—"no. . . to return and give praise to God"—"foreigner," thus letting us know what he emphasizes and which words are the real bear-ers of the message. "The ten" and "the foreigner" act like brackets at the beginning and the end of the three questions. In these questions, but especially in the third, Luke makes clear what theological message he intends to convey. The third question already shows what the faith of the Samaritan consists in: in his return to Jesus to give glory to God. The third question thus has, unlike the other two, the character of a real answer. Both vocabulary and style suggest that these verses may have been composed by Luke (Bruners, 1977: 246–280).

It is a "pagan" who praises God in Jesus' presence; the nine fail to come. That the Samaritan represents the pagans is clear from the fact that at the end of verse 18 Luke lets Jesus speak of "this foreigner." The return of the Samaritan seems here to be concerned only with "praising God." In the Old Testament, Israel was requested to proclaim the glory (*doxa*) of God and his miraculous deeds (Ps 96:2-3). But the pagan nations are also called to do this (Ps 96:7-9; Isa 42:12). In the New Testament, apart from Luke, the Book of Revelation speaks especially of giving praise to God (Rev 14:6f.; 16:9; 19:7).

In the context of a miracle, the expression "give God the praise" is also found in Jn 9:24. The cured man there designates Jesus as a prophet (Jn 9:17) and confesses him as being "from God" (Jn 9:33). Finally he reaches faith in Jesus and worships him (Jn 9:38). Here too we find a close connection between "giving praise to God" and faithful recognition of Jesus. Not simply praising God as such, but the combination of return to Jesus and praise given to God constitutes faith in the understanding of Lk 17:11-19. This is so because in Jesus God's salvation comes to people or, as Lk 17:21 expresses it, "(in him) the kingdom of God is in the midst of you" (compare Lk 11:20; 10:9, 11). The kingdom of God which has come near in Jesus is the real ground for returning to him and giving praise to God in his presence. This is the Christological affirmation of the account (Bruners, 1977: 397–401).

Verse 19:   Then he said to him,
             "Get up and go on your way;
             your faith has made you well.

Jesus now addresses the Samaritan. The expression "get up and go" presupposes that the Samaritan is still at Jesus' feet. Luke uses the verb *anistēmi*, "to get up, to rise," twenty-six times in the Gospel and forty-five times in Acts, and it is a favorite word of Luke's. The particular form of the verb used here, *anastas* (strong aorist participle), is found about thirty-five times in Luke-Acts. The verb also occurs often in the Septuagint. Luke apparently uses the expression "get up and go" in imitation of the Septuagint. He uses the same combination of verbs also in Lk 1:39; 15:18; Acts 8:27; 22:10 (compare Acts 8:26; 9:11).

The verb *poreuesthai*, "to go, to travel," occurs several times in Lukan miracle stories: Lk 5:25b and 8:48; see also Lk 7:8. In Lk 5:24 and 8:48 it is found in Jesus' final address to the healed person. The imperative "go" in Luke is used almost exclusively by Jesus. It has therefore a special importance. In the Septuagint, the imperative "go" is often combined with "in peace" (e.g., 2 Kgs 5:19). In Lk 17:19 "in peace" does not occur, most probably because the decisive statement follows in the enunciation about faith.

The words "made you well" are used in a double sense, for the Greek word for "make well" (*sōzō*) is the word ordinarily rendered "save" (Danker, 1988: 291; Stein, 1992: 434). The clause "your faith has made you well/has saved you" occurs four times in Luke (Lk 7:50; 8:48; 17:19; 18:42). In Lk 8:48 and 18:42 it is derived from Mark (Mk 5:34; 10:52). Elsewhere in the gospels the expression does not occur in exactly this form. It is a fixed motif of the literary genre of miracle stories. In Lk 17:19 it constitutes an inclusion with Lk 17:5, "Increase our faith!" In Lk 17:5 the apostles asked Jesus to increase their faith. The present story reveals that faith properly conceived is faith in Jesus (Danker, 1988: 290).

Luke likes to emphasize that faith saves (compare, e.g., Lk 8:50 and Mk 5:36). Besides Lk 17:19 Luke also speaks of "saving" in connection with healing and liberation from bodily defects and demons in Lk 6:9; 8:36, 48, 50; 18:42 (compare Acts 4:9; 14:9). Among the Synoptics, Luke has a special interest in "saving faith." See Acts 16:31, "Believe on the Lord Jesus, and you will be saved," where "believe" (*pisteuein*) and "to be saved" (*sōthēnai*) are almost identical. Salvific faith presupposes God's salvific activity in and through Jesus,

but equally includes thankful praise of God as well as turning to Jesus (Schneider, 1977: 252). The Samaritan now is
confirmed in his faith. He came to the right place. Thus
these words "Your faith has made you well" (see also Lk
7:50; 8:48; 18:42) do not say that exertion of faith spells
healing but that the one to whom the faith is directed has
spelled the difference for this man. Faith without an agent
who can respond to the faith is only a psychological phenomenon. Therefore the man's return to Jesus was of great
importance. He saw the Giver in the gift. The nine also
had faith that Jesus could heal them, but a plus accompanied the Samaritan's faith. He was made well in the profounder
sense of the word (see Lk 7:50; 8:12; 9:24, 56; 13:23; 19:10;
Danker, 1988: 291; Heutgen, 1977: 284). Against the backdrop of those who only want a healing (and those who are
not even grateful for that), this "foreigner" is an exemplar
of "saving faith" which "sees" the work and reign of God
(Tiede, 1988: 298). What we have, then, is a story of ten
being healed and one being saved (Craddock, 1990: 203).

Some commentators have said that verse 19 does not
entirely fit the account and would, therefore, be secondary.
But these commentators are not consistent, since the caesura of the account is found at the end of verse 14, and so
they should query not only verse 19, but the whole of verses
15-19. From verse 15 on, the account becomes a story about
faith. As already said, Luke distinguishes between "were made
clean"—"was healed"—"has made you well/saved you," and
uses them to indicate a progression. All ten lepers were
cleansed, but only one understood the meaning of this sign,
returned to Jesus and praised God. Together with verses 15-
18, verse 19 does therefore essentially belong to the account
and fits it perfectly (Bruners, 1977: 280–295).

Jesus dismisses the healed man with the formal assur-
ance, "your faith has made you well/saved you." Thus Luke
places the emphasis on the second part of the account. The
final stress is produced by the fact that expositional motifs

of approach (hindrance and faith) appear only after the miracle. Here the first outward approach is followed by a second, and it is only in this that the healed man breaks through the real barrier between himself and the miracle-worker (Theissen, 1983: 113–114).

In line with the train of thought developed in the previous verses, verse 19 speaks of the faith of the Samaritan. Obviously the promise of faith and salvation, while surpassing it, stands in parallel to the statement that the ten "were made clean." In the tension between bodily healing ("they were made clean") and the healing which encompasses the whole person ("made you well," "saved you"), it becomes once more clear what Luke intends to say by means of this account. Those who do not understand the cleansing as a sign of the dawning kingdom of God in Jesus may regain their physical health, but they pass by the real meaning of the miraculous event. Although unlike 2 Kgs 5:19-27, no punishing miracle follows, nevertheless the nine fail to experience salvation. Luke likes to speak of saving faith, especially in connection with Jesus' powerful deeds (Lk 8:48, 50; Acts 3:16; 4:5-12; Hendrickx, 1978: 243–244; Stein, 1992: 433).

A Christian community in which healing does not take place quietly but is placed in the center for its propaganda effect is a spiritually endangered community. Whether healing takes place through extraordinary means such as prayer or through "ordinary" means, such as the faithful ministrations of a doctor, is not the most important question. What matters is whether or not the bodily healing leads to a new life with God (Schweizer, 1984: 269).

PRESENCE OF THE KINGDOM AND COMING OF THE SON OF MAN
(LK 17:20–18:8)

According to some scholars, attention to the audiences specified by Luke in this section reveals that Lk 17:22–18:8 forms a unit of eschatological instruction addressed to the disciples. Lk 17:20-21, addressed to Pharisees, stands out as a separate piece, both on formal and material grounds. Nevertheless, Luke has left hints that instructions to Pharisees and disciples should be read together (Carroll, 1988: 72–76; 72 notes 129 and 130; Binder, 1988: 29; Green, 1997: 627–628). Verses 20-21 and 22-37 constitute a single text, although the audiences differ to some extent, and the first part introduces the theme of the kingdom of God while the second deals with the coming of the Son of Man (Hartman, 1992: 1665).

Although Lk 18:9-14 shares with Lk 18:1-8 the theme of prayer, Luke has specified for the parable on humble prayer (Lk 18:9-14) a new audience: "He also said to some who trusted in themselves that they were righteous and regarded others with contempt" (verse 9). "Pharisees" (then *and now*) are, beyond doubt, the target of this parable. The Pharisees of the text may also stand for an attitude in the reader's situation, viz. a failure to realize that God makes his reign effective in the reader's own time, in the Christian community, as he once did in Jesus' and his disciples' day (Hartman, 1992: 1666). Audience analysis isolates Lk 17:22–18:8 as an instructional discourse concerning eschatological themes. Nevertheless, Luke has left several clues that the juxtaposition of verses 20-21 and the ensuing instruction of disciples

30

is no accident. The most obvious link between the two sections is the verbal correspondence of verse 21a and verse 23a:

17:21a: Nor will they say, "Look, here it is!" or "There it is!"

17:23a: They will say to you, "Look there!" or "Look here!"

Moreover, the theme of the coming of the kingdom in Lk 17:20 (*erchetai*) and of the Son of Man in Lk 18:8b (*elthōn*) creates an *inclusio* setting apart the entire passage (Green, 1997: 628). To be sure, verses 20-21 mention the kingdom of God (three times), while Lk 17:22–18:8 revolves around the day of the Son of Man. However, these two concepts are closely related in Luke, as Lk 21:31 (alongside Lk 21:27-28, 36) shows. There Lukan redaction replaces the vague image of the Son of Man at the door (Mk 13:29b in light of 13:26) with the assertion: "The kingdom of God is near." While kingdom language and Son-of-Man language are not synonymous in Luke-Acts, it is likely that the two motifs serve to interpret each other in Lk 17:20–18:8 (Carroll, 1988: 72, 73; Hartman, 1992: 1665).

Only careful exegesis of the passage as a whole can answer the question of the relationship between verses 20-21 and the balance of the discourse (verses 22-37). At this juncture we can say only that our examination of the discourse must include verses 20-21, even though, on the basis of the distinction in addressees, these verses fall outside the discourse proper. Despite diverse origin, these traditional materials have been woven by Luke into one unit treating eschatological themes (Carroll, 1988: 74).

Our interpretation of the meaning and literary function of Lk 17:20–18:8 must be guided by its placement in the gospel narrative. The passage is the second of three large blocks of eschatological teachings located within the Travel Narrative (see Luke 12 and Lk 19:11-27). In addition, as recently as Lk 17:11 Luke has reminded the reader of Jesus' destination, Jerusalem. In view of Lk 9:31 and 13:31-35, the association of that city with Jesus' impending rejection and death is clear. Moreover, the Lukan Jesus' confrontation with the Pharisees has continued unabated, if indeed it has not escalated throughout the journey (Carroll, 1988: 74).

a. The Presence of the Kingdom (Lk 17:20-21)

Verses 20-21: (20) Once Jesus was asked by the Pharisees
                    when the kingdom of God was coming,
                    and he answered,
                    "The kingdom of God is not coming
                        with things that can be observed;
               (21) nor will they say,
                    'Look, here it is!' or 'There it is!'
                    For, in fact,
                    the kingdom of God is among you."

Few passages in Luke-Acts have proven as elusive as Lk 17:20-21. The occurrence of two Lukan *hapax legomena*, the noun *paratērēsis* ("observation"; NRSV: "things that can be observed"; verse 20) and the preposition *entos* ("within," "in the midst of," "among"; verse 21)—neither of which is transparent in sense—poses particularly difficult interpretive problems (Carroll, 1988: 76; Binder, 1988: 39–59).

Lk 17:20-21 is an answer which Jesus gives to some Pharisees who ask him about the coming of the kingdom of God. The setting for the Pharisees' question is left unspecified, and Jesus' answer is an isolated saying which might have been uttered by him at any time during his ministry. The saying is found only here in the canonical Gospels, but forms of it are to be found in the *Gospel of Thomas*. The first part is paralleled in # 113: "His disciple said to him, 'On what day will the kingdom come?' [Jesus said,] 'It comes not with expectation (of it).' They will not say, 'Look, here (it is)!' or 'Look, there (it is)!' Rather, the kingdom of the Father is spread out over the earth, and human beings see it not!" The latter part of it finds a parallel in both the Coptic and Greek forms of the *Gospel of Thomas*. The Coptic form of logion # 3 runs as follows: "Jesus said, 'If those who draw you on say to you, "Look, the kingdom is in heaven," then the birds of heaven will be (there) before you. If they say to you, "It is in the sea," then the fish will be (there) before you. But the kingdom is within you and outside you. . .'" The Greek form, preserved in OxyP # 654:9-16, is slightly different: "Je[sus] says, '[If] those who draw you on [say to you, "Look], the kingdom (is) in heav[en]," the birds of the heav[en will be (there) be]fore you. But if they say th]at it is under the earth, the fish of the se[a will be (there) before you; and the king[dom of heaven] is within you and outside you.'" None of these non-canonical forms, however, preserves a more primitive formulation of the canonical saying (Fitzmyer, 1985: 1157). The relation of Lk 17:20-21 to the following Lukan episode (Lk 17:22-37) is a matter of debate and affects the question of the source of verses 20-21. The treatment of verses 20-37 as a unit or as derived wholly from Q is not entirely convincing. Most probably verses 20b-21 should be understood as a saying detached from its original context and used here by Luke. Luke has probably composed the introductory question (verse 20a). Verses 20b-21, however, have probably been derived by Luke from his source "L" (Fitzmyer, 1985: 1158, 1159; Carroll, 1988: 76).

Thus far in the Lukan Gospel Jesus has spoken of the coming of the kingdom in teaching his disciples the Lord's Prayer (Lk 11:2, "Your kingdom come") and of the kingdom as something that could be seen (Lk 9:27). He has, moreover, instructed the disciples to announce that it "has come near" (Lk 10:9, 11) and has himself proclaimed that it "has come" to his hearers (Lk 11:20). Such remarks of the Lukan Jesus have to be understood as the background for the question now put on the lips of the Pharisees: "When does it come?" or "When is it going to come?" Jesus' answer to them is polemical in tone. In fact, it does not so much tell them when the kingdom will come as imply that they are misunderstanding what it is all about, that they fail to understand the eschatological significance of Jesus' ministry (Green, 1997: 628). His answer clearly tells them that they are not to look for the *time* of its coming or the *place* of its arrival. Jesus rejects all useless speculation about the coming of the kingdom (Fitzmyer, 1985: 1159).

This is the first of several places in Luke-Acts where a request for clarity regarding the kingdom leads to the correction of misunderstanding about the eschatological timetable and, then, about the nature of God's dominion (see Lk 19:11-27; 21:7-36; Acts 1:6; Fusco, 1992: 1677–1678; Carroll, 1988: 123–124). The line between the Pharisees and disciples is not hard-and-fast in the Lukan narrative [a reality that is overlooked in attempts to paint the Pharisees as "insincere" in their request (so Gowler, 1991: 263–266)]. But, as will become clear in Lk 17:22-37, the Pharisees are not alone in their failure to grasp Jesus' message about the character of God's reign (Green, 1997: 628, 629 and note 49).

The question posed by the Pharisees is wrongheaded on two counts. First, it assumes that God's reign is exclusively a future entity. Second, though more subtly, is the suggestion in Jesus' reply that the Pharisees are hoping to recognize the coming of God's dominion through scientific observation and assessment (Riesenfeld, TDNT 8: 148–149). Sign-watching has already been denounced in Luke (Lk 11:16, 29-32). Having negated the wrongheaded assumptions of the Pharisees' question, Jesus turns to his own concise but constructive message concerning the nature of the kingdom. He pronounces the kingdom as already active, present even where it is unacknowledged (Maddox, 1982: 134–136; Green, 1997: 629, 630 and note 53).

We proceed now to a more detailed discussion of the text, and first of all we try to unlock the meaning (in the Lukan context) of *meta paratērēseōs*, "with things that can be observed," one of the enigmatic expressions in the pericope.

It is found only here in the New Testament and, with the exception of a (later) occurrence in Aquila's translation of Ex 12:42, the noun *paratērēsis* appears nowhere in the Greek Bible (Stein, 1992: 437). One has therefore proposed to interpret the term in the light of Luke's use of the verb *paratēreō*, which does occur in Lk 6:7; 14:1; 20:20; and Acts 9:24. In each instance, the verb connotes a malicious watching directed at Jesus (or Paul). This proposal gains plausibility when we find the Pharisees as subject of the verb *paratēreō* on two of the four occasions (Lk 6:7; 14:1). The combination in Lk 11:14-32 of the motifs of hostile watching and signs from heaven—although the verb *paratēreō* does not appear—further supports this view. According to this proposal, then, *meta paratēreseōs* means "with malicious observation" (Carroll, 1988: 77, citing Farrell's Ph.D. Dissertation, 1972: 54–56).

This recognition of the nuance of hostility which colors the idea of "observation" in Luke-Acts should not be ignored. At the same time *Luke's* introduction of Jesus' saying with a question about the "When?" of the kingdom indicates that Luke understands *paratērēsis* along the lines of the Hellenistic usage of the noun denoting astronomical observation—that is, scanning the heavens for premonitory signs (Mussner, 1982: 107–111; Fitzmyer, 1985: 1160). The force of this first negative assertion about the kingdom would then be: God's kingdom does not come accompanying the search for signs that would announce its arrival. Lk 17:20 rejects all endeavors to forecast the advent of the kingdom of God by sign-watching. Lk 17:21a, "nor will they say, 'Look, here it is!' or 'There it is!'" brings geographical considerations into the picture. Jesus opposes not only temporal but also geographical pinpointing of the kingdom's arrival. The kingdom of God cannot be localized—except, that is, in its association with the figure of Jesus (verse 21b; Carroll, 1988: 77–79).

The *paratērēsis* in the sense of calculation (verse 20) is

contrary to the three comparisons (verses 24-30) with the lightning and with the unexpected catastrophes in the days of Noah and Lot, respectively, and also to the instruction in verses 31-35, which tells of, among other things, the man on the roof whom the sudden crisis does not allow to enter his house (Hartman, 1992: 1665).

Verse 21b appends a positive statement to the first two negations: "For, in fact, the kingdom of God is *entos humōn* [NRSV: 'among you']." The meaning of this much-discussed statement (see Carroll, 1988: 79 note 160) revolves around the sense of the preposition *entos*, which in the New Testament occurs only here and in Mt 23:26. The classical usage of *entos* is both spatial and relational; it indicates location within or inside certain limits, specified by the dependent genitive (Fitzmyer, 1985: 1160–1162). The meaning "within you" (NIV; see Stein, 1992: 438) falters on two impediments. First, nowhere else in Luke-Acts is the kingdom of God described as an inward, spiritual reality (Ringe, 1995: 222). Second, the object of the preposition (= the Pharisees) is incompatible with that reading, for Luke has portrayed the Pharisees in an increasingly negative light in the Travel Narrative (Fitzmyer, 1985: 1161). The context, the contours of Luke's view of the kingdom, and the presence of a plural object of the preposition combine to dictate the translation "among you" or "in your midst" (Craddock, 1990: 205; Danker, 1988: 292). The existence of something within the limits of a collectivity does not necessarily imply its presence inside the individuals who compose the collectivity. While *entos* with a plural object is uncommon in classical Greek, the reading "among" or "in the midst of" is attested (Carroll, 1988: 79 and note 160).

Jesus, then, issues in verse 21b a mandate to the Pharisees to look around them in order to discern the kingdom already at work in their midst (see Lk 11:20; Fitzmyer, 1985: 1159). In the light of verse 21b, the implied continuation of the saying is: "(Look! The kingdom of God is among you) *and you do not observe it.*" The kingdom of God is not discernible with the mode of observation practiced by the Pharisees (nor by the crowds in Lk 11:14-32).

The force of Lk 17:20-21 is to reject a particular strand of eschatological expectation, which searches for God's kingdom everywhere except where it is actually operative! The effort to pinpoint the date or locale of its manifestation misconstrues the nature of the kingdom. More to the point, because Jesus' hearers refuse to recognize the present activity of the kingdom in Jesus' teaching and healing ministry, they will not discern the future coming of the kingdom. How does this interpretation of verses 20-21 cohere with the general perspective on the kingdom of God in Luke-Acts (Carroll, 1988: 80)?

The complex picture of the kingdom in Luke-Acts has prompted a wide range of interpretations (see Carroll, 1988: 81 note 167). A distinct feature of the Lukan presentation of the kingdom is its association with verbs of proclamation. Fully one-fourth of all Lukan occurrences of the expression "kingdom of God" take this form (see Carroll, 1988: 81 note 168). This phenomenon leads Conzelmann to distinguish between the message of the kingdom and the kingdom itself. While the proclamation of the kingdom takes place in the present, after its initiation by Jesus (Lk 16:16), the kingdom itself remains a future entity (Conzelmann, 1960: 117, 122).

This two-sided image of the kingdom, as both present and future, is an aspect of the Lukan portrayal of the kingdom (E.P. Sanders, 1985: 150–156) that has evoked various explanations. Several scholars contend that the kingdom itself —not just its "picture" or "message" (Conzelmann)—is present in the person of Jesus: The presence of Jesus is the presence of the kingdom (Craddock, 1990: 205). Some go so far as to claim that Luke identifies the kingdom with the person of Jesus. After the ascension, Jesus would be present from heaven (as the enthroned king, so that the presence of the kingdom continues in the life of the Church (Carroll, 1988: 81 note 171). But the kingdom is not of human construction: "Do not be afraid, little flock, for it is the Father's good pleasure *to give you* the kingdom" (Lk 12:32).

EXCURSUS:

KINGDOM OF GOD: A SYMBOL FOR ASIANS?

The idea of God's rule, affirmed in various ways in the Hebrew Bible, reached its apogee in the New Testament. The expression "reign/kingdom of God" or "reign/kingdom of heaven" occurs more than 150 times in the New Testament and was, according to the Synoptic Gospels, the central focus of Jesus' preaching and ministry. Despite Jesus' frequent use of the symbol "reign/kingdom of God," he did not give it a clear definition. In summary form, it may be said that for Jesus the kingdom of God means the active presence of God his Father, inaugurated in his own life and death, which brought about a reign characterized by gratuitous forgiveness and reconciliation through universal justice and peace, in opposition to the anti-reign of division and hatred, injustice and oppression, and which calls for a radical conversion issuing in personal and social transformation.

The symbol of the kingdom of God as used in the New Testament poses many questions for a contemporary Asian theology. First, should the metaphors of king, kingdom, and monarchical reign continue to be used in speaking of God and God's rule? In the recent history of most Asian countries, experiences with emperors and kings have been by and large negative.

Second, Asia is the cradle of most world religions; presumably it is not difficult to convince Asians of the transcendent dimension of human existence. Rather, the challenge is to convince them that the reign of God demands not only individual conversion leading to salvation, but also that unjust and oppressive structures, both socio-political and economic, be removed and replaced with just and liberating structures.

Third, it has been argued that the addressees of the kingdom of God in the New Testament are the poor. In Asia the poor are characterized not only by abject poverty but also by their profound religiousness. How can the proclamation of the reign of God embrace both the poor and the religious?

Fourth, the New Testament presents the reign of God as a purely divine initiative and gratuitous gift (e.g., Lk 12:32). Many contemporary liberation theologians, however, insist that the gratuitousness of the kingdom is not opposed to but *requires* human action as response to God's free gift. How can this tension between gift and task be conveyed in an Asian context, in which salvation is seen to be the outcome both of pure grace from a compassionate being and of personal self-cultivation?

Fifth, one of the distinctive features of Jesus' understanding and practice of the kingdom of God is his opposition to the anti-kingdom. In proclaiming the kingdom of God to Asians, how can the forces of the anti-kingdom in Asia be identified and named? What liberating actions can and should the Christian Church undertake as an "option for the poor" so that the kingdom of God is truly "Good News" for the people of Asia?

Sixth, how can the final character of the kingdom of God be conveyed to Asians, who may believe only in limited salvation (e.g., Taoists, Confucianists, shamanists, and animists), or who may believe in absolute salvation—that is, the passing beyond all attachments into nirvana and the realization of emptiness? Furthermore, how can the personal nature of the union with God in the kingdom be maintained for Asians, some of whom believe that the self is illusion and that salvation is consequently the liberation of the self from the conditions of historical existence and personhood? (Phan, 2000: 21–22).

In reviewing the efforts of a number of Asian theologians, Peter C. Phan discerns the major contours, strengths, and weaknesses of an Asian "*basileia* theology" (Phan, 2000, 22–25). Tissa Balasuriya makes the kingdom of God the central symbol of his "planetary theology." For him "the most fundamental fact of Asia for Christianity and theology is human life itself. . . the struggle for life, which is the basic issue for the vast majority of Asia's massive and growing population." The answer to this challenge is Jesus' proclamation of the kingdom of God, since there is, according to Balasuriya, a similarity between Jesus' society and contemporary Asia: "Within a context of such deep-seated exploitation, Jesus presented a radical new teaching. He announced it as the 'kingdom of God.' In today's terminology we may say that he is speaking of a new person and a new society. . ." It is clear that Balasuriya is trying to translate Jesus' message about the rule of God into economic, political, and social terms and promote its implications for a social ethics.

Aloysius Pieris argues that the addressees of the kingdom of God in Asia are not only the economically and sociologically poor but also the religious, or more exactly, the poor who are religious and the religious who are poor. In Pieris' reading of the history of the Christian mission in Asia, the kingdom of God was not able to penetrate into Asia in the past because Christians failed to keep together the two poles of Asian reality, poverty and religiousness. To remain in Asia and to become a

part of Asia now, the kingdom of God must address together the religiousness of the poor and the poverty of the religious. This task is demanded not only by the peculiar situation of Asia but also by Jesus,
who, in Pieris' words, has undergone the double baptism of the "Jordan
of Asian religion" and the "Calvary of Asian poverty."

Whereas these two Sri Lankan theologians outline an Asian *basileia*
theology, a full-fledged version was elaborated in the 1970s by a group
of Korean theologians under the rubric of *minjung* theology. *Minjung* (literally, "the popular mass") refers to "the oppressed, exploited, dominated,
discriminated against, alienated, and suppressed, like women, ethnic groups,
the poor, workers and farmers, including intellectuals themselves." Ahn
Byungmu interprets the *ochlos* (the crowd) of Mark's Gospel to mean
the people who gathered around Jesus, i.e., the condemned and alienated.

Minjung theologians identify the *ochlos* of the New Testament with
the poor and oppressed Koreans throughout Korea's history, especially
during the colonization by the Chinese and the Japanese and under the
regime of Park Chung-hee. In the 19th century, Christianity was introduced into Korea not as the faith of the oppressing and exploiting colo-
nizers, as in many other Asian countries, but as a seed for liberation
from the Chinese and Japanese domination.

The *minjung* are thus the people of God or members of the kingdom
of God. Because of their prolonged unjust suffering, the *minjung* are weighed
down by *han*. *Han*, literally anger and resentment, is a mixture of many
things: a sense of resignation to inevitable oppression, indignation at
the oppressors' cruelty, and anger at oneself for allowing oneself to be
oppressed. These emotions, accumulated and intensified by injustice upon
injustice, can be a powerful source of psychological energy and an ex-
plosive potential for revolution if released in a socially organized way.

The process of resolving the *han* is called *dan*, literally cutting off.
On the individual level, it requires self-denial or renunciation of material wealth and comforts. This self-denial will cut off the *han* in our
hearts. On the collective level, *dan* can work towards transformation of
the world by raising humans to a higher level of existence. This process
consists of realizing God's presence in us and worshiping him, allowing
this consciousness of the divine to grow in us, practicing what we believe, and overcoming the injustices by transforming the world. Some
minjung theologians, especially Hyun Young-hak and the Korean femi-
nist theologians, advocate more traditional methods to release the *han*,
such as rituals, drama, mask dance, shamanism.

Minjung theology moves beyond both Balasuriya and Pieris by identifying the kingdom of God with a particular group of people. The *minjung*

are not only the addressees of the message of God's kingdom but constitute the kingdom itself. Jesus is identified with the *minjung*, and the various struggles for liberation in Korean history are identified as manifestations of the Jesus event.

However, some *minjung* theologians such as Suh Nam-dong find the symbol of the kingdom of God inappropriate. Suh draws a distinction between the kingdom of God and the millennium, between political messianism and messianic politics. According to Suh, the symbol of the kingdom of God has become abstract and other-worldly: it is the ideology promoted by dictatorial rulers practicing their "political messianism." On the contrary, the idea of millennium is concrete and this-worldly: it is the symbol of hope of the *minjung* in their "messianic politics."

For several years, C.S. Song, a Presbyterian Taiwanese, has been persistently advocating an Asian theology. The means with which to construct such a theology, Song suggests, are "imagination, passion, communion, and vision." The imagination is that in which we were created in God's image; passion enables us to feel the compassion of God in ourselves and others; communion makes us responsible for one another and for God; and vision perceives God's presence in the world and enables us to envision a new way of doing theology.

Among the immense and varied resources of Asia, Song privileges the personal stories of Asian people and their folktales, old and new. He believes that the most needed skill for Asian theologians is the ability to listen to the whispers, groanings, and shouts from the depths of misery of Asian humanity. This ability is the "third eye," that is, a power of perception and insight that enables theologians to grasp the meaning beneath the surface of things and phenomena.

Not surprisingly, Song grounds his theology of the reign of God in the message of the Hebrew prophets and the preaching of Jesus, especially the parables. From these sources he derives the conviction that salvation includes political and economic salvation. The God of the Hebrew-Christian faith, he says, is a "political God." "God's politics" means two things: it is a "politics against the barbarism of power," and it means that "the God of the prophets, and. . . the God of Jesus Christ, is a God who takes. . . the side of the poor against the rich."

Song is quick to point out that God's politics does not mean that Christians should replace secular power with another, perhaps sacred, power and government of their own to bring about the kingdom of God. Rather, "it aims at. . . the transformation of power. . . and in this transformation, or metanoia of power, is found the essence of God's politics."

God's politics which gives the people the power to challenge, criticize, and judge the abuses of those in power, naturally leads to what

Song calls the "politics of the cross." The politics of the cross does not dispense the people from organizing, becoming informed of the intricate power plays by which dictators seek to oppress and manipulate them, and employing the most effective means to achieve liberation.

The politics of the cross, however, does not mean weakness and ineffectiveness. Indeed, the powerless cross proves so powerful that throughout the centuries it has empowered countless persons to struggle for justice and freedom. It has encouraged them to use nonviolence, not just for tactical reasons but out of love, to carry the cause of the people to the court of rulers.

Song holds that "the vision of God's reign is like the magnifying lens that gives us an enlarged picture of life and the world as Jesus sees them and. . . as we must also see them." This vision of the reign of God as comprehensive inclusiveness and sociopolitical and economic liberation must, he insists, be rooted in the reality of the present world and must not be pictured as a purely eschatological event. Though the reign of God is God's deed, it needs eyewitnesses, people who sight it, identify it, and distinguish it from its counterfeits; and it needs people who embody it by their personal involvement in it. Like Jesus, people of today must bear witness in a situation of conflicts and struggle for freedom, justice, love, and life over against slavery, injustice, hate, and death.

Finally, it is important to note that Song does not forget that God's reign also brings forgiveness of sin and deliverance from demonic powers and that, after all, it reaches its fulfillment only in the eschatological resurrection. However, he hastens to add that the resurrection is not an event unrelated to what we are doing now (Phan, 2000: 22–25).

In the light of the theologies of the reign of God proposed by Asian theologians, Phan addresses the six issues raised by the symbol of the kingdom of God outlined above.

First, to preach and witness to the reign of God is the primary mission of the Christian Church, even in Asia. The first challenge to this mission is to convey the substance of the biblical message of the reign of God and to strip away the distortions of its interpretation that have accrued through history. One persistent distortion is in the patriarchal and authoritarian connotations attached to the symbol of the kingdom of God. For cultures heavily influenced by Confucianism, the dangers of patriarchalism and hierarchical authoritarianism, and correlatively those of blind obedience and preservation of the status quo, are particularly acute. In this cultural context it is vitally important to affirm the basic equality of all persons in the reign of God and to stress the prophetic character of the reign of God as well as the duty of speaking truth to power.

Second, Hinduism and Buddhism tend to foster disregard for and escape from the present world and everyday life, which is considered as illusion or suffering. Taoism's ethics of non-contrivance, and its insistence on the duty of following non-deliberate and non-purposive intuition or spontaneity in nature, society, and individuals may foster passivity in the face of evil and injustice. Confucian ethics focuses primarily on self-cultivation, though individual behavior is acknowledged to have an impact on social units such as the family and the state. To this apparent lack of social concern and ethical individualism, a Christian theology of the reign of God brings a message about the God who takes sides, about social justice and liberation, and about the necessity of overcoming oppressive structures, even by means of revolution as the last resort. Furthermore, it can help Asian religions retrieve potential for the social transformation of some of their teachings. Pieris has reminded us of the political and economic implications of the case of the Buddhist monk, who embodies in himself both religiousness and poverty. He is quintessentially one who has renounced mammon for religious reasons so that he may help the socioeconomic poor. With the former the monk achieves interior liberation from greed and acquisitiveness, and with the latter he brings about social emancipation from structured poverty imposed upon the masses. Similarly, in the light of the theology of the reign of God, Confucius's teachings regarding the "Mandate of Heaven" of the king, and the duty of the ruler to practice virtue to preserve the mandate of heaven, can be retrieved for the common good and social transformation. Confucius repeatedly emphasized the duty of the king to lead the people with virtue and propriety.

Third, because the vast majority of Asian people are both religious and poor, the message of the kingdom of God, if it is to become a life-giving truth not only *in* but also *of* Asia, must primarily address the religious poor. Furthermore, Christians should jettison the notion that they have a well-formulated and universally valid theology to teach the Asian religious poor and nothing to learn from them.

Fourth, it is in the experience of liberation that the gratuitousness of the kingdom of God can best be understood and lived. Once conscientized of their plight as the result of oppression, the poor will eventually make claim to what is rightfully theirs and will take part in actions that bring about their liberation. It is here that the theology of the kingdom of God will help confirm the poor's sense of gratuitousness of their liberation by showing them that they can achieve freedom and justice for themselves because God has taken their side first, because, as Song has argued, God is not neutral but has made "an option for the poor." Confucianism has widely been characterized as humanism engaged in moral self-cultivation, with its prescriptions for a good society based on virtue, just government, and harmonious human relations. The experience of liberation of the poor in the kingdom of God can convincingly show that human effort and divine grace are not mutually contradictory. In the kingdom of God as experienced by the poor, human effort and divine grace are not in inverse but direct proportion: the more human, the more divine; and the more divine, the more human.

Fifth, the message about the kingdom of God will be ethereal and abstract unless the signs of the anti-kingdom are clearly identified, named, and exorcised: those who continually seek to oppress God's people for personal (political and economic) gains, the pervasive patriarchal and androcentric social and moral system both in the Christian Churches and in many Asian countries, and the demons of sex tourism, cheap labor, and ecological destruction.

Sixth, and finally, the nature of salvation, which is the goal of the kingdom of God must be broached. Confucianism does not propose belief in a savior or a messiah who would bring supratemporal or transcendent salvation. Rather it acknowledges the importance of a good teacher who exemplifies his teachings in his own life and who, ideally, should also be a ruler, a sort of Platonic philosopher-king, in order to put his teachings into practice for the good of the state. Despite fundamental differences in their visions of what constitutes the ultimate happiness for humankind, there are many commonalities between Confucian and Christian construals of the "messianic age": common possession of earthly resources, good faith, universal love, care of the weak in society, justice, peace, work for the common good, and absence of evil. To this list of innerworldly blessings the Christian faith adds the personal union of humans with the triune God in grace as an essential element of the reign of God. But this union with the divine must not be viewed as something antithetical to or transcending the earthly blessings. Rather, the latter must be seen as "sacraments," i.e., instruments and signs of the personal union between humans and the triune God. In this way, the symbol of God's reign, though not identical with the Confucian utopia of the "great Unity," can find deep resonances or "tick resemblances" with what constitutes for Confucianists the ultimate happiness for humankind (Phan, 2000: 25–26).

b. The Coming of the Son of Man (Lk 17:22-37)

This section has a substantial parallel in Mt 24:26-27, 37-39, 17-18 (this piece is paralleled in Mark and presented in the Markan sequence of the earlier part of the chapter),

40-41, 28. A Matthean parallel is lacking for verses 22, 25, 28-29, 33 (but Matthew has a parallel to this last verse in Mt 10:39), 34, 37a (Nolland, 1993: 856–857).

In chapter 21 Luke records the apocalyptic discourse of Jesus which is prompted by questions about the destruction of the temple. In that discourse the end of the temple and the destruction of Jerusalem are historical events to which the discussion of the end of history and the coming of the Son of Man is tied (Mark 13; Matthew 24). In 17:22-37, however, Luke separates the parousia (coming of the Son of Man) from the fate of Jerusalem (Ernst, 1977: 487–488). This discourse is also free of references to cosmic convulsions and other signs of final travail. The questions and issues here have to do with the coming of the kingdom and the sudden parousia of the Son of Man (Craddock, 1990: 204).

Having answered the Pharisees' question about the coming of the kingdom, Jesus now addresses the disciples, instructing them about the day when the Son of Man is to be revealed (Fitzmyer, 1985: 1164). In Lk 17:22-37 the Pharisees have disappeared as conversation partners, and the disciples play that role instead. One gets the impression that Jesus realized his disciples could easily have misunderstood his words to the Pharisees. If the kingdom of God is in our midst, then is here and now all there is? Granted, some marvelous experiences have been made possible by the presence of Jesus: the poor, the maimed, the crippled, and the blind have found relief, but this has been but a beginning, the front edge, as it were, of the reign of God. So much pain, oppression, poverty, and grinding hardship remain: surely we will see its final eradication. Is there not to be a final consummation which has long been associated with the coming of the Son of Man? (Craddock, 1990: 205–206).

The topic is now the day(s) of the Son of Man. Verses 22-37 give instruction on that topic. First, in verses 22-23, Jesus predicts a future critical situation in which the audience is warned against heeding people saying "look here, look there." In verses 24-35 follow the reasons (*gar*) for this warning. After three comparisons of the coming day of the Son of Man with the lightning and with the days of Noah and Lot, respectively (verses 24-30), verses 31-35 add further admonitions concerning "that day" and "that night." Verse 36 in the traditional text is to be regarded as secondary. Verse 37, finally, adds a saying, introduced by an intervening question from the disciples, "where?" (Hartman, 1992: 1665 and note 9).

Verses 22-37 depict the "day" of the Son of Man as a sudden, inescapable, and ubiquitous invasion of the world to effect a final separation among people. The essential criterion of inclusion among the "saved" is single-minded readiness for the appearance of the Son of Man. In contrast, other persons are so absorbed in the routines of life that destruction overtakes them unawares (Carroll, 1988: 89).

Verses 22-23: (22) Then he said to the disciples,
"The days are coming
when you will long to see
  one of the days of the Son of Man,
and you will not see it.
(23) They will say to you,
'Look there!' or 'Look here!'
Do not go, do not set off in pursuit.

After the introductory setting of the problem through the Pharisees' question and Jesus' answer, verses 22-23 sketch the future situation of the disciples, that is, of the readers, when they will "long to see one of the days of the Son of Man" and the "look there" people will appear. The warning not to pay heed to them is explained (*gar*) by three comparisons. What do they tell the reader concerning "that day"? (Hartman, 1992: 1667; see below).

Verse 22, which is almost certainly from Luke's hand (Carroll, 1988: 92 note 210; Jeremias, 1980: 33: certainly verse 22a), presupposes a period of time of sufficient duration and difficulty that believers will yearn for "just one" of the days of the Son of Man. Some scholars hold that verse 22 presupposes a long time of waiting (Grässer, 1957; Carroll, 1988: 93 note 211). The phrase "the days are coming" ["days will come"] occurs also in Lk 5:35 and 21:6 and is a common designation in the prophetic literature for a future time of judgment and distress (Amos 4:2; Jer 7:32; 16:14, etc.; Fitzmyer, 1985: 1168; Ernst, 1977: 488). Such an era has come; it represents the past and present of Luke's community. The coming of the Son of Man has been eagerly awaited, yet has delayed (Carroll, 1988: 93).

The phrase "one of the days of the Son of Man" is not easy to understand and its meaning is disputed (Marshall, 1978: 658; Fitzmyer, 1985: 1168–1169; Bock, 1996: 1427–1428). Part of the problem is the fluctuation within this discourse between the plural "days" and the singular "day" (Green, 1997: 632) and the eventual transition to "night" in verse 34. The "day" (singular) seems to refer to what Acts 1:11 describes (i.e., the parousia of Jesus, even if Luke never uses that term). Then what is meant by the "days of the Son of Man"? A period? And what is "one of" them? Given the fluctuation in the passage, it seems likely that Luke has made "the days" of the Son of Man into a phrase to parallel "the days of Noah" (verse 26) and "the days of Lot" (verse 28), and that he has also introduced here his favorite expression "one of. . ." (Fitzmyer, 1985: 1168; for other explanations, see ibidem, 1168–1169; Ernst, 1977: 488; Kremer, 1988: 172; Stein, 1992: 438). "One of the days" appears to be an expression for "the first of the days" (see Lk 24:1; Acts 20:7, or the commencing of the End; Tiede, 1988: 301).

"You will long to see. . . and you will not see it." "You will not see," i.e., physically observe. These words indirectly allude to the first part of Jesus' answer to the Pharisees in verse 20d, "the kingdom of God is not coming with things that can be observed." The Lukan Jesus alludes to the longing of the evangelist himself and of his contemporaries, expressed in "your kingdom come" (Lk 11:2) and in "Maranatha" (1 Cor 16:22). In their eagerness for that day, they search high and low for signs of it. "And you will not see it," i.e., not that the disciples will not live that long or that it will never come, but rather that it does not come "by observation" (Fitzmyer, 1985: 1169; different, Green, 1997: 632–633) or in answer to a longing.

The clause "they will say to you" refers to the seduction to be proferred to disciples during the Period of the Church, "Do not go, do not set off in pursuit," i.e., do not have anything to do with such seduction; your salvation does not depend on such titillating declarations about the place where the revelation is to be made (Fitzmyer, 1985: 1169).

When hope is delayed, one is tempted to grasp at any straw: here the possibility that the Son of Man might have turned up in some remote place. A coming of this kind (with its evident similarity to the way that Jesus had been present as Son of Man in his historical ministry) is being rejected as a possible path to the fulfillment of the longing of verse 22 (Nolland, 1993: 859).

Verse 24:   For as the lightning flashes
              and lights up the sky from one side to the other,
              so will the Son of Man be in his day.

The image of lightning or meteorological phenomena in the Old Testament (e.g., Ex 24:15, 18) and Judaism (2 Bar 53:8-9) is tied to theophany (Geiger, 1976: 67), so that the figure suggests that the coming involves God acting on behalf of his people (Marshall, 1978: 661; Bock, 1996: 1429).

Verse 24 employs the metaphor of lightning for the Son of Man on his day. This image grounds the imperative of verse 23 not to stray after persons who localize the kingdom "there" or "here." That is, the saying assumes that the appearance of the Son of Man will be everywhere visible, even as lightning illumines the whole sky. There will be no mistaking the advent of the Son of Man in glory (Carroll, 1988:

89; compare Fitzmyer, 1985: 1170). The stress falls on the visibility of the coming (Plummer, 1901/1977: 407; Marshall, 1978: 661; Bock, 1996: 1429), not its suddenness (Ernst, 1977: 488: moment of surprise; Grässer, 1960: 170) or brightness (Leaney, 1958: 231). Visibility is the point, given the contextual emphasis on not needing to go and find the day when it comes (Bock, 1996: 1429). Exhortations to go somewhere to see a secret coming are deceitful and absurd and must be rejected (Stein, 1992: 439).

The comparison with the lightning obviously says that when the Son of Man comes, there will be no doubt. This is to be held against the "look there" people, and against the reader's temptation to replace the watchful hope with something more "objective." The comparisons with Noah's and Lot's days (see below) add that, to the majority, the day will come as an unexpected catastrophe, when the Son of Man is "revealed."

Verse 25:   But first he must endure much suffering
             and be rejected by this generation.

To the first comparison is added something of a parenthesis, "but first (that is, before the appearance of the Son of Man) he must endure much suffering and be rejected by this generation." Most scholars regard the saying as a Lukan insertion into Q material, with ties to Lk 9:22 (Zmijewski, 1972: 406–410; Geiger, 1976: 76 note 68; Ernst, 1977: 489). To the reader the Son of Man had not yet appeared like the lightning, and his suffering had occurred long ago. Was the effect of this statement that the reader was informed that in Jesus' days there were people who held Messianic ideas, represented also in Lk 19:11 and 24:21, not to mention Lk 17:29 (see also Acts 1:6)? That is, ideas which did not include that the Messiah had to suffer "before entering into his glory" (Lk 24:26). Jesus' suffering was a divine "must," belonging to the divine counsel (Ernst, 1977: 489); any idea of a glorified Messiah or of the Son of Man coming in glory presupposed that he had suffered and died (Lk 9:44; 18:31-33; 24:6-7; Acts 2:23-31; 3:18; 13:27-29; Hartman, 1992: 1667, 1668).

Therefore, verse 25 reassures Luke's generation that the divinely willed course of history has been proceeding according to plan: Jesus knew that his glorious parousia would have to wait. Nothing is amiss! At the same time, the note of warning is clear: for those who live during the "days before the day," aligning oneself with the Son of Man is everything (Carroll, 1988: 94). The phrase "this generation" has appeared earlier in Lk 7:31, echoing the portrayal of the people of God in the Exodus material as stubborn, stiff-necked, and rebellious, as people who resist God's purpose and God's representatives (Ex 32:9; 33:3; Deut 10:16; Lk 9:41; Acts 7:51-53; Green, 1997: 634).

Verses 26-27:   (26) Just as it was in the days of Noah,
                         so too it will be in the days of the Son of Man.
                 (27) They were eating and drinking,
                         and marrying and being given in marriage,
                         until the day Noah entered the ark,
                         and the flood came and destroyed all of them.

The Noah and Lot stories (verses 26-30) sharpen the above picture of the universal impact of the coming of the Son of Man, adding the hues of catastrophic judgment. In contemporary Palestinian Judaism Noah was known as a paragon of righteousness. In contrast to him, his contemporaries, not so upright, are introduced to describe "this generation" (verse 25). Verses 27 and 29 give emphatic final position to *pantas*:

                 Verse 27b: ". . . and the flood came
                 and destroyed all of them."
                 Verse 29b: ". . . it rained fire and sulfur from heaven
                 and destroyed all of them."

Verses 26 and 30 indicate that the advent of the Son of Man will have analogous effects (Carroll, 1988: 90).

Noah's and Lot's days are compared with the days of the Son of Man, and with the day of his revelation, respectively, for which the readers are supposed to long (verse 22). That for which they yearn is hardly the destruction of those others, but their own "redemption" (see Lk 21:28). Thus the three comparisons all confront the reader with the question of how to behave in order not to be overtaken unawares. Noah stands for righteousness (Gen 6:9), and Lot may be understood in a similar manner (Wis 10:6-9; cf. 2 Pet 2:7). So the comparisons should have an exhortative function over against the reader (Hartman, 1992: 1667–1668).

In spite of the proverbial wickedness of the people of Noah's day and of Lot's townspeople (see, e.g., Gen 6:1-8; 18:16-21; Schlosser, 1973: 13–36), such concerns do not at all seem to occupy center stage here. Eating, drinking, marrying, and giving in marriage (verse 27)—these are the stuff of everyday life and are not inherently wicked. To these are added commercial practices (verse 28), again not problematic in themselves. Though not intrinsically evil, within their immediate context these practices are deemed as potential diversions, potential distractions from the necessity of one's fundamental orientation toward the purpose of God (see Lk 8:14; 12:19, 29, 45; 14:18-20). Luke knows some of these activities as potential distractions from what human existence should be about (Fitzmyer, 1985: 1171). With these parallels from Israel's past, Jesus warns his followers about the dangers of the period before the End. This will be a time when life will be easily occupied with the everyday and the urgency of faith will easily be replaced with laxity (Green, 1997: 634–635; Stein, 1992: 439). The real danger is that we will continue to live our inoffensive everyday lives of middle-class propriety, closing our eyes to God's future (Schweizer, 1984: 277).

Verses 28-30:   (28) Likewise, just as it was in the days of Lot:
                      they were eating and drinking,
                      buying and selling, planting and building,

(29) but on the day that Lot left Sodom,
it rained fire and sulfur from heaven
and destroyed all of them
(30) —it will be like that on the day
that the Son of Man is revealed.

The Lukan Jesus refers to another Old Testament figure, Lot, in wording parallel to Lk 17:26-27a. Both passages use *kathōs* to state the comparison with the days of the Old Testament figure, and they share references to eating and drinking, but Lk 17:28 also refers to buying, selling, planting, and building. The new activities are laid out in two pairs (Zmijewski, 1972: 437–439). The portrayal of life's activity matches Gen 19:15-23 (Fitzmyer, 1985: 1171; Bock, 1996: 1431).

Verse 30 is likely to be a Lukan inspiration, pulling together the thrust of the two preceding similitudes. The language of "revealing" in this verse picks up on the language of "seeing" in verse 22: here will be the fulfillment of the disciples' longing. Luke sees deliverance as well as judgment imaged in these two similitudes: it is only when Noah and Lot have been taken out of the firing line that the others find that they have been left to the ravages of judgment. Verse 31 will develop this two-sidedness (Nolland, 1993: 861).

In "it will be like that. . ." the main comparison is not that the Son of Man's coming brings certain and horrendous judgment. While this may be true, the main point of comparison here is that it will catch people just as unprepared (Stein, 1992: 440; Bock, 1996: 1434).

The last of the three comparisons in Lk 17:24-30 ends in a reference to "the day that the Son of Man is revealed." The governing motif from verse 29 through the end of the passage is "the day." Lot was the son of Haran, brother of Abraham (Gen 11:27). Sodom was one of the "cities of the valley" (Gen 13:12) through which the Jordan River flowed. It was notorious for its pride, its consumerism, and its lack of concern for the poor and the needy (Ez 16:49). "Fire and sulfur" alludes to Gen 19:24. The Matthean counterpart of verse 30 makes a more explicit reference to the parousia of the Son of Man (Mt 24:39, using *parousia*).

The verb that Luke uses, *apokaluptetai*, is cognate to the noun (*apokalupsin*) employed by Paul in 1 Cor 1:7, when he refers to the "revealing" of the Lord Jesus Christ. Though Luke studiously avoids the word *parousia*, the verb used here is one of the reasons for thinking that he understands "the day(s) of the Son" as a reference to what other New Testament writers call the parousia (Fitzmyer, 1985: 1170–1171 passim; Bock, 1996: 1434).

Verses 31-33: (31)   On that day, anyone on the housetop
          who has belongings in the house
          must not come down to take them away;
          and likewise anyone in the field
          must not turn back.
       (32)   Remember Lot's wife.
       (33)   Those who try to make their life secure will
          lose it,
          but those who lose their life will keep it.

Lest one gain the impression from verses 26-30 that such daily routines are intrinsically problematic, Jesus goes on to use them for illustrative purposes in a way that disallows any such understanding. This issue does not revolve around who has belongings, labors in the field, sleeps at night, or works at the grinding stone. What is at stake is not whether one is engaged fully in the routinization of life. Rather, the question is whether, in the midst of life, one maintains a single-minded orientation toward the aim of God and its realization at the eschaton (Green, 1997: 635).

The day on which the Son of Man will be revealed (*apokaluptetai*, verse 30) will demand detachment from the things of this life, and it will do so suddenly, with no provision for hesitation, no opportunity for escape (verses 31-33). If one should find oneself on the rooftop—that is, the flat roof of the typical Mediterranean-area house, access to which was normally gained by an exterior staircase—when that day arrives, separated from one's belongings, then the wise course is to leave them behind, and to flee from the roof by the exterior staircase and leave directly, without entering the house itself to get belongings (Fitzmyer, 1985: 1172). If that day overtakes one in the field, then the attempt to return to the household from which one is separated will prove disastrous (verse 31). Lot's wife is the negative role model (verse 32); on such a day, to turn back (*eis ta opisō*) is to invite disaster. That day reverses the customary strategies of life preservation (verse 33); only those who are willing to leave life behind will find it. The parenetic force of all these sayings is that the eschatological perspective—the standpoint of the day of the Son of Man—forever rules out "business as usual." The disciples (Luke's fellow believers) are to live in such orientation toward the kingdom and away from the cares of life, that they will be ready —and willing—to abandon all on that day when the Son of Man comes. Only so will they live "into" the benefits of the consummated kingdom (Carroll, 1988: 90–91).

Lk 17:31-33 presents three admonitions concerning how it will be precisely "on that day." Of the three, the first two appear as concrete examples, one concerning a man on his roof and the other mentioning a man in the field; the first "must not" (third person imperative) enter his house, the latter "must not" return (also third person imperative). Both admonitions (or maybe only the latter) are in some way illustrated by a reference to Lot's wife: she should be remembered (second person imperative). The third admonition is held in a general key (*hos ean*). The three admonitions are actually very tightly held together: "anyone who is on the housetop. . . must not come down, and likewise anyone in the field must not turn back." Hereto is added asyndetically "remember Lot's wife," on which follows, also asyndetically: "those who make their life secure. . . ." On the other hand, the verses give a somewhat uneven impression; the clause on Lot's wife breaks the flow, and one may be uncertain how to relate it both to what precedes and to the following saying on securing and losing one's life.

When we ask ourselves which pictural value to assume for the admonitions not to enter the house or to return (verse 31), and how to relate this to the third admonition on securing and losing one's life, we start with the admonition which is addressed directly to the audience, i.e., both to the narrative audience and to the one in the reading situation, viz. "remember Lot's wife" (Hartman, 1992: 1668–1669).

"To remember" signifies more than a cognitive act in the biblical tradition, but is typically the precursory mental act leading to related activity. The admonition, "Remember Lot's wife" (see Gen 19:26), then, both interprets her action as the manifestation of an unwillingness to relinquish everything at the time of judgment and serves to warn Jesus' followers against similarly displaced values (Green, 1997: 635).

According to Gen 19:26, Lot's wife "looked back" (*epeblepsen eis ta opisō*) which is suggestive (but not more!) of Lk 17:31, "anyone in the field must not turn back" (*epistrephein eis ta opisō*). Some commentators suggest that the one who enters his house and the one who returns home do so because of attachment to earthly property (Marshall, 1978: 665; Schweizer, 1984: 275; Talbert, 1984: 167). Such understanding may have some support in the wording of the text: the first person has his "belongings" (*skeuē*) in his house and he enters in order to "take them away" and the second returns "likewise." Then one has to assume that this was the sin of Lot's wife. This interpretation need not, however, be the most natural. For the reader who "remembered" Lot's wife would not only recall her turning back but also that in the story of Genesis the angels told Lot: "Flee for your life; do not look back or stop anywhere in the Plain; flee to the hills. . ." (Gen 19:17). That is, the reader would realize that she disobeyed the command to the family and was not saved. In other words, the Lot story focuses on the same motif as the third, general admonition, viz. on saving one's life. Then it is a reasonable conclusion that the imagery of the two exemplary admonitions should be understood in the light of the generalizing saying on saving and losing one's life. This is at stake "on that day" (Hartman, 1992: 1669).

If somebody holds to the interpretation that Lot's wife must be remembered because she wanted to fetch the belongings from her house, then this should color the understanding of the saying on winning and losing one's life, i.e., one loses one's life through clinging to earthly goods. If, however, we let the Genesis context of the statement on Lot's wife together with the saving-losing saying determine the understanding of the two former admonitions, the accent becomes somewhat different. Then the fault of the man who enters the house and of him who turns around (or: returns home) is a hesitation which becomes fatal to their lives. A possible, coherent understanding of the three admonitions would then be that what is at stake is an obedient, unhesitating resolution, even if one's life appears to be endangered, because this is the life-giving resolution (Hartman, 1992: 1669–1670).

These admonitions can be understood in two ways by the Lukan reader. The exemplary admonitions are said to apply to how to act "on that day." A natural understanding of the instructions might then refer to some action to be taken on that very day, i.e., then one should act obediently and with resolution, even risking one's life. One may, however, be doubtful what the advice to perform such action might mean at the parousia. Commentators sometimes refer to the flight motif in Mk 13:14-20: one shall flee to the mountains when seeing "the abomination of desolation" (Ernst, 1977: allegorically interpreted; Marshall, 1978: 664: "precipitate flight," but taken metaphorically); note, however, that we read in Luke of a flight to the mountains when Jerusalem is besieged (Lk 21:20-21). The scope may, however, also be less precise in terms of time: the instruction concerns a way of resolute action, already in the present, but having "that day" in mind, which will occur as unexpectedly as the sinners were overtaken by the Flood and the rain of sulphur and fire. Earlier in the Gospel the reader has met a similar exhortation to show resolution: "No one who puts the hand to the plow and looks back (*eis ta opisō*) is fit for the kingdom of God" (Lk 9:62). Someone may feel that this interpretation rather reflects a will to make a knotty text more comprehensible by a modern mind than a natural understanding of Luke. But we suggest that the wider literary context in Luke 18 favors this understanding. Lk 9:23 and 21:34-36 also demand an attitude which corresponds to this choice (Hartman, 1992: 1670).

Verses 34-35: (34) I tell you,
   on that night there will be two in one bed;
   one will be taken and the other left.
(35) There will be two women grinding meal together;
   one will be taken and the other left.

Verses 34-35 assume a sudden and unforeseen intrusion of the eschatological day, rounding out the picture with a graphic depiction of the division effected by the eschaton. Of two men sleeping in a bed at night, one will be taken and the other left behind (verse 34). The night imagery should not be pressed, so that one concludes that Luke expects the parousia to occur at night (so, e.g., Strobel, 1961) or at the arrival of the Messiah on the night of Passover ("on that night"!; so Ernst, 1977: 491). It has been suggested that this "being taken up" (*paralēmphthēsetai*) connotes salvation conforming to the pattern of Jesus' exaltation (*analēmpsis*; Zmijewski, 1972: 505; Fitzmyer, 1985: 1172).

Of two women grinding at the mill, one will be taken and the other left behind (verse 35). Normally it took at least two persons to manipulate the ancient Palestinian mill, unless an animal was used. The preceding Noah and Lot allusions indicate that the fate of being taken away denotes rescue, while being left behind means destruction. When the Son of Man comes, an irrevocable division of humankind will occur. The provision provoked by Jesus' mission (continued by his followers) is set in concrete at the eschaton (Carroll, 1988: 91 and notes 205, 206).

Whereas that which is said concerning "that day" in verses 31-33 is openly admonitory, the saying concerning "that night" seems, on the surface, to be only foretelling: in the two pairs, one is to be "taken away," the other to be "left." But we are still under the spell of the three comparisons, and thus the reader easily realizes that the fates are similar to those told in the Noah and Lot stories: some are left, some are taken away. In addition, their activities are of the same everyday life type.

It is reasonable to assume that the cases adduced tell the reader something, and the commentaries suggest that this "something" is the division among people (Marshall, 1978: 667; Schneider, 1977: 357) or the suddenness of the judgment (Kremer, 1988: 173). But to the readers both possibilities should have the same effect: they should ensure that they belong to those taken away. Their affinity to this group is not the result of a lottery on that day, but—as in the cases of Noah and Lot—depends on being righteous, i.e., a concern for the present time (Hartman, 1992: 1670–1671).

[Verse 36: Two will be in the field,
        one will be taken and the other left].

Some manuscripts and ancient versions add this verse, which has traditionally been numbered. All the good Greek Lukan manuscripts, however, omit this verse. Moreover, it spoils the symmetry and was undoubtedly added to some manuscripts by assimilation to Mt 24:40 (Fitzmyer, 1985: 1173; Kremer, 1988: 173; Danker, 1988: 294; Ringe, 1995: 222; Bock, 1996: 1443).

Verse 37:   Then they asked him, "Where Lord?"
               He said to them,
               "Where the corpse is,
               there the vultures will gather."

Luke places in climactic position the enigmatic Q say-ing, "Where the corpse is. . ." (verse 37b; cf. Mt 24:28). By introducing this saying with the disciples' question, "Where, Lord?," Luke apparently connects the image of the carrion with the fate of those left behind. That is, persons not seized from their worldly existence and thrust into the benefits of the kingdom life will find destruction as certainly as the dead body is found by the vultures. The comparison sug-gests the certainty and universality of judgment for those who are not taken into salvation (Carroll, 1988: 91–92).

To anybody who does not read the text in a synopsis, the saying about the vultures, gathering to the body, is not automatically associated with the coming of the Son of Man in verse 24 which will be clearly as observable as the light-ning. The disciples of the text ask in terms reminiscent of verse 23, where people say "look there" to those who long for one of the days of the Son of Man. Are the disciples just depicted as stupid (Fitzmyer, 1985: 1173) so that they ask for the place of the coming of the Son of Man/the judg-ment/the kingdom of God? Or do they ask whither those taken away are brought (Zmijewski, 1972: 513–517)?

However the question is to be understood, it receives a restraining answer: there is no need to know anything about this in the present—and when the day comes, there will be no need for foreknowledge. The saying's semantic function is non-informative, in the sense that it refuses to give infor-mation on the topic introduced (Hartman, 1992: 1671).

From earlier times the Greek noun *aetos* designated the "eagle." There may be an allusion in this reference to "eagles" to the image of an eagle carried by the Roman armies: "Next (came) the ensigns (*sēmaiai*) surrounding the eagle (*aetos*), which in the Roman army precedes every legion, because it is the king and bravest of all birds" (Josephus, *Jewish War* 3.6, 2 # 123; Fitzmyer, 1985: 1173; Danker, 1988: 294; C.F. Evans, 1990: 633: "improbable"). The force of the proverbial saying is that two things belong inevitably together, or that to find the one you must look for the other; but, as often with such sayings, its application is enigmatic (C.F. Evans, 1990: 633; for the various interpretations of this saying, see Bock, 1996: 1439–1440).

Using a variety of images, Lk 17:22-37 presents the day of the Son of Man as an inescapable event, which will disrupt the normal course of things suddenly, ubiquitously, and unmistakably. It will mean a final separation of humankind by God, and only an alert manner of living oriented toward the eschaton will equip one for its onset. The urgent tone of this parenetic instruction is evident, but just when will this sudden arrival of the Son of Man occur? Apart from the necessity to be ready at any moment, does the discourse offer additional clues? (Carroll, 1988: 92).

Luke 17:22-37 urges the necessity of eschatological faith. The need to be expectant and ready is all the greater during a protracted time of waiting for the day of the Son of Man. Delay (the present experience of the Church) and the imminent expectation (the present obligation of the Church) go hand in hand. Living during the "days of the Son of Man," Luke and his community must be kept ready and waiting (Carroll, 1988: 94).

c. **The Parable of the Widow and the Unjust Judge** (Lk 18:1-8)

The kingdom of God or related themes are in the center of interest from Lk 17:20 and through Lk 18:31. This means that in the immediate context the reader encounters some further aspects of the kingdom of God, present and coming. Thus Lk 17:20-37 is followed by the parable of the Widow and the Unjust Judge (Lk 18:1-8) which is the climax of the former (Mattill, 1979: 89; Kremer, 1988: 174).

It is introduced by a sentence which tells the reader what kind of text is coming up (a parable), and what is its moral: one should persevere in prayer. The sentence forms a certain boundary to the preceding text, but does not really mark that which follows as a new episode, since there is no new action, no new place, no new constellation of characters, no new time. This soft dividing line is made even less divisive when the finale in Lk 18:8 asks: "And yet, when the Son of Man comes, will he find faith on earth?" Regarded within the theme indicated on the meta-level in Lk 18:1 it is not too far-fetched to assume that the faith sought is one expressed in faithful and steadfast prayer in the time when the disciple longs for the days of the Son of Man (Fitzmyer, 1985: 1181; Schneider, 1977: 362; Kremer, 1988: 174).

The similarity between Lk 18:2-5 and Lk 11:5b-8 has repeatedly been pointed out. Some have even spoken of twin parables, which Luke found together in his source, but which he separated to use at different stages of his Gospel (different: Binder, 1988: 13). The similarity of the two passages is indeed striking. Just as Lk 18:2-5 begins by focusing attention on the judge, who is also center stage in the parable's finale, so Lk 11:5b-8 focuses on the friend, and concludes with an observation about this friend. In both parables, therefore, the main character was originally the one petitioned, not the petitioner. This means that the main point of these parables was originally not (persevering) prayer, but rather that the one petitioned—God—will certainly listen. In both passages the central concept of "bothering" or acting importunately is expressed by the Greek verb *parechein*, Lk 11:7; 18:5 (found four times in Luke and five times in Acts, against once in Mark and Matthew). It is only because of the pre-Lukan or Lukan arrangement of the texts (Lk 18:1 in the case of the parable of the Widow and the Judge, and the insertion of the parable of the Friend at Midnight between the Lord's Prayer, Lk 11:2-4, and the admonition about asking, seeking, and knocking, Lk 11:8-9) that the attention goes now more to the petitioner (and to prayer; Binder, 1988: 13). It is not necessary to accept the opinion that the two parables originally formed a pair and that Luke or the pre-Lukan tradition separated them to use Lk 18:2-5 in its present context. But it may be interesting to note that Lk 11:1-13 and 18:1-14 seem to occupy parallel positions in the Travel Narrative (Bailey, 1980: 79–82).

Verse 1:   Then Jesus told them a parable
            about their need to pray always and not to lose heart.

Luke indicates the onset of this narrative unit with no change of scene, topic, or character, thus intimating its immediate connection to the preceding discourse (Lk 17:22-37). Jesus' audience remains the disciples, though his instruction is hardly privileged, since the Pharisees remain in the extended audience (though temporarily outside the narrator's focus—see Lk 17:20-21; 18:9). The possibility of "losing heart" was raised implicitly in Lk 17:22-37—wherein anticipation of a delay in the fulfillment of God's eschatological purpose is coupled with an experience of opposition to provide a setting for a loss of eschatological perspective and the concomitant growth of a business-as-usual attitude. "Lose heart" may be too passive a way to understand Jesus' concern that his followers not begin to behave remissly (Freed, 1987: 40); in any case, it appears in the context as the opposite of "faith" (verse 8b), itself manifest in deeds of faithfulness (Green, 1997: 638).

Verse 1 is clearly a Lukan introduction (Ott, 1965: 19; Zimmermann, 1977: 79; Binder, 1988: 12; Nolland, 1993: 866; Herzog II, 1994: 218; Reid, 1999: 290; for a detailed analysis, see Freed, 1987: 39–42). This statement directly concerns the nonappearance of the parousia (Conzelmann, 1960: 95–136; Talbert, 1984: 169), and any question that this is the case is answered by Luke's interpretation of the story in verses 6-8 (Hedrick, 1994: 187–188). The verse unequivocally states that the disciples' prayers are to offset cowardly resignation in the face of hazards they will run (see Lk 11:4b and 22:46).

The narrative aside in Lk 18:1 comments on the story by interpreting the parable for the reader. Fitzmyer notes that "the purpose of the parable as stated by Luke in this verse does not suit perfectly the thrust of the parable itself. . ." (Fitzmyer, 1985: 1178). Since this is the case the reader will mold the parable to fit the interpretation, rather than ignore the narrator's authority. The interpretation given by the narrator governs the way in which the reader will read the parable, which may explain why the narrator chose to provide the interpretation as the beginning of the parable, in the form of an aside, rather than wait until the end (Sheeley, 1992: 110).

It is increasingly recognized today that what has traditionally been labeled Luke's parable of the Importunate Friend (Lk 11:5-8) does not concern itself with persistence in prayer (for a comparison of the two parables, see Ott, 1965: 23–31). For the purpose of the present argument it is enough to note that, depending upon whom the quality of "shamelessness/ boldness" is referred to, the petitioner or the householder, this parable deals with either the faithfulness of God in hearing prayer, or the confidence with which the praying disciple may approach God, or both (Marshall, 1978: 465). All suggestions that the parable would be first of all about "persistence" in the interpretation are unwarranted. Luke is not teaching that one may bend God's will by first bending his ear. Prayer offered repeatedly enough is no more guaranteed to effect the desired result than prayer offered faithfully enough (Crump, 199: 131; Hendrickx, 2000: 115–119).

Having once eliminated ideas of persistence from the interpretation of Lk 11:5-8 it becomes even easier to see them as rightly excluded from the interpretation of the parable of the Persistent Widow and the Unjust Judge. The concern over "justice" (verses 3, 5, 7, 8) and the anticipated-yet-delayed retribution (verses 4a, 7-8) indicate, first of all, that the scope of this instruction concerns perseverance amidst oppression; it does not offer generalized teaching on all petitionary prayer (Zimmermann, 1977: 94). Secondly, Luke's introduction (verse 1) is therefore concerned with bolstering belief in the value of prayer itself, not enjoining repetition of the same prayers over and over to achieve a desired end. Luke uses *ektenōs* (Lk 22:44; Acts 12:5) to refer to "persistence." *Pantote*, which we find here, answers the question "How long?" by replying "All the time." The repetitive approach to prayer has already been made by the oppressed, without success (verse 7). Indeed, it is the fact that repeated prayers for justice are not immediately answered (verse 7) which gives the parable its pastoral relevance. According to Luke, the timing of God's will does not ignore the disciples' prayers, but it is established independently of such prayers. It is the crisis of faith which may result from this collision between divine sovereignty and a naive belief in the immediate efficacy of persistent prayer that elicits Luke's exhortation to "pray always and not lose heart" so as to "be found faithful" by the Son of Man (verse 8). Thus the parable of the Widow and the Unjust Judge not only does not teach that God's intentions may be immediately influenced by persistence in prayer, but it actually addresses the pastoral problems which may result when persecuted Christians approach God with just such ideas about prayer in mind. The parable promises that God does answer prayer, but also warns of the dangers inherent in believing that prayers offered often enough will invariably be answered as and when requested (Crump, 1992: 131–132).

Although Luke says that the parable is about praying always, the story itself appears to be about obtaining justice through perseverance. With his introduction, however, Luke intimately links prayer with the relentless pursuit of justice. Both are constitutive of Christian ethics. Jesus' followers are to sustain both a personal relationship with him in prayer and to bring that to expression in their deeds. Another way this is often expressed in the Third Gospel is "hearing and doing the word of God" (Lk 6:27, 47; 8:15, 21; 11:28; Reid, 1993a: 286).

The contrast to prayer is to "lose heart." The Greek verb *egkakeō* is used in an unusual sense in the New Testament. Etymologically it is made up of *eg-* ("in") and *kakeō* ("[behave] badly"). Properly *egkakeō* means "to behave badly or remissly in" as, e.g., in "they culpably neglected to send aid." Usually, *egkakeō* is used to signify "to be faint-hearted, lose heart, grow weary." In Lk 18:1 it may have the sense of becoming so weary that one behaves badly (Spencer & Spencer, 1990: 43).

Verse 2:   He said,
             "In a certain city there was a judge
             who neither feared God nor had respect for people.

The parable proper is contained in verses 2-5 (Ott, 1965: 21; Zimmermann, 1977: 81; Reid, 1993a: 284). It is a surprising story in which, according to many scholars, a model of unrighteousness is used to speak indirectly and by contrast of God. Of course he yields to pressure (verse 5), but to suggest that this means that believers must bang on heaven's door until God relents is to miss the point (see also the "shameless friend" in Lk 11:5-8; Tiede, 1988: 304–305).

The reader knows nothing about this judge or about the city in which he administers justice. He is simply "a certain judge" (*kritēs tis*). What must a reader think about this figure to make his role in the story sensible? It is probably not a Roman court setting, since the judge is apparently not removed from plaintiffs and defendants but is readily and regularly accessible. Little is known of the administration of justice in Palestine during the time of Jesus. Generally the Romans did not interfere in the internal administration of provinces and vassal states but allowed them to conduct their own affairs with the least possible intervention.

Derrett describes two different "judicial" systems in Palestine: what he calls "customary" law courts (i.e., religious courts in which pious Jews brought a complaint before pious judges) and "administrative" courts (i.e., courts of the ethnarch/ tetrarch and governor that assisted in the maintenance of law and order, applying the ordinances that came from the political authorities and overseeing the collection of revenues). In other words, there were the "synagogues" with their "rulers," on the one hand (customary), and the "authorities" with their "kings" and "governors," on the other (administrative; cf. Lk 12:11 and 21:12; Derrett, 1971-1972: 180–186). The royal administration of Herod the Great proceeded on the basis of "administrative" divisions in the country, down even to the level of the villages. The Romans later divided the province of Judea into eleven administrative toparchies, small states or districts of a few cities or towns (Josephus, *Jewish War*, 3.54–55). Derrett concludes that the widow in the story had taken her case before a civil court (Derrett, 1971-1972; compare Plummer, 1901/1977: 41; disputed by Price, 1996: 197–198). Indeed, characterizing the judge this way better fits such a situation than assuming that he was a religious leader administering the "customary" law (Hedrick, 1994: 1993–1994).

Lk 18:1-8 is one of the few parables of Jesus where the word "God" is mentioned (Via, 1976: 4–5). The clause, "who neither feared God nor had respect for people" (see Freed, 1987: 42–43) is quite obviously important since it is applied to the judge in the story not once but twice, once by the narrator (Lk 18:2) and once by the judge himself in a soliloquy (Lk 18:4). Most commentators take the expression as a negative description. For example, Marshall describes the judge as "corrupt" (Marshall, 1978: 672), and Scott says, "for the judge neither to fear God nor to have respect for men (sic) makes him without honor, shameless. In a dyadic society this is a severe description, for in essence it describes a person outside the bounds of society, who is determined by no significant other, whether God or man (sic). He is an outlaw judge" (Scott, 1989: 180). Both Marshall and Scott derive this rather severe view of the judge from a series of Hellenistic parallels. All but two of these are derived from the Greek and Roman traditions, and are quite similar, though not identical, to the expression in Luke's story. Josephus also describes King Jehoiakim ("Joakeimos") as "unjust and wicked by nature; he was neither reverend toward God nor kind to man" (Josephus, *Antiquities* 10.83; Tiede, 1988: 305). These expressions have a "formulaic" character in that they seem to be a standard way of discrediting someone. The present expression is, therefore, a piece of stock rhetoric (Danker, 1988: 294). With the exception of Josephus (who does not use the language of Luke), none of Wettstein's examples come from a Jewish setting, and other examples in Jewish texts are elusive (Hedrick, 1994: 195).

The expression "fear of the Lord" is a technical expression in Jewish literature (and in Luke probably because of the Septuagint); it would have been heard in a pious Jewish context as meaning the judge was an impious or irreligious man who made no pretense of following the Torah. That is somewhat different from "corrupt" or "shameless." Nor should one automatically assume that it is equivalent to "immoral." Further, Luke's use of the term elsewhere suggests that he understands its use here as meaning this judge gave no evidence of traditional religious piety. A person who "feared the Lord" would have expressed that piety in concrete ways as did Cornelius (Acts 10:2, 22, 35; cf. 13:16, 26). But the judge was not "religious" in the sense of traditional Jewish piety (Hedrick, 1994: 195).

Verse 3:   In that city there was a widow
            who kept coming to him and saying,
            'Grant me justice against my opponent.'

The widow in the Old Testament is a typical symbol of the innocent, powerless oppressed (see Ex 22:22-23; Deut

10:18; 24:17; 27:19; Job 22:9; 24:3; Isa 10:2, etc.; see also Spencer & Spencer, 1990: 50–51). In the Hebrew scriptures and ancient Judaism widows were accorded privileged status by the devout Israelite. He saw God as the protector of widows. Hence it was clear to the pious Jew that the God who protected widows expected that his people would, following his example, also give them preferential treatment. The description of the divine judge and the widow in Sir 35:13–18 quite probably was common knowledge in the time of Jesus (and Luke). One discovers a number of important parallels in word and thought from the text, which is dated in the second century B.C.E. (Young, 1998: 55–56; Nolland, 1993: 865–866).

Widows were regarded as a special protected class and were to be treated differently from other women (Hedrick, 1994: 197; Ringe, 1995: 224). Isa 1:17 calls on the rulers and the people to "learn to do good; seek justice, rescue the oppressed, defend the orphan, *plead for the widow*." Then, in verse 23, we are told, "Everyone loves a bribe and runs after gifts. They do not defend the orphan, and *the widow's cause does not come before them*." In our parable the widow is the embodiment of the poor and unjustly treated (Kremer, 1988: 174). The Jewish legal tradition required that on the basis of Isa 1:17 "the suit of the orphan must always be heard first; next, that of the widow. . ." Thus the woman of the parable had legal rights that were being violated. She had neither a protector to coerce nor money to bribe (Plummer, 1901/1977: 412). It has been suggested that a debt, a pledge, or a portion of an inheritance was being withheld from her (Jeremias, 1963: 153). The issue is clearly money because, according to the Talmud, a qualified scholar could decide money cases sitting alone (Bailey, 1980: 133).

But the widow in Lk 18:1-8 is not exactly powerless. She persistently makes her complaint in a courtroom until justice prevails. Her portrayal departs from the stereotypical or traditional picture of widows as poor, defenseless women

(Praeder, 1988: 56). The parable (verses 2-5) is indeed about the granting of justice (Ringe, 1995: 124; Spencer & Spencer, 1990: 47). Although most present-day readers may not see any incongruity, Jesus' first audience would have been startled at the thought of a woman arguing her own case in court. Such a duty would ordinarily have been assumed by her nearest male relative, who would have taken responsibility for her at the death of her husband. This may have led the audience to assume that her complaint was against the very man who should have been her protector (Reid, 1993a: 284; 1999: 289).

The widow "kept coming" to the judge. The imperfect tense (*ercheto*) stresses that this was not a single request; rather, she had made numerous requests; she "kept on" coming to him with her petition. This is a persistent and repeated action (Freed, 1987: 45). The image of the widow's continual requests created by the imperfect tense is reinforced in Lk 18:4 with the judge's equally persistent rejection of her plea (*ouk ēthelen epi chronon*, "for a while he refused"; Hedrick, 1994: 198). The widow's resource is not power or property but legal persistence. She knows her rights and how to exercise them (compare Ruth 4; Benjamin, 1990: 216). It is ironical that a person of such helplessness in her society should turn out to be a figure of power (Via, 1976: 25).

The parable thus far makes three assumptions. First, the widow is in the right (and is being denied justice). Second, for some reason, the judge does not want to serve her (she has paid no bribes?). Third, the judge prefers to favor her opponent (either the opponent is influential or has paid bribes). Some scholars surmise that the widow's opponent may be a powerful citizen whom the judge did not want to alienate (Ryan, 1987: 353). In biblical stories the widow's opponents are always those who deprive defenseless people of their land and children (compare Ruth 1:1-22; Benjamin, 1990: 214).

Yet there is a crucial element in the parable that has

gone unnoticed. Ordinarily women in the Middle East do
not go to court. The Middle East was and is a man's world
and women are not expected to participate with men in the
pushing, shouting world described in several descriptions of
court cases (compare Green, 1997: 640; Reid, 1999: 289).
There is, furthermore, Jewish evidence from talmudic times.
Tractate Shebuoth reads: "Do, then, men come to court, and
do not women ever come to court? . . . —You might say, it
is not usual for a woman, because 'all glorious is the king's
daughter within' (note Ps XLV, 14; the king's daughter [i.e.,
the Jewish woman] is modest, and stays within her home as
much as possible)." In the light of this reticence to have
women appear in court one could understand her presence
here as meaning that she is entirely alone with no men in
an extended family to speak for her. This may be the assumption of the story. In such a case her total helplessness
would be emphasized (Bailey, 1980: 133–135). But in the
end it must be noted that most of the particular assumptions frequently made about the legal and personal circumstances involved here, play no real role in the dynamic of
the story (Nolland, 1993: 867).

Verses 4-5:   (4) For a while he refused,
                   but later he said to himself,
                   'Though I have no fear of God
                   and no respect for anyone,
              (5) yet because this widow keeps bothering me,
                   I will grant her justice,
                   so that she may not wear me out
                   by continually coming.'"

The judge is unwilling to heed the widow's demands
to act against her opponent. Matching her persistence, he
resists (the imperfect *ēthelen* answers the imperfect in verse
3: *ērcheto*), at least "for a while" (*epi chronon*). "Though I
have no fear. . ." introduces a concessive clause: "despite
the fact that." How long he holds out is unclear (*epi chronon*
could mean a rather long time). This indication of time is

important for the further development of the story because it motivates the persistent coming of the widow mentioned in verse 5. But it is even more important as opposite of "quickly" (*en tachei*) in verse 8a (Zimmermann, 1977: 84). Speculation about why the judge refused is misguided, since this is a parable and not an actual incident. The judge refused because the storyteller wanted him to (Stein, 1992: 445).

The transitional phrase *meta tauta* (literally, "after these [things]," found nine times in the Lukan writings [Freed, 1987: 47]), signals a major shift in the narrative's action (Fitzmyer, 1985: 845; Spencer & Spencer, 1990: 51–52). It focuses the reader's attention on the judge's soliloquy (Young, 1998: 58–59) —as transition to a separate and distinct element of the narrative. Hence the judge's soliloquy takes place apart from the nagging demands of the widow. Not only is he alone with his thoughts in this moment, he is away from the irritation that drove him to ponder his situation (Hedrick, 1994: 199, 200). The story thus far has set us up for a failure of justice, but in verse 4 we are prepared for a surprising development (Nolland, 1993: 868).

The translation "bothering" for *parechein. . .kolpon* fails to do justice to the sense of physical debilitation conveyed by the expression (Green, 1997: 640 note 92). The woman's constant badgering was actually "wearing him down" physically. She was (by this expression) considerably more than a "bother" or minor annoyance: her persistence had begun to drain his energies (Hedrick, 1994: 200).

The expression here translated "wear [me] out" (*hupopiazō*) is borrowed from the boxing ring for a blow under the eye (cf. 1 Cor 9:27) and has led many commentators to suggest that the judge is fearful lest the woman get violent (Linnemann, 1966: 185; Hedrick, 1994: 200). The narrator does not portray this widow as acting in a violent way, only in a way that departs from her culturally scripted role. The notion of violence derives from the judge, who may inter-

pret her persistence as an act of violence against the system
(Schottroff, 1995: 104). In fact, the language does not require the interpretation which suggests physical violence, and
the cultural milieu of the Middle East excludes it. The widow
can shout all kinds of insults at him, but if she tries to get
violent she will be forcibly removed and not allowed to return. Derrett argues that the term *hupopiazō* means "to blacken
the face" (Derrett, 1971-1972: 189–191). He correctly observes that the phrase is common throughout the East. However, it means "to destroy the reputation of" and describes
people with a sense of personal honor which they are anx-
ious to preserve. But our judge has no such personal honor.
Derrett observes this objection and tries to defend his interpretation by suggesting that the phrase "have no respect for
anyone" is really a compliment offered to an impartial judge.
Against Derrett, Bailey argues that "I have no fear of God
and no respect for anyone" is clearly meant as a double-
edged negative statement, not part compliment and part insult
(Bailey, 1980: 136; Catchpole, 1977: 88–89; Green, 1997:
639). What the judge wills is not the widow's vindication
but to get rid of her (Via, 1976: 14).

Verse 6:   And the Lord said,
              "Listen to what the unjust judge says.

With regard to verses 6-8, opinion is divided among scholars between those who see these verses as Jesus' own interpretation and those who read them as the interpretation of
the early Church (Binder, 1988: 14–15). With Bultmann,
many scholars have regarded the opening phrase of verse 6,
"And the Lord said," as an attachment formula providing a
transition from the parable (verses 2-5) to the sayings in
verses 7-8 (Bultmann, 1963: 175; Nolland, 1993: 869). Verse
6 may be either a Lukan editorial comment calling attention to the following interpretation of the parable or, ex-
cluding "and the Lord said," be part of the parable itself
(Stein, 1992: 445).

The absolute use of *ho kurios* ("the Lord") is out of step with the narrative flow and is a sign of later interpretation. Calling Jesus "Lord" is a post-resurrection insight that has been retrojected into the time of Jesus' earthly ministry (Zimmermann, 1977: 88; Reid, 1999: 291). When the Lukan Jesus, "the Lord," speaks, he interprets the parable with three distinct comments (Lk 18:6, 7-8a, 8b). First, in verse 6, he tells his hearers/readers, "Just listen what the judge of unrighteousness says!" The phrase may be translated as "the unjust/unrighteous judge" indicating that he is unjust, but this judge is not just personally unjust. He is actually adjucating "injustice" rather than justice (see also "the manager of unrighteousness" = "unrighteous manager" in Lk 16:8). That is how the word of the "mammon of unrighteousness" (Lk 16:9) works (Tiede, 1988: 305).

The injunction "listen" (*akousate*) reminds us of the injunction at the beginning of the parable of the Sower: *akouete* ("listen"; Mk 4:3) and of the "eschatological call" at its end (Mk 4:9; compare Lk 8:8; Zimmermann, 1977: 88).

Verses 7-8a: (7) And will not God grant justice to his chosen ones who cry to him day and night?
Will he delay long in helping them?
(8a) I tell you, he will quickly grant justice to them.

The second comment states that God's reign of righteousness is the exact contrast, and the Lukan Jesus develops the contrast in verses 7-8a. Verses 7b-8a constitute a unity of thought. This is supported by the analogy found in Baruch 4:25, "My children endure with patience (*makrothumēsate*) the wrath that has come upon you from God. Your enemy has overtaken you, but you will soon (*en tachei*) see their destruction and will tread upon their necks" (Schneider, 1975: 74). The widow could not get prompt justice, but the two questions in verse 7 indicate that God's elect will not receive such disregard. The text introduces a straightforward analogy between the widow of the parable and God's "chosen ones who cry to him day and night." (Binder, 1988: 18). This is consistent with the portrayal of the widow Anna in Lk 2:37, who worshiped in the temple with fasting and praying "night and day" (compare the characterization of exemplary widows in 1 Tim 5:5 as those who continue in prayer "night and day"). The idea of "the elect" (i.e., God's chosen ones) is traditional in the Old Testament and early Christianity (see, e.g., Deut 4:37; 7:7; Pss 77:31; 88:3; Isa 43:20; Rom 8:33; Col 3:12, etc.). Here Luke designates as the elect those who adopt the manner of this widow caught in unjust circumstances; on the strength of this metaphor, "crying out to God" must be correlated with practices consistent with the dogged pursuit of justice (Green, 1997: 642).

(For the different interpretations of verse 7c, "Will he delay long in helping them?," see Ott, 1965: 48–54). The word translated "delay" in the NRSV (*makrothumei*; for an extensive discussion, see Catchpole, 1977: 92–101; Zimmermann, 1977: 89–90; Binder, 1988: 19–20; Spencer & Spencer, 1990: 59–61) could also mean "to be forbearing" or "to be patient" (see Danker, 1988: 295), but the issue is how "long" they must endure injustice. The close parallels with Sir 35:18 (35:19 LXX) suggest that this may be a traditional phrase, but then the issue is still that God will not delay. And verse 8a confirms that the point of the whole is that God will deal speedily to vindicate those who cry out in prayer (Tiede, 1988: 306).

The parable finds its application to God's action on a "how much more" basis, that is, an argument from lesser to greater: now we are dealing with the judgment of God, not with an unjust judge; now we have the elect ones to whom God is pledged, not a widow who is unknown to the judge (Kremer, 1988: 174). It is more than likely that an eschatological vindication is intended, even without the specifically eschatological setting provided by verse 8b and by the larger Lukan structure (Nolland, 1993: 869).

God will "quickly" (*en tachei*) grant them justice. *Tachos* is a noun signifying "swiftness and speed." In the plural *tachos* refers to "velocities." *Tachos* can refer to quickness of temper or apprehension. The adjective *tachus* also signifies quickness of motion as opposed to *bradus*, "slow." *Tachus* is usually translated in the New Testament "quickly, without delay" or "soon, in a short time" (Spencer & Spencer, 1990: 62; Binder, 1988: 21 refers to Sir 27:3, "If a person is not steadfast in the fear of the Lord, his house will be quickly [*en tachei*] overthrown"). Which of the two meanings is to be preferred? Scholarly opinion is divided over the matter, but "soon" seems to be preferable (Mattill, 1979: 91–94).

Verses 6-8a give reassurance to those who may grow weary in their daily pursuit of justice. Justice is rarely achieved instantly but demands a commitment that can seem to drag on endlessly. The judge expected that the widow would hurt him verbally or even physically before long. But the parable illustrates the achievement of justice by nonviolent persistent presence and vocal demands (Reid, 1993a: 286).

Verse 8b: And yet, when the Son of Man comes,
              will he find faith on earth?"

The third comment turns the whole discourse back to the coming "day of the Son of Man." No, the faithful need not fear that God will delay or disdain their petitions. Heroic efforts are not necessary to catch God's attention, even in prayer. The problem of "losing heart" (verse 1) or "losing faith" before the day of the full public revelation of God's judgment is the real issue, and the reason why people must continue in prayer. God will never fail or be distant, but the elect must pray that their faith not fail (see Lk 22:32, 40; Tiede, 1988: 306).

The verb *heuriskō* ("find") occurs eighty times in Luke-Acts as compared with Matthew, twenty-seven; Mark, eleven; and John, nineteen. *Pistis* ("faith") occurs twenty-six times in Luke-Acts, against eight in Matthew; five in Mark, none in John (Mattill, 1979: 89).

The final question appears to be almost an aside to the disciples, or, more precisely, an aside from Luke to his community. God's timing is different from that of the seeker (Reid, 1999: 291), and the passing of time with no glimmer of the longed-for days may be threatening the persistence of the Church's prayers. The widow's untiring pursuit of justice is translated into the "faith" that should mark the Church's welcome of the awaited Son of Man (Ringe, 1995: 224).

The concluding future Son of Man saying in the form of a question ("when the Son of Man comes, will he find. . ?") is best illustrated by the conclusion of the apocalyptic discourse, "Be alert at all times, praying that you may have the strength to escape all these things that will take place, and to stand before the Son of Man" (Lk 21:36). The phrase "on earth" in Lk 18:8b indicates the arena of the Son of Man's activity and authority at the end time (Praeder, 1988: 69).

The urgency of Jesus' question about faithfulness resides in the fact that it finds its sharpest expression in a discourse aimed at his own disciples, and even more so because Luke relates Jesus' question without reference to a particular group of people: Will this sort of faith be found on earth? In this way, Jesus' warning about persistence in the face of injustice speaks at all times, everywhere, to all, until the coming of the Son of Man (Green, 1997: 643).

Lk 18:1-8 can be considered a parable about today's bureaucracy and red tape, bribery of people in administration and venality of judges. The widow is simply the injured party in our society, the person who cannot succeed because she or he lacks the things which give people a real chance: money and connections, influence and power, health and charm (Hendrickx, 1986: 231). In the Bible, the widow (and the orphan) stand for the defenseless, and therefore, if we want to "apply the biblical texts to today's situation," we should first establish who in the situation we are dealing with are the defenseless. Most of the time we will come to the conclusion that many if not most of the defenseless are not widows, whereas we may at times encounter situations in which we tend to say, "God help those who fall into the hands of this widow!" This should warn us for the complex character of applying biblical texts to today's situation.

The widow in the parable is not unlike the widows and mothers of Argentina who, for twenty years have continued their weekly march in the Plaza de Mayo in the heart of Buenos Aires. Every Thursday afternoon they still gather to demand investigation into the "disappearance" of their husbands and sons during the military regime of the 1970s. So far they have succeeded in discovering the fate of about one-third of the men. Luke's first conclusion in Lk 18:6-8 affirms that God rewards unflagging petition, day and night, with justice.

The story is one of hope. Followers of Jesus have, by their attitudes and actions, the power to transform not only individual situations but unjust structures as well. This power rests with people who persist in prayer and undaunted action for justice. Like the widow, these people are more likely to be found in low positions than in high places (Reid, 1993a: 286–287).

Most commentaries on the parable turn instinctively to the character of the judge as the figure who reveals something about God (but see Via, 1976: 4: "the judge is not an image of God"). All of them struggle to make sense out of the parable, because the judge clearly does not reflect what we believe about God's hearing and responding to the cries of the poor. But there is a far simpler way to understand the parable. It is the widow who is cast in the image of God and who is presented to the disciples as a figure to emulate. When the widow is seen as the God-like figure, then the message of the parable is that when one doggedly resists injustice, faces it, names it, and denounces it, until right is achieved, then one is acting as God does. Moreover, it reveals godly power in seeming weakness. The persistence of one apparently powerless widow achieves the victory for right:

the power of one! Followers of Jesus are invited to take up this same stance: to draw on the power of apparent weakness to overcome death-dealing powers (Reid, 1999: 294).

ENTERING THE KINGDOM LIKE A CHILD
(LK 18:9-30)

The toll collector lacks any claim upon God but calls upon his mercy and is heard (Lk 18:9-14). Children are free from all the barriers that adult self-importance and self-sufficiency place between an individual and the approach to the kingdom of God, so the kingdom of God is for them and for those who will become childlike (Lk 18:15-17). While the commandments retain their validity as the path to life, in the presence of the call of Jesus, there must also be a radical turning away from security based upon the possession of material resources. But no one will be the poorer for giving anything up for the kingdom of God (Lk 18:18-30; Nolland, 1993: 872).

a. The Pharisee and the Toll Collector *(Lk 18:9-14)*

The parable of the Pharisee and the Toll Collector is usually thought to be the last of the exemplary stories peculiar to the Third Gospel (Bultmann, 1963: 178–179; but its status as exemplary story is contested by a number of scholars; see Schlosser, 1989: 275–278). The parable is traditionally called either the parable of the Pharisee and the Tax Collector or the Pharisee and the Publican, both of which are misnomers. It has been shown that the *telōnēs* of the parable is a toll collector, not a tax collector (Donahue, 1971; Herzog II, 1994: 173). Whereas most commentators tend to link the parable to the preceding context, specifically Lk 18:1-8, as two parables about prayer, some relate it to the following (e.g., Bossuyt and Radermakers, 1981: 400–401; Hedrick, 1994: 208).

The story proper consists of only Lk 18:10-13. What is meant by "story proper" is the self-contained narrative that shows the actions of the Pharisee and the toll collector in the temple. Usually a redactor intervenes most extensively at the fringes of the traditional unit, at the beginning and at the end. This is verified in the present pericope (Schlosser, 1989: 273). Lk 18:9 is clearly not a part of that fictional "world." It belongs to the agenda and world of the Lukan Jesus, and as such is part of a literary frame telling the reader how Luke wants the story to be read (for details, see Jeremias, 1980: 272–273). Lk 18:14b is also not a part of the fictional world of the story. Rather it is a traditional saying that Luke uses as a moralistic interpretation of the story. By means of this introduction and conclusion Luke places the story in the context of a later rabbinic debate as to which type of person should be ranked over the other: the nominally righteous or the penitent. Luke's sympathy is decidedly with the penitent in this regard (Lk 18:14a). The status of Lk 18:14a (i.e., is it part of the fictional story or part of Luke's conclusion?) is problematic. Most commentators never address the issue directly, but simply assume that Lk 18:14a is the original conclusion of the historical Jesus (Donahue, 1988: 187; Fitzmyer, 1985: 1183; Bailey, 1980: 154–155; Talbert, 1982: 170; Gourgues, 1997: 233). Others take Lk 18:14a as part of Luke's conclusion and hence do not regard it as a saying of the historical Jesus (Crossan, 1975: 82; Scott, 989: 97).

Most interpreters of Lk 18:9-14 have tended to view the parable as one which is based on a representation of the actual practice of Pharisaism in Jesus' day. According to this interpretation, the point of the parable was to criticize the flawed piety of Pharisaism, represented by the Pharisee, and to show how true piety functions, as seen in the actions of the toll collector. While I. Howard Marshall concedes that the portrait of the Pharisee is "slightly overdrawn" it is nevertheless "drawn from life. . . Jesus is attacking the Pharisaic religion as it was, not an exaggeration of it" (Marshall, 1978: 677–680). For Fitzmyer, the Pharisee is "a type or representative of faithful Jewish observers of Mosaic regulations" and Luke "scarcely caricatures the Pharisaic type" (Fitzmyer, 1985: 1186–1187). The important implication of this interpretation is that Jesus brings a new way of approach to God in contrast to the flawed status quo represented by the Pharisees (Neale, 1991: 167).

Jewish interpreters have understandably been less enthusiastic about the summarily negative representation of Judaism implied in this interpretation of the Pharisee in Lk 18:9-14. C.G. Montefiore, for example, has called the Pharisee a "caricature." More recently, other commentators have expressed a similar view that the Pharisee of this parable is a "caricature" (e.g., Schottroff, 1973: 439–461; Tiede, 1988: 307; Downing, 1992: 80–99; Ringe, 1995: 225; Holmgren, 1996: 253; McBride, 1999: 182; disputed by Schnider, 1980: 42–56; Schlosser, 1989: 285; Gourgues, 1997: 241–242). This interpretation is, in Neale's view, the correct one and is fully consistent with the way he has suggested that Luke uses the Pharisees for the purposes of telling his Gospel story, but he also introduces some nuances to the use of the term "caricature" (Neale, 1991: 167–168, 172–173). The "historical" Pharisees have not been in evidence so far in the Third Gospel and this remains true with regard to this parable.

The first response to Jesus' story about two men who went up to the temple to pray is, "I am certainly glad that I am not like those Pharisees." But that is exactly what the Pharisee said about the toll collector! What did Jesus really desire to communicate when he told this example story? The parable of the Pharisee and the Toll Collector frequently is interpreted in a way which vilifies the Pharisees but extols the preeminence of Christianity over Judaism. Is this what Jesus wanted? The original message of Jesus is lost when we as Christians give praise to ourselves that we are not like the Pharisees. The obvious problem with an understanding that sharply contrasts Judaism and Christianity emerges from the drama of the parable itself. As a result, we as Christians ironically behave in a manner nearly identical to the dramatization of the Pharisee in the parable. In Luke's words, we trust in ourselves that we are righteous and despise others (Lk 18:9). As a result of our religious bias, we allow the first-century context of the parable to fade from view (Young, 1995: 181–182).

The parables of the Persistent Widow and the Unjust Judge and the parable of the Pharisee and the Toll Collector appear on the surface to represent a pair of simple instructions for effective prayer for different categories of people. Those whose cause is legitimate have only to persist in prayer for it (Lk 18:1-8). Sinners have only to throw themselves on God's mercy and not try to make excuses or seem better than they are (Lk 18:9-14). On a deeper level, though, both prayers bring the attention of Luke's readers back to the issue of justice. The widow is granted justice in her case, and the toll collector returns to his home "justified" (Lk 18:5, 14a; in Greek, as in English, the two words share a common root). Both verdicts are portrayed as coinciding with God's will, and both fly in the face of the judgment of the judge and the Pharisee, who are locked into the system of social and economic competition and the hierarchy of honor and prestige that favor the dominant classes in their society. In both parables, prayer is about the reversal of the rules of those systems, as the concluding proverb confirms (Lk 18:14b; see also Lk 14:11; Mt 18:4; 23:12; Ringe, 1995: 225).

Verse 9:   He also told this parable
             to some who trusted in themselves
             that they were righteous
             and regarded others with contempt:

The audience shifted from the Pharisees back to the disciples in Lk 17:22, but the parable of the Pharisee and the Toll Collector is directed "to some who trusted in themselves that they were righteous and despised others." The pattern of switching audiences back and forth from the disciples to the Pharisees suggests that the Pharisees are the ones primarily addressed here (Neale, 1991: 170; compare York, 1991: 72). But the text itself which has "some" is vague. The persons who are thus identified can belong to the crowd, to the disciples (Danker, 1988: 296; Tiede, 1988: 307; Heininger, 1991: 209; different: Joji, 1997: 474: "some" certainly refers to the Pharisees), or to Jesus' opponents (Gueuret, 1989: 291; Holmgren, 1994: 252). The possibility that Luke focused his discussion on a problem within his own church should not be too quickly dismissed (C.F. Evans, 1990: 642). His own church, like every other institutional church, faced the possibility of reading the gospel in a way which encouraged pride in personal piety and its concomitant tendency to see people who are not obviously *inside* to be *outside* God's chosen people (Doble, 1996: 113).

Luke's editorial construction inevitably leads the readers of the parable, as opposed to Jesus' listeners, to judge the Pharisee before the parable begins, a judgment that Luke repeats in his editorial conclusion in verse 14b, "for all who exalt themselves will be humbled, but all who humble themselves will be exalted." The portrayal of the Pharisee in the parable is not restricted to Pharisees as a group (Green, 1997: 646)— hence the power of the parable—but the Pharisees have come to represent those attributes and are the paradigm for others having the same traits (Fitzmyer, 1985: 1185; Gowler, 1991: 266). Although the description seems to fit the historical Pharisees, they were not the Pharisees, for Luke would not have had the Pharisees in mind. Lenski saw the group being addressed as either having the Pharisaic spirit or followers of Jesus who are still affected by that spirit (Lenski, 1964: 899). The address was directed not only to the contemporaries of Jesus but also to Christian disciples (Fitzmyer, 1985: 1189; Tan, 2000: 287). We should emphasize that Luke's purpose is not to condemn a particular group but to warn against a particular attitude in light of the present and impending reign of God (Green, 1997: 646).

The adverb "also" connects the parable with that of the Widow and the Judge (Green, 1997: 645), while the adjective "this" highlights their distinctiveness. The point and audience of each parable are different. The Greek word for "rely" is *peithō*, allied with the noun "faith" (*pistis*), which comes from "to bind." The transitive verb signifies "to persuade," "to make friends of." The intransitive verb signifies "to trust, have confidence, obey, rely on." A warrior can rely on armor, and without it is defeated (Lk 11:22). In effect, *peithō* in Lk 18:9 has the sense of trusting or having confidence in oneself so as to rely on oneself (Gourgues, 1997: 235). Luke specifies exactly which kind of self-reliance Jesus has been discussing, "that they were righteous." Jesus here disparages not so much self-reliance in general but a very specific type of self-reliance, relying upon oneself for righteousness. Luke carefully explains the audience of this parable as "the ones relying upon themselves that they are righteous and despising the rest (*tous loipous*)." Relying and despising are participles indicating that these people continue regularly to rely and to despise (Spencer & Spencer, 1990: 64, 65, 66).

Verse 10:   "Two men went up to the temple to pray,
             one a Pharisee and the other a tax collector.

Jesus does not use the sex-specific term "male" (*anēr*), but the generic term "human" or "person" (*anthrōpos*). However, in Lk 18:13 the masculine pronoun is used for the toll collector. Moreover, very few women would ever become Pharisees because women were exempt from studying the law. Jesus speaks generically of two men because what he says is true of men and women (Spencer & Spencer, 1990: 67).

These two people "went up" to pray in the temple because the temple was built on a hill, Mount Zion. Jerusalem
itself, built on a plateau 2500 feet above sea level, was sur-
rounded by hills, forcing people to go up to Jerusalem (see
Ps 125:2; Lk 10:30). Although it is not explicitly stated,
one may surmise that the Pharisee and the toll collector
went to the temple to pray during one of the three times of
daily prayer, where the prayer of the people "ascended up"
to God in conjunction with the offerings of the people. The
morning prayer was shortly after sunrise at the time of the
burnt offering. It included the *Tefillah* (benedictions) and
the *Shema* (Deut 6:4-9; 11:13-21; Num 15:37-41). The
afternoon or ninth hour of prayer (3:00 P.M.) included only
the *Tefillah*. The evening or sunset prayer included the *Tefillah*
and the *Shema*. A priest would announce these three hours
of prayer by blowing the *shofar*, a ram's horn, which was so
loud it could be heard as far as Jericho, over 10 miles away.
These two people came up to the temple to pray at one of
these three times (Spencer & Spencer, 1990: 69).

The construction, "one a Pharisee. . . the other a tax
collector,"—which indicates an antithesis (see Heininger, 1991:
210–211)—is significant for the way it sets two already well-
defined images in stark ideological contrast. The phrase could
not be more economically expressed, yet it brings together
all that Luke has been developing in his story in a single
parabolic confrontation (Neale, 1991: 171; compare Gueuret,
1989: 297–300). Luke often works with "extremes": first and
last, humble and prideful, poor and rich, insider and outsider. In the present parable, the same contrast of extremes
occurs, namely, the comparison between the very religious
Pharisee and the very sinful toll collector. We are dealing
here with hyperbole. The hyperbolic nature of Jesus' parable makes us aware that we are not to take the story literally (Holmgren, 1996: 253).

The Pharisees were devout lay people very influential in
daily life. The original audience listening to the story did

not consider the Pharisee to be a stereotype of the self-righteous hypocrite. A Pharisee in the mind of the people of the period was far different from popular conceptions of a Pharisee in modern times (see further Young, 1995: 183–189; compare Doble, 1996: 113–116). "Pharisees" is a Greek transliteration (*pharisaioi*) of the Hebrew *perushim*, "the separated ones." They obtained ritual purity by separation from uncleanness and unclean persons.

The *telōnēs* or toll collector was the highest local bidder for the right to collect indirect taxes. Roman censors were appointed every four years to collect the direct taxes or *tributum*. They delegated the collection of provincial taxes to *publicani*. However, the *publicani* would farm out to private citizens the collection of indirect taxes for a prescribed locale. For instance, Zacchaeus was the controller of customs for the Jericho area (Lk 19:2-10). Most toll collectors were detested by Jews and other nationalities as well. They were considered robbers and robbers of the worst type. They robbed their own people by selling their services to a foreign oppressor. They were robbers and traitors (Spencer & Spencer, 1990: 69, 70-71). Luke's picture of the toll collectors (*telōnai*) is complex, concentrated in a few passages (see Doble, 1996: 116–118).

The setting of the parable in the temple precincts is important because the temple was the primary place where the redemptive media of Palestine were institutionalized. Together with the Torah, which provided ideological support for the role of the temple and spelled out the nature of obligation to it, the temple dominated the life of the people of the land, whether they lived in Galilee or Judaea. Indeed, the temple's ideological reach extended throughout the Diaspora, as the collection of the temple tax from every observant Jewish man so clearly indicated (Herzog II, 1994: 178; compare McBride, 1999: 182–185).

During Jesus' time, Palestine was under a heavy burden of taxation. Imperial Rome exacted tribute from Judaea directly through its colonial bureaucracy and, in Galilee, indirectly through their client, Herod Antipas. The poll tax and the land tax were the two primary taxes collected by the Romans. The purpose of taxation was not social well-being but enhancement of the position of elites. In addition to collection of direct taxes, Roman occupiers and internal Jewish rulers alike collected a vast array of indirect taxes in the form of tolls, imposts, duties, tariffs, and so forth. Because the collection of direct taxes was in the hands of the social elites and their hirelings, and because the process was protected by the military power of the state, tax collectors, whether Roman or Jewish, would live beyond the reach of most popular hostility, though they would be hated nonetheless. In his investigation of the relevant terms for officials participating in the system of exacting tribute, Donahue (1971: 53) noted that the Talmud could waver in its evaluation of tax collectors but not in its estimation of toll collectors, who were universally despised. Toll collectors, who actually staffed the booths and cheated the public on behalf of the chief toll collectors or toll farmers whom they served, were visible and socially vulnerable. On them fell the full force of popular resentment toward the whole oppressive system in which they were but minor functionaries (Herzog II, 1994: 180).

Roman taxation was not the sole burden in the land. Temple taxation was equally oppressive, although it was mystified and represented in the form of religious obligation. Twelve different taxes are prescribed in the Torah. The total on agricultural produce was between 21 and 23 percent. Given the fact that most peasant farmers existed at the subsistence level, the sum total of religious obligations levied upon the people was nothing short of enormous. But the temple authorities were not about to lessen the burden and forfeit their privileges. The temple system was no less oppressive than Roman occupation, but the combination of the two systems of tribute produced a crisis among the peasant population base (Herzog II, 1994: 180–181).

Understood in this context, the parable of the Pharisee and the Toll Collector is "the parable of the two toll collectors." Like the toll collector who is a functionary in the Roman system, the Pharisee is a retainer in the temple system. Through the network of synagogues, the Pharisee and his faction participated in efforts to enforce the collection of tithes, but their major role was ideological, as reflected in their polemics and rhetorical efforts to persuade. The Pharisee's emphasis on tithes in his prayer indicates his role in sanctioning tithes and placing them at the center of the requirements for ritual purity (Herzog II, 1994: 182).

Verses 11-12:   (11) The Pharisee, standing by himself,
                        was praying thus,
                        'God, I thank you that I am not like other people:
                        thieves, rogues, adulterers,
                        or even like this tax collector.
                 (12) I fast twice a week;
                        I give a tenth of all my income.'

The phrase *statheis pros heauton tauta proseucheto* can (note the repeated *pros: pros heauton. . . proseucheto*; Gueuret, 1989: 292) be translated several ways (Hedrick, 1994: 217-218; Schlosser, 1989: 282–283; Heininger, 1991: 214–215). A definite conclusion cannot be reached, but some of the possible readings are: "prayed thus with himself" (RSV; Schweizer, 1984: 281), "prayed thus about himself" (Fitzmyer, 1985: 1182), "stood by himself" (Bailey, 1980: 142), "he took up a prominent position" (Jeremias, 1963: 140). The phrase cannot mean that he prayed silently, as custom required him to pray aloud (C.F. Evans, 1990: 643). The emphasis, whatever the translation, should be upon his accentuation of his piety in contrast with his opinion of the toll collector (Donahue, 1988: 76–77; Gowler, 1991: 268 note 186).

"Others" (*hoi loipoi*) in verse 11 corresponds to the "others" (*tous loipous*) of verse 9. According to some commentators, the comparison of the "other people" to the toll collector (*ē kai hōs houtos ho telōnēs*) shows that the toll collector is presented as exceeding and embodying all the qualities of impiety already listed (Neale, 1991: 173). But it is not clear how the narrator intends the toll collector to be understood in connection to this list (for a discussion, see Hedrick, 1994: 221–222).

In the Hebrew scriptures the custom of fasting played a significant role in the religious life of ancient Israel. Fasting was a custom whereby one deprived oneself of food for a limited period of time, humbled oneself, repented, prayed, and hoped that God would be moved by this display of repentance, self-humiliation, and physical self-deprivation so as to act differently toward the individual/nation. According to Torah, only one fast day a year was required: the Day of Atonement (Lev 16:29, 31; 23:27-29, 32; Num 29:7). But other special days of fasting were observed through the years (Hedrick, 1994: 222–223).

According to Torah, a tithe, or a tenth of the produce of one's fields, seed, grain, wine, oil, and the firstborn of herds and flocks was required (Deut 14:22-23). Torah did not require tithing of garden herbs, however. The Pharisees in Jesus' day apparently, however, tithed even herbs (Mt 23:23), though it was not required for all herbs. Later the general rule evolved that one must tithe "whatever is used for food, and is kept watch over and grows from the soil." The Pharisee in the story apparently does not concern himself with exceptions and specifically claims that he pays tithes on everything he acquires (*ktōmai*)—with no exceptions (Hedrick, 1994: 223, 224).

The Pharisee's direct definition of the toll collector reinforces the initial description of him by the narrator. The Pharisee places the toll collector in the same category as extortioners (*harpages*), the unjust, the adulterers. The speech of the Pharisee, of course, does not carry much weight, and readers may even be amused at the Pharisee's pious words contrasting himself with such sinners. Jesus—whose voice has utmost authority and reliability—had already informed the reader that the Pharisees are "full of greed [extortion]" (*gemei harpagēs*, Lk 11:39). Thus the Pharisee's words in this parable are almost entirely vacuous (Gowler, 1991: 267).

The Pharisee stands and prays in the temple, and his lengthy prayer—in contrast with the toll collector's shorter prayer—is filled with first-person singular verbs. In fact, the prayer contains five first-person verbs: "I thank," "I am," "I fast," "I give," and "I get" (Gowler, 1991: 268; Holmgren, 1994: 254). After (routinely?) addressing "God," he says five times "I." One may get the feeling that this is not a prayer, but the expression of a "one man mutual admiration society" or "spiritual navel gazing"!

But the "I have—I have not" prayer of the Pharisee is grounded in the covenant relationship and in liturgies that illustrate the nature of this relationship. For example, Deut 26:1-15 describes a ritual that a farmer is to perform in harvest time. The farmer is to take a portion of the first harvest of grain, bring it to the sanctuary, and present it to the priest who is to place it before the altar. Following this act, the farmer is instructed to give witness concerning *what God has done* (verses 5-9) and to confess his gratitude for what God has given him (verse 10). By the same token, *the farmer is to give witness of what he has done or not done* as a responsible member of the covenant community:

> I have removed the sacred portion out of my house, and moreover I have given it to the Levite, the sojourner, the fatherless, and the widow, according to all your commandments which you have commanded me; I have not transgressed any of your commandments, neither have I forgotten them... I have obeyed the voice of the Lord my God, I have done according to all that you have commanded me (Deut 26:12-15).

The repeated use of "I have" and "I have not" in the above confession makes us somewhat uncomfortable; they appear to be the words of a self-satisfied person. But such is not the case. The confession is not a free prayer of the individual; it is a part of a liturgy that takes place when the worshiper brings to the sanctuary an offering from his harvest. In addition, it is important to observe that before the farmer speaks of what *he* has done, he witnesses to God's initiating grace:

> A wandering Aramean was my ancestor; he went down into Egypt and lived there as an alien, few in number, and there he became a great nation, mighty and populous. When the Egyptians treated us harshly and afflicted us, by imposing hard labor on us, we cried to the Lord, the God of our ancestors; the Lord heard our voice and saw our affliction, our toil, and our oppression. The Lord brought us out of Egypt with a mighty hand and an outstretched arm, with a terrifying display of power, and with signs and wonders, and he brought us into this place and gave us this land, a land flowing with milk and honey. So now I bring the first of the fruit of the ground that you, O Lord, have given me (Deut 26:5-10).

Following these words, which praise God for his goodness, the worshiper speaks about himself, that is, about himself as a responsible community member or covenant partner of God. The worshiper stands before God, and in this holy moment he speaks to God of the kind of person he is. He confesses that he has done what God expects of him; he has been sincere and responsible. It is likely that these words were spoken in the presence of a priest and a congregation made up of neighbors. This latter part of the liturgy, which focuses on what the worshiper has or has not done, underscores the teaching that God will receive offerings only from persons who are responsible members of the covenant community. The worshiper is to be identified, must step forth as an individual from the congregation to be seen by all. The liturgy in Deuteronomy 26 rejects anonymous gifts to God. When an offering is brought to the sanctuary, it is expected that the giver will stand up and affirm a partnership with God that is expressed in a humane lifestyle and in specific deeds.

Religious words and religious experiences can easily lose their meaning and become a means of self-promotion. The perversion of something good is well known to each of us. It happened in ancient times and it occurs yet today. The Pharisee in the parable typifies (in the mind of Luke) one for whom sacred confession has become a means of exalting self and demeaning others. The form of the confession found in Deuteronomy 26, and elsewhere, may easily be transformed from a confession before God to self-congratulation. With this parable, the Lukan Jesus joins with the prophets and rabbis in condemning such posturing, and the story concludes with a threat directed at those who exalt themselves (Holmgren, 1994: 257–258).

What is so terrifying about our Pharisee when we look at him attentively is that he errs in the very process of trying to be pious. He had the right name for God. He avoided greed and adultery, the overpowering of others economically or sexually. He gave of his time and his wages to God's work. He was aware of the need for holiness. Basically, he remembers God's covenantal laws without remembering God. His prayer, although perfect in form, was not directed to the God who sees and rewards in secret (Mt 6:6; Spencer & Spencer, 1990: 76). Instead of taking the high road of Deut 26:12-15 and remaining on the level of thanksgiving, the Pharisee feeds on his own virtues and makes odious comparisons (Danker, 1988: 297).

The Pharisee's outward form of religious piety was not acceptable to God because of the attitude of his heart. Like the prophets before him, Jesus teaches that sacrifices are not enough in the absence of true heartfelt devotion to God. God desires worship from the heart.

The Hebrew word *kavanah* means the intention or true desire of one's heart. Literally it refers to direction. Often the term means concentration. The supreme importance of *kavanah* in the prayer life of the people is emphasized in Jewish literature. The application of the parable of Jesus must be studied in the light of *kavanah*, namely, the direction of one's heart. In the Jerusalem Talmud, the sages of Israel discussed the duty of each individual to recite the *Shema*, "Hear O Israel, the Lord our God, the Lord is one." The rabbis taught that it is not enough just to repeat the words. The intention of the heart is of paramount significance. They taught, "The recitation of the *Shema* must be accompanied by the intention of the heart (*kavanah*)." The word *kavanah* denotes concentration; it refers to heartfelt sincerity. The words of the Jewish rabbis, that a person must "direct his or her heart to God in awe, fear, trembling, and quaking," make the meaning of prayer in Hebrew thought clear. The sincere intention of the heart is needed (Young, 1995: 191, 192).

Verse 13:   But the tax collector, standing far off,
                would not even look up to heaven,
                but was beating his breast and saying,
                'God, be merciful to me, a sinner!'

The toll collector "stands far off (*makrothen*). But is he far away from the Pharisee (Plummer, 1901/1877: 418)? From others praying in the general vicinity (Donahue, 1988: 189; Bailey, 1980: 152–153)? From the altar? From the temple itself (Linnemann, 1966: 60)? The fact is, it is unclear what the narrator is using as a point of reference for the measurement of distance. It is unlikely, however, that the toll collector is standing "far away" from the Pharisee and other worshipers, since the toll collector is near enough for the Pharisee to recognize him as a toll collector and to refer to him as "this" (*houtos*) toll collector (i.e., over here, near) rather than "that" (*ekeinos*) toll collector (over there, i.e., afar; Hedrick, 1994: 225–226).

If the Pharisee is a caricature, can the same be said of the toll collector? Certain aspects of the portrayal of the toll collector are also exaggerated for effect. Indeed, the very selection of the toll collector for the role as the repentant counterpart to the Pharisee is an indulgence in caricature for the narrator of the parable. The whole juxtaposition of the Pharisee and the toll collector is, in itself, something of a parody. But the toll collector differs from the Pharisee in that his actions commend themselves to the reader as being the more appropriate way to address oneself to God in the temple; common sense demands a verdict in favor of the toll collector (against Linnemann, 1966: 60). The reader may even respond to the parable by proclaiming, "The tax collector—it is I!" (Schottroff, 1973: 453). It is not "logical judgment" which adjucates the decision but "understanding" (Schottroff, 1973: 441–442; Neale, 1991: 176–177).

The Pharisee's speech is longer than the account of his actions in the parable (Schlosser, 1989: 281: "bref élément narratif"), but the situation is reversed with the toll collector. The more lengthy account of the toll collector's actions contains the key to the parable's portrayal of the characters (Tolbert, 1979: 76–77; Gourgues, 1997: 239). The fact that he stood "far off" is a description of physical environment that clearly displays his humble attitude. The toll collector also refuses to lift his eyes to heaven, and he beats his breast in sorrow (see Lk 23:48). The man's prayer is terse and brutally honest with not one first-person singular verb (Gowler, 1991: 268). If the Pharisee says, "God, I thank you...," the toll collector says, "God, be merciful to me."

The difference between the Pharisee and the toll collector was the *kavanah* of their hearts. As a Jewish theologian, Jesus calls each individual to a genuine heart-controlled relationship with God. The beauty of the story is seen in the image of the toll collector. God's grace cannot be earned. Even a wicked toll collector is accepted by God when he cries out for divine mercy. It is the same for both the religious and the unholy. Both are needy but in different ways. God loves the toll collector. He loves the Pharisee. But no matter how sinful or impious the individual may appear in the eyes of the good religious people, God's favor possesses no limitation. He loves the toll collectors and the sinners. His grace is given to everyone who directs his or her heart to God in sincere prayer (Young, 1995: 193).

Genuine religion, however, is threatened not only by the "works program" of the Pharisee but also by "tax collector theology." It is not healthy or helpful to go through life with eyes to the ground, hands striking the breast, and crying out, "God be merciful to me a sinner!" This portrayal of the toll collector, like that of the Pharisee, is hyperbole; nevertheless, it may speak to us of the danger of a "one-note" theology. People who go about lamenting their sinfulness may manage, at times, to slide away from responsibility for their actions because, as they say, "We are only sinners saved by grace." Approached in this way, religion becomes too simply the celebration of God's grace, which is an emotional substitute for the call to do what is found in the teaching of the prophets and Jesus (Holmgren, 1994: 259).

Verse 14a: I tell you,
            this man went down to his home justified
            rather than the other;

Structurally, the "explanation" of the parable is found in verse 14 with the pronouncement of Jesus. Here much of what was left unsaid or merely implied in the parable is given its meaning (Neale, 1991: 172). Jesus repeats the authoritative "I tell you" (Lk 18:8) before the significance of the story. The two humans had ascended (*anebēsan*) up the temple mount, up to the temple courts to pray. Now the effects of those prayers in their lives are symbolized by their descent (*katebē*) from the temple mount into their homes. Their prayers, according to the Lukan Jesus, had to do with justice (Spencer & Spencer, 1990: 79; see Rayan, 1981 below). The verbs *anabainō* and *katabainō* clearly indicate the beginning and the end of the story. The passive *dedikaiōmenos* is undoubtedly a divine passive: God has justified the toll collector rather than the Pharisee (Schlosser, 1989: 278).

Verse 14b: for all who exalt themselves will be humbled,
              but all who humble themselves will be exalted."

Verse 14b is best seen as a "floating" saying (it also appears in Mt 18:4; 23:12 and Lk 14:11) which has been attached to the parable either in the tradition or by Luke himself (McBride, 1999: 181; Gourgues, 1997: 244; Schlosser, 1989: 274). The phrase *par' ekeinon* (NRSV: "rather than the other"; see Fitzmyer, 1985: 1188; Jeremias, 1963: 141–142; Marshall, 1978: 680) leaves no doubt that the prayer of the Pharisee was rejected (Jeremias, 1963: 142).

The aphorism, "for all who exalt themselves...," also affects the meaning of the following verses in Luke 18 (Talbert, 1982: 170–171). Luke illustrates the nature of the humble and the self-exalted with the pericope on little children (Lk 18:15-17—the humble who enter the kingdom) and the narrative of the rich ruler (Lk 18:18-30—one who has kept the law from his youth but is apparently excluded from the kingdom due to his unwillingness to part with his wealth; York, 1991: 75).

Originally Lk 18:10-14a did not deal in the first place with "moral" categories, with moral virtues and vices, such as pride and haughtiness, or awareness of sin and repentance, but with basic attitudes before God (McBride, 1999: 192). In the prayer of the two men the parable described the attitude of two people before God (Gourgues, 1997: 234–236). Lk 18:10-14a, therefore, shows two images of God, and by saying that one man went home justified while the other did not, it also passes judgment on both images of God. Consequently, it is first of all proclamation and revelation of God. It may rightly be said, then, that the parable seeks to illustrate and teach what God's grace is.

The actualization of this parable is not as obvious as is often thought. Nowadays self-righteousness is no longer the exclusive domain of the devout who would despise sinners. There is in intellectual circles a radically impious self-righteousness which at times asserts itself very consciously.

The present parable resists hurried attempts at identification. What we are told here is not easily arranged according to groups: here the pious, there the enlightened; here the progressives, there the reactionaries. The denunciation of others with whom we do not want to have any dealings, whom we despise or secretly fear, this beloved perennial attitude of self-affirming accusation of others, shows the Pharisee in our own heart. The parable holds up a mirror to us, pious and impious, progressives and reactionaries, Marxists and capitalists. All without exception we are placed by Jesus in God's own presence; that is why he situates this scene in the temple. And he asks us which righteousness, which justice we want to choose: our own, which allegedly entitles us to denounce and despise others, or the altogether different, real righteousness.

The Indian theologian Samuel Rayan, reading the parable in the light of the caste system, states the following: "The ideology of spiritual superiority and holier Karma yielding high caste birth is held up to ridicule. Its holiness is exposed without pity. Two men went up to the temple to pray. One was a pure upper caste man, the other a polluting *candala*. The pure caste man told God how good he was, how much better than the other man, for unlike the other he knew the Vedas, recited the mantras and revered brahmins. The candala stood far away outside the temple precincts, bowed his head, beat his breast and confessed himself an impure outcast due to his evil Karma and sought God's mercy. This man God befriended, said Jesus, not the other. Everyone who exalts himself and considers himself spiritually superior, karmawise higher and caste-wise upper, is, in God's estimate, of low human quality and least promising for the future of the earth. The promises are with those who opt to suffer and struggle with and for the deprived, despised and rejected outcasts; the pulaya, the paraya, the chamar, the wankar, the kurava, the veda, the bhangi, the musahar, the dusadh" (Rayan, 1981: 217).

While several modern salvation theories abolish all sense of guilt, at no other time does there seem to have been so much denunciation and condemnation. Groups and parties level massive accusations at each other. The theatrical scene has been turned into a permanent "tribunal." Nothing surpasses the critique of society, and the self-righteous is always a potential public persecutor of his/her fellow human being. The story of the Pharisee and the toll collector repeats itself time and again in constantly new forms. People appeal to their own achievement and righteousness and condemn others whom they consider as to be written off. The number of cleaning-up actions or purges in the name of higher ideals is interminable (Hendrickx, 1986: 245–247 passim).

b. *Entering the Kingdom of God Like a Child* (Lk 18:15-17)

At this point Luke resumes following Mark. After a long departure from using Mark as a source (Lk 9:51–18:14). Luke picks up almost where he left off in Mk 10:1 (Tiede, 1988: 309). Some scholars have pointed out connections between the parable of the Pharisee and the Toll Collector (Lk 18:9-14) and the incident of the children (Lk 18:15-17). The remark that some people "despised others" (Lk 18:9) is echoed in the disciples' treatment of the children (Lk 18:15b; Sellin, 1976: 111–112). The reversal of position of humble and exalted that is announced in the proverb concluding the preceding parable (Lk 18:14b) is dramatized by Jesus' welcome of the little children (Ringe, 1995: 226). For Marshall, there is a "neat link" between the two stories by means of the theme of humility (Marshall, 1978: 681; Nolland, 1993: 880; different: Joji, 1997: 471, who holds that they are not related). Eugene A. LaVerdiere sees a similarity between the toll collector and the child: receiving the kingdom in faith without pretense (LaVerdiere, 1980: 219). The story of the children and the incident of the rich man/ruler (Mk 10:17-31//Lk 18:18-30) were already together in the Markan context. In Mark they were part of a *Haustafel* ("house rules") which may have come to the evangelist from the tradition (Schweizer, 1976: 114); but Luke has omitted the exchange about marriage and divorce (Mk 10:2-12), thus putting the emphasis on the contrast between the two episodes, which he thus highlights by omitting the change of scene between the two (Mk 10:16-17; Kodell, 1987: 415–416; compare Craddock, 1990: 211–212). One has referred to the stories found in Lk 18:9-25 as "exemplary pairs." The Pharisee and the Toll Collector of Lk 18:9-14 are paralleled with the rich ruler and the children of Lk 18:15-25 (Kodell, 1987: 417–430).

Talbert parallels verses 15-17 with Lk 10:21-24 (the kingdom revealed to babes, *nēpioi*), though the order of the parallel passages at this point is not strict (Talbert, 1974: 51). Kodell questions Talbert's point that Luke has "in effect said that the disciples are the babes, while the prophets who desired to see and did not are the wise and understanding" (Talbert, 1974: 53). Kodell holds that it is more probably a subtle reproof aimed at the disciples because of their rejoicing over their power against demons (Lk 10:17 indicates that they are still concerned about personal greatness; cf. Lk 9:46 and 10:20). This coordinates with the attitude of the disciples at the beginning and the end of the great interpolation (Lk 9:51–18:14; Kodell, 1987: 425).

It has been suggested that Jesus blessed the children analogously with Jacob's blessing of Ephraim and Manasseh (Gen 48) in somewhat parallel circumstances, and that thereby he developed further the theme once enhanced by Jacob (Derrett, 1983: 1–18).

Verse 15:   People were bringing even infants to him
                that he might touch them;
                and when the disciples saw it,
                they sternly ordered them not to do it.

Some scholars have taken Lk 18:14 as the end of Luke's Travel Narrative (e.g., C.F. Evans). But there is no new beginning here; the journey goes right on. In Mark, this story of the children and the following story of the rich man/ruler are part of a *Haustafel*; but Luke has altered this pattern, not only omitting the divorce question at this point (Mk 10:2-12; cf. Lk 16:18) but also changing the emphasis of the children story (by juxtaposition with the parable of the Pharisee and the Toll Collector) to lowliness as a mark of discipleship (Marshall, 1978: 681; Fitzmyer, 1985: 1191).

The custom of blessing children is referred to in the Old Testament (Gen 9:26-27; 27:28-29; 49), and its importance is emphasized in the literature of the Second Temple period (Sir 3:9). Even today in a Jewish home the father often will lay his hand upon his child's head and say a blessing over him/her. The occasion may be on the eve of the sabbath or a holiday, or prior to the child's wedding, or even at the deathbed of the parent. In the Jewish prayer book the blessing of family is described by quoting from Psalm 128. The psalm is recited for a family blessing, and the custom is practiced in many Jewish homes where the child is dedicated to the Lord at the beginning of the week at the conclusion of the sabbath.

While the custom is not fully attested in the early sources, the gospels give us here an account where children were brought to Jesus for his blessing. Today a father will place his hand upon the head of his son and pray that he would be like the sons of Joseph and ask the Lord to bless him with the blessing of Aaron (see Gen 48:20; Num 6:24-26). Likewise, he will bless his daughter, praying that she would be like Sarah, Rebekah, Rachel, and Leah and be preserved in the peace and grace of the Lord. Jesus was asked to bless the children. He desired to bless them. But the disciples tried to stop the children from coming (Young, 1995: 98).

In the ancient world, where many children did not even survive infancy, rituals welcoming a child into the larger community often took place only when he or she reached the threshold of adulthood, and after the worst of the threats to survival were past. Infant mortality rates sometimes reached 30 percent. Another 30 percent of live births were dead by age six, and 60 percent were gone by the age of sixteen (Malina & Rohrbaugh, 1992: 383). Only at adulthood did the child become a person to be reckoned with. In terms of common values, then, the disciples' attempt to protect Jesus and his important mission from interruptions by children is understandable. In terms of the reign of God, however, the disciples have missed the point. Children, who possess nothing and bring no merit or claim to privilege, are in a position to "receive" God's reign in the only way it can be received, as a gift (Ringe, 1995: 226). But merit and achievement, two words not applicable to small children, are apparently very much in the disciples' minds as they think about God's reign (Craddock, 1990: 212).

Verse 16:   But Jesus called for them and said,
            "Let the little children come to me,
            and do not stop them;
            for it is to such as these
            that the kingdom of God belongs.

The text, as found in the best manuscripts (see Nestle) can be translated: "But Jesus called them (the babies) to him, saying. . ." "Saying" is a subordinate clause of "called the babies to him." Thus the addressees are those who brought them and possibly other people as well, as well as the disciples who rebuked them (Patte, 1983: 15).

Jesus used the opportunity of conflict with his inner circle of followers to teach his message of the kingdom. Jesus said, "Let the little children come to me. . . ." He wanted to make

a point about entering the kingdom. To come into the kingdom means to join in the flow of God's reign among his
people. Jesus continues, " ... do not stop them; for it is to
such as these that the kingdom of God belongs." Jesus recognized the qualities and the characteristics of the children
as being the desired approach to life for the disciples. What
qualities did Jesus see in children? (Young, 1995: 98).

Although it is easy to romanticize about children with
respect to this pericope, such qualities as "innocence," "openness to the future," and "trusting" are not the first ones that
come to mind when reviewing general perceptions of children in the first century. One has noted the high mortality
rate among young children; added to this is the simple observation that children were viewed as "not adults." They
might be valued for their present or future contribution to
the family business, especially in an agricultural context, but
otherwise they possessed little if any intrinsic value as human beings. Luke's phrase "even infants" draws attention to
the particular vulnerability of the smallest children perhaps
accounting for the widespread practice of infanticide and
child abandonment—and, thus, for the suitability of the infant as a particularly effective example of lowliness accented
in verses 9-14 (Schneider, 1977: 2.366–367). "Little children," on the other hand, translates a term used for household slaves and children, those maintained in a relationship
of subordination in a Greco-Roman household. Against this
cultural horizon, the response of the disciples is easily understood, even justifiable. Why should Jesus' time be taken
up with persons of such little importance, especially when a
"ruler" was waiting in the wings (verse 18)? On the other
hand, Jesus has already called into question this way of con-
structing human relations—explicitly in Lk 9:46-48, most
recently in Lk 18:9-14 (Green, 1997: 650–651).

Hospitality has also played an important role in the Lukan
narrative (e.g., Lk 7:36-50), and it is central to this pericope.
As Jesus makes clear in his response to the disciples, in deny-

ing children access to Jesus, the disciples have refused to welcome children. Yet, "receiving the kingdom" is intimately tied to "receiving little children." That is, the wording of verse 17 masks an ellipsis: "Whoever does not receive the kingdom of God *as one receives* a little child will never enter it" (Green, 1997: 651 note 131). "Receiving little children" is tantamount to granting them hospitality, performing for them actions normally reserved for those of equal or higher status. That is, Jesus is asking his followers to embrace a topsy-turvy system of values and to extend respectful service to that social group most often overlooked (Green, 1997: 651).

> Verse 17: Truly I tell you,
> whoever does not receive the kingdom of God
> as a little child
> will never enter it."

The pronouncement about receiving the kingdom like a child (Mk 10:15 = Lk 18:17) is omitted by Matthew, probably because he had used a similar saying in Mt 18:3 (and the present episode can be considered complete without it). The interpretation in Mt 18:4 points to lowliness as the childlike attitude needed for entry into the kingdom. That is the sense here, especially under the aspect of powerlessness, defenselessness, or availability without claim (see Lk 18:13; Schweizer, 1976: 206–207). Some have argued that *dexētai. . . hōs paidion* should be interpreted "as one receives a child" (e.g., Patte, 1983: 34), but "as a child receives" is the natural sense flowing from verse 16c (Taylor, 1957: 423; Kodell, 1987: 425 and note 52).

In Luke it is no longer said that Jesus touched the children (babies) after the interruption by the disciples. Thus the space "near Jesus" is not as intimate as in Mark (see Mk 10:16), and more like in Mt 18:1-5. Mk 10:16 is totally missing (Patte, 1983: 15, 16). In contrast to Mark and Matthew, Luke composes the story in the form of a sayings-chreia without pointed action. [The term chreia covers aphorisms, dialogues, actions, or stories as long as the climactic saying is attributed to some historical personage (Robbins, 1983: 78)]. Instead of exhibiting the *ethos* of Jesus through both action and speech, the Lukan story contains speech that includes the maxim along with the specific saying, without adding any comment about Jesus' action after the saying. The Lukan form results from removing the action to emphasize the speech of Jesus. When the action is removed from the end of the story, a specific saying followed by a general maxim concludes the unit. This phenomenon emphasizes the speech of Jesus in such a manner that the unit contributes well to the argumentation about the kingdom of God that has been introduced in Lk 17:20 with the question about the time when the kingdom of God would come. By allowing the sayings to stand at the end of the story, Luke has created a sequence of three stories (Lk 18:1-8; 18:9-14; 18:15-17) that end with a maxim. These maxims, with their supporting statements, represent a sequence of argumentation that describes the means by which a person may enter the kingdom (Robbins, 1983: 60, 61).

Jesus relates to the children as if the disciples—who are part of the situation that Jesus interprets—were not present. This characterization of Jesus has several effects. First, it is consistent with his role of enticing his addressees to participate actively in the establishment of their own will: a call demands a response. Second, the disciples are no longer under a fundamental reproof. Their misinterpretation and mishandling of the situation does not jeopardize their status as disciples belonging to the kingdom (as was the case in Mark). Third, the pronouncement is less directly related to the concrete situation of "people bringing babies to Jesus." In fact, Lk 18:17 becomes a quite general statement concerning the way in which the kingdom should be received (like a child), which does not need to be interpreted any longer in terms of Jesus' concrete involvement with children (Patte, 1983: 16).

As modern readers we need to be wary of lapsing into the very modern practice of sentimentalizing our views of children and then reading such views into Luke's account of Jesus' command to receive the kingdom of God as a child. Reducing this demand to an attitude of openness and trust seems to be unable to account for the particularities of this story and its connections to the paragraphs which follow. Likewise, to see receiving the kingdom of God as a child in terms of humility would be to read Luke in a decidedly Matthean fashion (Fowl, 1993: 153) thus also obscuring the particularities of Luke's account. Instead, if we read Lk 18:15-17 in the light of the paragraphs that follow, seeing the rich ruler, the disciples, the blind man and Zacchaeus as exemplars of either failure or success in regard to receiving the kingdom as a child, we will see Jesus' command as a call to single-minded, unrelenting pursuit of an object of desire (Fowl, 1993: 158).

c. *The Rich and the Kingdom* (Lk 18:18-30)

Luke found the story of the rich man/ruler and the second episode about children (the first being Lk 9:46-48) already joined in the earlier tradition (compare Trilling, 1969: 141). In using these stories as "exemplary pairs," the evangelist has changed their relationship, making them now contrasting examples of the attitudes exposed in the parable of the Pharisee and the Toll Collector. He has also made changes within the text and context of the present narrative, such as removing the travel detail of Mk 10:17 in order to heighten the contrast between the two episodes (Trilling, 1969: 127; Marshall, 1978: 684; Fitzmyer, 1985: 1196), describing the inquirer as a "ruler" and directing Jesus' comments on riches to the man rather than to the disciples (Lk 18:24; see Mk 10:23; Kodell, 1987: 426).

Like many of the pericopes in Luke's Travel Narrative, this one begins without specifying the time or place of the incident, and it appears as one of the many events on Jesus' journey to Jerusalem (see Mk 10:17). The account summarizes one of Jesus' exegetical discussions on the kingdom of God and has a two-part structure. As such, it begins with a dialogue between Jesus and a rich ruler on how to inherit eternal life (verses 18-23) and ends with a subsequent conversation between Jesus and his disciples on the relation of riches to the kingdom of God (verses 24-30; Kimball, 1884: 139–140).

Verse 18:   A certain ruler asked him,
             "Good Teacher, what must I do to inherit eternal life?"

Luke drops the Markan introduction, which refers to Jesus making his way along the road—in this Gospel Jesus has been at it since Lk 9:51! (Fitzmyer, 1985: 1196). Luke's omission of the Markan introduction here connects the present verse's interest in what is needed for eternal life more closely to the interest of verse 17 in conditions for entry into the kingdom of God (Nolland, 1993: 885). As in Mark and Matthew, Luke's placement of the account of the rich man/ruler after verse 17 creates a contrast with *hōs paidion* ("as a little child"; Johnson, 1977: 144).

The ruler's question matches almost word for word the lawyer's question in Lk 10:25 (the only difference is the addition of "good" to describe the teacher; Bock, 1996: 1476; for Jesus' rejection of "good," see Ibidem, 1477–1478). The word *archōn* ("ruler") is a favorite word of Luke's (six/seven times in Luke, ten/eleven in Acts, nine in the rest of the New Testament). Luke heightens the tension by identifying the person coming to Jesus as an *archōn* ("ruler"; cf. Lk 8:41; 14:1; 23:13, 35; 24:20; Acts 3:17; 4:5; 13:27; 14:5); all of these uses refer to Jewish leaders in contexts which portray the *archōn* negatively in some sense opposed to Jesus or his followers (Tannehill, 1986: 144; York, 1991: 155 note 3; Bock, 1996: 1476). Fitzmyer refers to him as a "Palestinian magistrate" (Fitzmyer, 1985: 1196, 1197). The question is debated whether Luke is implying a hostile attitude toward Jesus by substituting this title for *heis*, "one," (Mk 10:17; Krodell, 426 note 56). However, Luke may simply be underlining the comparison between the Pharisee in the temple and this rich ruler. The first unqualified (unlike Lk 8:41; 12:58; 14:1) use of the term "ruler" provides a transition to the use of the term in connection with the role of the Jewish (lay-)leadership in the trial and execution of Jesus (Lk 23:13, 35; 24:20; Acts 3:17; 5:26). The present pericope makes its own modest contribution to Luke's view that by and large the Jewish leadership had vested interests that kept them from embracing Jesus' proclamation of the kingdom of God (Nolland, 1993: 885).

The mention of his position is no accident (Johnson, 1977: 145), for it enhances the man's social and economic status (Pilgrim, 1981: 120). He is a man of recognized honor and authority in his community. He comes to Jesus, whom he recognizes as a person of religious authority (York, 1991: 155).

The rich ruler begins by asking Jesus an exegetical question on how to inherit eternal life. That he is asking an exegetical question is suggested by the facts that it is the same question asked by the lawyer in an expository discussion in Lk 10:25, that the rabbis deliberated this topic (e.g., *b. Ber.* 28b) as they also did the similar one on the greatest commandment (e.g., *b. Sab.* 31a; Mt 22:36; Mk 12:28), that this pericope has parallels in form to certain rabbinic patterns, that he addresses Jesus as teacher, and that he appears to be a religious ruler (Kimball, 1994: 140; Marshall, 1978: 684; Stein, 1992: 456; Ellis, 1966: 217; different: Fitzmyer, 1985: 1198: uncertain).

Luke makes it easy to view the ruler as a Pharisee, so that the statement *tauta panta ephulaxa* (Lk 18:21) is a clear echo of the recital of the Pharisee in Lk 18:11-12. The addition of *panta* ("all") in verse 22 and the description of the man as *plousios* ("rich") are both customary Lukan usages in the question of riches (Lk 5:11; 6:24; 16:1-19 (Fitzmyer, 1981: 247–248; Krodell, 1987: 426).

Verse 19:   Jesus said to him,
             "Why do you call me good?
             No one is good but God alone.

First, Jesus rejects the description of himself as good; he appears to refrain from being called "good" because this appellation must be viewed from the perspective of God and belongs to God alone (Johnson, 1991: 276; York, 1991: 155). Thus, he is not saying anything about himself (as to his deity or sinfulness) but emphasizing the goodness of God and pointing the ruler to him (Marshall, 1978: 684; Fitzmyer, 1985: 1199; Ellis, 1966: 216; but see Danker, 1988: 299: Jesus renounces such praise for himself; Nolland, 1993: 885–886). However, Jesus' answer has proved to be a difficult christological problem to many commentators (see Fitzmyer, 1985: 1199; Kimball, 1994: 140–141 note 208).

Verse 20:   You know the commandments:
             'You shall not commit adultery;
             You shall not murder;
             You shall not steal;
             You shall not bear false witness;
             Honor your father and your mother.'"

Jesus answers the ruler's question by quoting commandments five through nine of the decalogue. He introduces them with the formula "you know the commandments" (cf. Lk 10:26), which is equivalent to an order to obey them (Marshall, 1978: 684–685; Fitzmyer, 1985: 1197; Kimball, 1994: 141). It is uncertain why he only cites the second half of the decalogue, those concerned with relations to people, but does not also quote the first half, those concerned with relations to God; perhaps it is because these commandments could be outwardly judged (for various conjectures see Kimball, 1994: 141 note 210; see also C.F. Evans, 1990: 651). Deut

30:15-20 makes a nice commentary on Jesus' reply (Danker, 1988: 300; Bock, 1996: 1479). Elsewhere Jesus (Mt 22:37-39 = Mk 12:29-31) and the lawyer of Lk 10:25-37 whom he affirmed, combined commandments to love God and neighbor.

Verse 21: He replied,
          "I have kept all these since my youth."

Although the ruler's claim that he had obeyed all the commandments throughout his lifetime appears absurd at first glance, it is paralleled in the rabbis (e.g., *Ab*. 3:15; cf. Lk 18:11; Marshall, 1978: 685; Plummer, 1901/1977: 423) and even in Paul (Phil 3:6) and Lk 1:6. The ruler believed that he had kept all these commandments since he became accountable (Fitzmyer, 1985: 1200; Stein, 1992: 457). In his fidelity to the Law, he demonstrates that his piety is just cause for honor along with his social standing. He no doubt expects praise for his diligence from the honorable teacher. Instead of receiving praise and honor, however, he is faced with a terrible dilemma (York, 1991: 156).

Verse 22: When Jesus heard this, he said to him,
          "There is still one thing lacking.
          Sell all that you own
          and distribute the money to the poor,
          and you will have treasure in heaven;
          then come, follow me."

The ruler had asked for further guidance. Jesus takes him at his word. He strikes first at the center of the man's security—his material possessions (Danker, 1988: 300). Despite his response of total obedience, Jesus gives him a further command to enable him to receive treasure in heaven (i.e., eternal life; Marshall, 1978: 685; different: Fitzmyer, 1985: 1200; Nolland, 1993: 887). Sell all you have and give the proceeds to the poor and follow me (For a discussion and critique of the major views, see Seccombe, 1982: 118–130).

Luke heightened Jesus' teaching here by adding "all" (*panta*; cf. Mk 10:21; Mt 19:21). He gives this particular command because he recognized the ruler's true need and the commandment he had been breaking. Jesus always requires from one just that earthly security upon which one would lean (Ellis, 1966: 217; Schweizer, 1984: 285). The ruler was breaking the first commandment, "You shall have no other gods before me," because he allowed his wealth to become an idol that he loved more than God (Ex 20:3; Deut 5:7; Kimball, 1994: 142; Schmithals, 1980: 182; Talbert, 1984: 172).

The rich man/ruler must sell all that he has and distribute to the poor and then come and follow Jesus. He proves incapable of doing so. Luke omits Mark's "Jesus, looking at him, loved him" (Mk 10:21). It seems that Luke could not write that Jesus loved a person who immediately afterwards would prove incapable of selling what he owned and distributing the money to the poor (Lk 18:22). But the omission has also been attributed to Luke's (and Matthew's) hesitation to attribute emotions to Jesus, and that, therefore, it should not be taken as indicating a more critical stance (Nolland, 1993: 886).

Jesus' answer to the ruler's question takes seriously how wealth is intricately spun together with issues of status, power and social privilege (Green, 1995: 113–117; as to the question why Jesus gave this ruler such a radical command, see Bock, 1996: 1481–1482). His answer has the dual effect of defining the commitments and behaviors characteristic of the community of his followers and of undercutting completely the social conventions that governed the ruler's life and community. The kingdom of God calls for including the marginalized in one's circle of kin, for the abolition of status disjunctions, for giving without expectation of return —deviant behavior all, behavior that would lead to the ruler's loss of social standing and to his capacity to identify with the poor for whom the good news has come (Lk 4:18-19; Green, 1997: 656–657).

"The poor" as a typical term serves to give Jesus' command a certain moral legitimacy. Making the poor the potential beneficiaries of the ruler's assets at least eliminates controversy over where the assets should go. The authorial audience knows of God's desire for beneficence toward the poor. The poor, then, would be judged by Luke's audience to be scripturally appropriate recipients (Roth, 1997: 198).

Verse 23: But when he heard this,
he became very sad;
for he was very rich.

At that news, the man is dejected (*perilupos egenēthē; perilupos* is used only here by Luke; compare Mk 14:34; Mt 26:38) because he is exceedingly rich (*plousios sphodra*). The man/ruler is described as "rich" only by Luke; Mark and Matthew both say that he had "many possessions" (*ktēmata polla*). Jesus' announcement that the *archōn* must sell all his possessions would not just mean the loss of wealth, but the loss of honor and importance as well (Ringe, 1995: 227–228). More than possessions are at stake—he must sacrifice his status as well. In distributing his wealth among the poor he must associate himself with the social outcasts—the beggars like Lazarus (Lk 16:19) who cannot reciprocate and are of no social value (Lk 14:13). Perhaps worse, he must follow after a man who consistently spends his time with such people (Danker, 1988: 118).

Though he attempted to worship God and mammon at the same time, when the test was put to him he saw that his wealth was really his god. Luke says that the man became sad upon learning that he could not have both his money and eternal life (Craddock, 1990: 213). He did not really keep the first and greatest commandment so his lack of faith was exposed (Talbert, 1982: 172; Kimball, 1994: 142 and note 215).

The dialogue with the ruler is often terminated in verse 23 (Fitzmyer, 1985: 1196; Marshall, 1978: 683), and thereby separated from the rest of the discussion, although Luke has erased all mention of the departure of the ruler. This insinuates that Jesus does no longer speak for him although he remains among the hearers. One should, however, ask oneself if it would not be better to treat Lk 18:18-30 as a whole. In fact, the ruler who enters the scene at verse 18 is clearly excluded from the audience only in Lk 18:31, "Then he [Jesus] took the twelve aside and said. . ." Until that moment all that is said concerns him (Gérard, 1995: 86–87).

Verses 24-25:   (24) Jesus looked at him and said,
                      "How hard it is for those who have wealth
                      to enter the kingdom of God!
                 (25) Indeed, it is easier for a camel
                      to go through the eye of a needle
                      than for someone who is rich
                      to enter the kingdom of God."

It is little wonder that Jesus *looks at him* [Jesus speaks to the disciples in Mark and Matthew, after *the rich man has walked away*; York, 1991: 157 note 7], and says: "How hard it is for those who have wealth (*hoi ta chrēmata echontes*) to enter the kingdom of God! . ." (Lk 18:24-25; York, 1991: 157).

In response to the ruler's reaction (verse 23), Jesus gives *him* (and his disciples) a lesson on how wealth can hinder people from entering the kingdom of God. Indeed, while in Mk 10:22 and Mt 19:22 we read that "he [the ruler] went away sorrowful" before Jesus addressed the disciples, in Lk 18:23-24 the ruler stayed and "Jesus looking at him said, 'How difficult it is. . .'" In Luke, Jesus' words are, therefore, first of all addressed to the ruler (Schweizer, 1984: 286; C.F. Evans, 1990: 652).

Jesus then illustrates the problem by the hyperbolic comparison of a camel going through the eye of the needle, a comparison of Palestine's largest animal trying to get through its smallest opening. Compared to verse 24, verse 25 states

Jesus' thought even more radically: "hard" becomes now "impossible" (Ernst, 1977: 504; Kremer, 1988: 178; LaVerdiere, 1980: 222). Some have sought to soften this hyperbole by suggesting (1) camel (*kamēlos*) should be rope (*kamilos*; rejected, e.g., by Stein, 1992: 458) or (2) eye of the needle refers to the name of a small entrance in a city wall through which a camel might squeeze with difficulty (for representatives of these views, see Fitzmyer, 1985: 1204). Many scholars have stressed that both camel and eye of a needle should be understood literally (Marshall, 1978: 687; Ellis, 1966: 218; Jeremias, 1963: 195; Fitzmyer, 1985: 1204; Tiede, 1988: 312–313; Kremer, 1988: 178; Nolland, 1993: 890; Kimball, 1994: 143; Ringe, 1995: 228; Bock, 1996: 1485). Jesus similarly contrasted a camel and a gnat, the largest and smallest creatures in Palestine, when rebuking the Pharisees in Mt 23:24, and the rabbis used a parallel hyperbole of an elephant passing through a needle's eye to illustrate a teaching (*b. Ber.* 55b; *b. B. Mes.* 38b; Strack-Billerbeck Vol. I, 828; Kimball, 1994: 143).

The phrases "to enter the kingdom" and "to enter through the eye of a needle" [NRSV: "to go through the eye of a needle"] are set in parallel (both use the verb *eiserchomai*) in order to underscore the sheer impossibility of pulling away from the gravity of wealth in order to embrace a world order in which status distinctions are irrelevant on account of the prevenient extension of God's graciousness to everyone (Green, 1997: 657–658).

Verse 26: Those who heard it said,
          "Then who can be saved?"

The hyperbole creates tension for the rest of Jesus' audience. Upon hearing Jesus' statement, "those who heard it" (the disciples in Mk 10:24, 26 and Mt 19:25; but the disciples are not mentioned in Luke; does the latter suggest that the disciples understand and, therefore, should not ask such question?) asked Jesus, "Then who can be saved (i.e., enter the kingdom of God)? In the present pericope it seems that "to inherit eternal life" (verses 18, 30), "have treasure in heaven" (verse 22), "to enter the kingdom of God" (verses 24-25, 29), and "to be saved" (verse 26) are used synonymously (see, e.g., Marshall, 1978: 683–689; Tiede, 1988: 313; Stein, 1992: 456, 458; Bock, 1996: 1484; Green, 1997: 658; Fitzmyer, 1985: 1200 sees some differences). Luke derives this reward language ("treasure in heaven") from Mk 10:21; it echoes moreover the Q-saying of Lk 12:33 (Fitzmyer, 1985: 1200). "Those who heard it" implies that "if the rich (whose wealth is generally seen as a sign of God's blessing) cannot enter the kingdom, how can anyone enter it? (Marshall, 1978: 688; Geldenhuys, 1951/1988: 460; Stein, 1992: 458–459).

Verse 27:   He replied,
             "What is impossible for mortals
             is possible for God."

Jesus responds to their bewilderment by telling them, "What is impossible for mortals is possible with God"; that is, God can break a rich person free from his riches (or anyone free from what enslaves him) and save him (Kimball, 1994: 143). By leaving the rich man on the scene (unlike Mark and Matthew), Luke keeps him within hearing distance of Jesus' remarks and reminds his audience that hope does exist for all—including the rich—because God does the impossible (see Lk 1:37). That it is indeed possible to leave his possessions behind is seen in the verses that follow (York, 1991: 157).

Verse 28:   Then Peter said,
             "Look, we have left our homes
             and followed you."

Peter, as the disciples' spokesperson (Schneider, 1977: 371; note the "we"), reminds Jesus that they had left their possessions (ta idia) and followed him; in effect, they had done what the rich ruler could not do (York, 1991: 157). In

Luke, it is only at this point that the disciples come to the fore (Ernst, 1977: 501). The *archōn* comes to Jesus as a man of great wealth and honor seeking eternal life. When told he must abandon his wealth—which ultimately means loss of honor—he is unable to respond. The disciples, on the other hand, with less honor to lose and a belief that through Jesus honor will be gained, have left their possessions to follow Jesus. It is to them that the promise of eternal life is given (York, 1991: 158). Peter seems to imply "will we enter the kingdom?" or "what will we receive in return?" (Marshall, 1978: 688; Kimball, 1994: 143). In terms of an expression of fundamental loyalties, there is some genuine similarity with Jewish conversion motifs (see especially *Joseph and Asenath* 13:2: "I left behind all the good things of the earth and fled to you, Lord"), but this hardly amounts to a demonstration that this is how the origin of the text is to be accounted for (Nolland, 1993: 891–892).

Verse 29-30:   (29) And he said to them,
            "Truly I tell you,
            there is no one who has left house
            or wife or brothers
            or parents or children,
            for the sake of the kingdom of God,
        (30) who will not get back very much more in this age,
            and in the age to come eternal life."

Jesus responds favorably to Peter. Those who have humbled themselves for the sake of the kingdom will be exalted. Jesus promises them that those who have left their homes and families for the sake of the kingdom will receive "much more in this age and eternal life in the age to come." Instead of "for the sake of the kingdom of God," Mk 10:29 has "for my sake and for the sake of the good news" (cf. Mt 19:29, "for my name's sake").

Only Luke included "wife" in the list of relatives. He also did this in Lk 14:26 (Stein, 1992: 459). Luke omits

Mark's "with persecutions" (Mk 10:30), for although the church undergoes persecution in Acts, this does not arise over its life of poverty and communal possession, which is represented as an ideal and untroubled state (C.F. Evans, 1990: 654). Some scholars find that Luke, unlike Mt 19:29 and Mk 10:30, does not promise wealth but only community (i.e., the church family; Talbert, 1982: 173; C.F. Evans, 1990: 654; similarly Fitzmyer, 1985: 1206; Stein, 1992: 459; Kimball, 1994: 143 note 222). The kingdom is received, not gained through shabby trade. And standard societal structures are not primary instruments for determining the identity of God's people (Danker, 1988: 301).

Unlike Mt 19:30 and Mk 10:31, Luke's account does not conclude with the saying about the first and the last (cf. Lk 13:30) but ends with the promise of eternal life as it had begun with a question on how to inherit eternal life (Lk 18:18; Kimball, 1994: 144; Stein, 1992: 459; Bock, 1996: 1491).

FROM THE FINAL PREDICTION OF THE PASSION
TO THE ENTRY INTO JERUSALEM
(LK 18:31-19:44)

Prior to the account of Jesus' entry into Jerusalem, Luke relates four events in the ministry of Jesus: the final prediction of the passion (Lk 18:31-34), healing of a blind man near Jericho (Lk 18:35-43), dining with Zacchaeus at Jericho (Lk 19:1-10), and telling the parable of the Pounds to those who thought arrival at Jerusalem meant the arrival of the kingdom (Lk 19:11-28). This section begins and ends with the expression "going up to Jerusalem." Jericho really gives us a clue to the progress of the journey. It was the last town of significance before one left the Jordan Valley to make the ascent to Jerusalem. Since Jesus is moving toward the city in a large crowd of pilgrims (Lk 18:36; 19:3), one needs little imagination to sense the expectations, the arguments over the nature of the kingdom, the confusion, the rumors, and the predictions of what will happen once they arrive in Jerusalem (Craddock, 1990: 215). The rest of the Travel Narrative consists in two subsections: the approach to and arrival at Jerusalem (Lk 19:29-40) and Jesus' lament over the city (Lk 19:41-44).

a. The Final Prediction of the Passion (Lk 18:31-34)

The saying found in Lk 18:31-33(34) is the last of a series of three programmatic passion predictions, the other two being Lk 9:22, 43b-45. Although Luke has given his reader a number of other allusions between chapters 9 and 18 (Lk 12:50; 13:31-33; 17:25) to Jesus' impending fate, these three are particularly related by their close similarity. All three have the "Son of Man" as their subject (Cunningham, 1997: 116; compare Danker, 1988: 302).

In the Gospel of Mark, Jesus, while on his way to Jerusalem, makes three solemn predictions that he will have to suffer and die at the hands of his enemies but will rise again "after three days" (Mk 8:31; 9:31; 10:33-34). Matthew and Luke repeat these predictions (Mt 16:21; 17:22-23; 20:18-19; Lk 9:22, 43b-45; 18:31-33) but agree against Mark that Jesus said he would rise "on the third day" (*tēi tritēi hēmerai*) instead of "after three days" (*meta treis hēmerais*). Matthew, however, does agree with Mark's formulation in one other instance (Mt 27:63). Commentators agree for the most part that the synoptic passion predictions are *vaticinia ex eventu* ("predictions after the facts"), and there can be little doubt that the specific historical details in these predictions found their way there from the memory of the early Church rather than from the mouth of Jesus (Perry, 1986: 638).

The mention of the killing and the resurrection on the third day in Lk 9:22 is repeated in Lk 18:32. The idea of divine necessity, conveyed in Lk 9:22 by the use of *dei*, finds expression here in the fulfillment of the things written by the prophets. The use of *paradidōmi* is common to Lk 9:44 and 18:32. The disciples' failure to understand the necessity of the Son of Man's suffering is emphatically stated in both Lk 9:45 and 18:34. Whereas the first two predictions stand immediately before the beginning of Jesus' journey to Jerusalem, the present prediction stands just before the end of that journey and the actual entry into Jerusalem. The close parallel between the first pair and this one forms a literary inclusion framing the entire Travel Narrative and orienting it toward the passion (Cunningham, 1997: 116–117).

Verse 31:   Then he took the twelve aside and said to them,
             "See, we are going up to Jerusalem,
             and everything that is written about the Son of Man
             by the prophets will be accomplished.

A few observations are now in order that are relevant to this particular prediction. There is a focus on Jerusalem as the place of Jesus' death that is absent from the other two passages (see Lk 13:32-33).

Previous indications of the divine necessity of Jesus' suffering were expressed by the use of *dei* (Lk 9:22; 13:33; 17:25) or the divine passive (Lk 9:44; 13:32). At this point a new element appears in terms of the fulfillment (but see Fitzmyer, 1985: 1209) of the writings of the prophets (absent from Mk 10:33; Mt 20:18, the synoptic parallels of this passage). "Everything" (*panta*) is to be understood in an encompassing way: In Jesus the times are fulfilled (Büchele, 1978: 132). The point explains why Jesus' suffering and death is necessary from a divine point of view. The coming passion relates to the execution of God's plan *as it is revealed in the Scriptures of Israel*. This theme becomes more prominent during the passion (Lk 22:22, 37), in Jesus' explanation to the disciples after the resurrection (Lk 24:25-27, 44-46), and in the preaching of the disciples (Acts 3:18; 17:3; 26:22-23; Cunningham, 1997: 117).

Verses 32-33:   (32) For he will be handed over to the Gentiles;
                 and he will be mocked
                 and insulted and spat upon.
                 (33) After they have flogged him,
                 they will kill him,
                 and on the third day he will rise again."

In this final prophecy of the passion, details are added. That Jesus' death and resurrection were according to the law and the prophets was dramatized in the conversation with Moses and Elijah at the transfiguration and stated repeatedly in both the Gospel and Acts (Lk 24:25, 27, 44;

Acts 3:18; 8:32-35; 13:27; 26:23). In addition to specifics of Jesus' shameful treatment, Luke for the first time implicates the Gentiles. In fact, no reference is made here to religious authorities (Büchele, 1978: 132). No doubt, Luke is looking back on the event, with the conspiring of Herod Antipas and Pontius Pilate and the participation by both Jews and Gentiles in Jesus' death (see Ps 2:1-2 as quoted in Acts 4:25-26). For these details of the passion, notice that there are six statements of mistreatment, suffering, and death, and only one about the resurrection. The first six (in Greek: five) verbs describe how people treat Jesus; their actions lead to suffering and death; the seventh, on the other hand, speaks about God's action on behalf of Jesus: it leads to glorification (Büchele, 1978: 133). This apparent imbalance is not due to a love of the tragic but rather to a recognition that the suffering of Jesus constituted the major theological problem in the proclamation that Jesus of Nazareth was God's Messiah. If there is a tendency of denial in every death, this was specially so in the death of Jesus. Whole theologies were built around denials of his death. Simon of Cyrene was mistakenly crucified instead of Jesus; the vinegar offered to Jesus contained a drug and he only appeared to be dead; and so the stories went. In the ancient church, the denials were answered by a return to the insistence on texts like Lk 18:31-34 in the Apostles' Creed: "Suffered under Pontius Pilate, was crucified, died, and was buried" (Craddock, 1990: 215–216).

The human agents who carry out God's plan in the crucifixion shift in the three predictions. In Lk 9:22 it is the Jewish religious leadership who rejects the Son of Man. More generally, in Lk 9:44 the Son of Man is betrayed (*paradidosthai*) into the hands of men (with no mention of who does the betraying). And in this passage the Son of Man will be betrayed (*paradothēsetai*) to the Gentiles. Just as Luke has earlier prepared the reader for the involvement of the crowds in the passion of Jesus by noting their increasing opposition to Jesus, so this prepares the reader for the involvement of the Gentiles generally (Acts 4:25-27), and of Pilate in particular (Lk 20:20 in contrast to Mk 12:13).

This prediction also differs from the other two in that it contains more elaborate detail referring to mocking, insulting, spitting and flogging. This follows the apparent literary trend in the Third Gospel whereby additional detail is increased as the reader nears the event of the crucifixion (Cunningham, 1997: 117–118).

It has been observed that elements of the prediction find specific fulfillment in the later narrative, which gives the prediction the character of programmatic prophecy. The use of *paradidōmi* to refer to the handing over of Jesus will later be frequently used in the crucifixion narrative itself (Lk 22:4, 6, 21, 22, 48; 23:25) as well as reflections upon it (Lk 24:7, 20; Acts 3:13). The mention of the Gentiles, as explained above, finds fulfillment in the involvement of Pilate (Lk 20:20) and probably Herod (which is unique in the Gospels, cf. Acts 4:25-27). Of the four specific actions that the Gentiles commit between the handing over and the killing, only mocking is specifically fulfilled later in the narrative (Lk 22:63; 23:11, 36). It is possible that the reference to insulting which is not found in the synoptic parallels, anticipates the involvement of Herod and his soldiers and is also found only in Lk 23:11. Besides the killing and the resurrection on the third day, which finds obvious fulfillment, the other feature that anticipates events of the later narrative is the statement concerning the disciples' inability to understand (Tannehill, 1986: 254). This contrasts with the Emmaus episode, where the disciples finally understand the necessity of Jesus' suffering in God's plan (Lk 24:45; Fitzmyer, 1985: 1208; Cunningham, 1997: 118–119).

Verse 34:   But they understood nothing about all these things;
             in fact, what he said was hidden from them,
             and they did not grasp what he said.

Luke alone strongly emphasizes in this third prediction of the passion the disciples' lack of understanding in a pleonastic threefold statement (Büchele, 1978: 133). Luke says not only that "they understood nothing about all these things" but also that "what he said was hidden from them." The combination recalls the similar mixture in Exodus: "Pharaoh hardened his heart" and "God hardened Pharaoh's heart." Logic breaks down in the Bible's struggle to relate human failure and divine purpose. Luke is not reticent to see God's hand in both not seeing and seeing by the disciples. At Lk 9:45 and 24:16 similar statements are made. In Luke's theology, what is really going on in Jesus' death and resurrection is not grasped by human intelligence but comes by revelation. That revelation must now wait until after the resurrection. At that time the risen Christ will open the eyes and minds of the disciples, not only to who he is but to the fact that his passion fulfills the Scriptures (Lk 24:16, 25-27, 31-32, 44-45; Craddock, 1990: 216–217; Büchele, 1978: 133).

The RSV and NRSV obscure the distinction in the clauses by the rendering "this saying" and "what he said" respectively. The Greek (to rhēma) for this expression is used frequently in Luke in the sense of "this thing" or "this event" (Lk 1:37, 65; 2:15; 19:51; Acts 10:37, "What happened," NEB). In brief, such an outcome as Jesus described lay outside the comprehension of the disciples. But Luke offers a theological interpretation. The thing or event "was hidden from them," namely by God (Danker, 1988: 302).

b. Healing of a Blind Man near Jericho (Lk 18:35-43)

Luke draws his story from Mark without use of any other source (Schramm, 1971: 143–145) but his dependence on Mark does not control his usage of the episode. Having followed Mark quite carefully since Lk 18:15, Luke now takes more initiative with his source, dropping a major section (Mk 10:35-45), placing the healing within Jesus' entrance to Jericho rather than his departure (Mk 10:46), and supplementing this healing with another encounter in Jericho (Lk 19:1-10) and the stern warnings of the parable of the Pounds (Lk 19:11-27). Some commentators have observed only Luke's omission of the words in Mk 10:45 concerning giving his life as "ransom for many," as if Luke had selectively omitted just this detail to alter Mark's "theology of the cross."

It might be closer to the mark to suggest that Luke's omission of Mk 10:35-45 is consistent with Luke's depiction of the disciples. While they did not understand Jesus' passion prediction (see Lk 18:34), neither did they misinterpret his words so extremely as Mark suggests. Some traces in Mk 10:41-45 seem to show up in Lk 22:24-37 where Jesus is both correcting and instructing the Twelve, and Luke agrees that a proper understanding of discipleship is immediately linked with understanding Jesus' identity and dominion. But arguments as to why Luke did not use a portion of Mark will remain speculative and may distract from more concrete observations of the testimony which Luke's narrative offers (Tiede, 1988: 317).

This is the last major miracle story in Luke, and in all three synoptic gospels it is the very last miracle Jesus performs before his entry into Jerusalem (Breck, 1994: 107). Still journeying toward Jerusalem, Jesus meets a blind man on the outskirts of Jericho (Lk 18:35). The importance of this story to Luke can be judged not only by its being the last full miracle story before Jesus arrives in Jerusalem but also by being Luke's only story of the healing of a blind person (discounting the general reference to Jesus giving sight to many who were blind in the presence of the delegation from John the Baptist; Lk 7:22). This healing demonstrates the arrival of the time of fulfillment, as Isaiah prophesied: "Then the eyes of the blind shall be opened, and the ears of the deaf unstopped" (Isa 35:5; Mirro, 1982: 224; Danker, 1988: 303).

This episode is bordered by shifts in the narrative setting signaled in Lk 18:35 and 19:1. Yet repetitions and allusions harken back to earlier points in the narrative (Roth, 1997: 198). The context of this story is particularly telling in that what Jesus has just said about his impending death, he also says is hidden from the disciples, who are not able to grasp what he said (Lk 18:31-34). Therefore, the story of this blind man being healed and immediately following Jesus highlights not just the blindness of the uncomprehending disciples but also how obvious to their sight ought to have been Jesus' identity and power (Twelftree, 1999: 163).

Since Luke omits Mk 10:35-45 (the request of the sons of Zebedee), including the reference to the Son of Man's death as a "ransom [redemption] for many" (Danker, 1988: 303; Fitzmyer, 1985: 1212), the story of Zacchaeus now immediately follows that of the blind man near Jericho, suggesting that Jesus cures two men from their respective blindness.

Verse 35:   As he approached Jericho,
             a blind man was sitting by the roadside begging.

Jericho is the first town to be mentioned since the beginning of the Travel Narrative (Ellis, 1966: 219; Bock, 1996: 1505). It was a major city at the southern end of the Jordan valley, a mile south of the ancient Israelite town. It had been built by Herod as his winter capital, with a fortress to guard the road from Jericho to Jerusalem (C.F. Evans, 1990: 657, 658; Marshall, 1978: 692–693).

The blind man would belong to the five or ten percent of the population known as "expendables," for whom society as a whole had no need. He is clearly one of the "poor" as this is understood within the Lukan narrative (Green, 1997: 663). The man's blindness "paralyzed" him; he can only sit by the roadside (in Mk 11:1 explicitly the road to Jerusalem; Kirchschläger, 1992: 1112; compare Lk 19:11:

"because he was near Jerusalem"). Before returning his sight to him, Jesus makes him walk. He orders the man to be brought to him. He approaches but has still to be guided by others. It is only when he will have recovered his sight that he will be able to walk and follow Jesus by himself (Meynet, 1981: 704).

It has been suggested that the apparent contradiction (as to the location of the healing—nearing or leaving Jericho) of Lk 18:35 with Mk 10:46 and Mt 20:29 is caused by failure to appreciate the semantic range of Luke's use of *eggizō*. This may be a verb of motion for Luke, but it seems much more likely that it is primarily a verb of location. Thus Lk 18:35 should be rendered: "When he was in the vicinity of Jericho" (Porter, 1992: 91–104).

Verse 36-37:   (36) When he heard a crowd going by,
                              he asked what was happening.
                         (37) They told him,
                              "Jesus of Nazareth is passing by."

The blind man "heard a crowd going by," like a group of pilgrims making their way to Jerusalem (Bock, 1996: 1506; Ernst, 1977: 509 [possibly a popular gathering to see the great prophet]), and "asked what was happening," literally, "inquired what this might be" (Fitzmyer, 1985: 1215; for the explanation of the name *Nazoraios*, see *ibidem* and Bock, 1996: 1507). Because of the identification of the blind man as "poor," and especially because Luke has underscored the efficacy of the good news in providing recovery of sight for the blind (Lk 4:18-19; 7:21-22), the simple news that "Jesus is passing by" such a person may be enough to give Luke's readers an inkling of the outcome of the scene the evangelist has begun to paint (Green, 1997: 663). Provided that by "passing by" Luke picks up a term used in theophanies (cf. Ex 12:23; Mk 6:48), the evangelist therewith indicates Jesus' salvific significance (Kremer, 1988: 180; Ernst, 1977: 510).

Verse 38:   Then he shouted,
               "Jesus, Son of David, have mercy on me!"

The crowd proclaims that "Jesus of Nazareth is passing by," but the blind man "sees" much more (Danker, 1988: 303). He sees what the crowd cannot (Craddock, 1990: 217). Physical blindness masks insight about Jesus' identity (Ringe, 1995: 230). The implicit trust of the blind man in the "Son of David" is a kind of "seeing" which brings him to the healing he sought (Tiede, 1988: 319). The blind man's re-action is reminiscent of that of the lepers in Lk 17:11-19, and of God's "chosen ones" in Lk 18:7 (Green, 1997: 663). In the Septuagint the verb *boaō* was used for the needy cry of the oppressed and downtrodden to God. So by using *boaō* ("to cry," or "to call out") instead of *krazō* (also "to cry," or "to call out"), Luke is probably signaling to his readers that this man is calling out to God for help (Twelftree, 1999: 163).

The blind man's plea is forceful and direct. It is highly evocative in content as well as in style. "Son of David" re-calls not only the prediction of the angel to Mary: "The Lord God will give him the throne of his father David" (Lk 1:32), but also the Septuagint hope for an ideal king, a royal messiah. Luke had already described Jesus as the "Son of David" (Lk 1:27, 32, 69; 2:4, 11; 3:31) and was preparing the reader for Lk 19:28-40 (Stein, 1992: 463; C.F. Evans, 1990: 658–659; in Mark only in Mk 10:47-48 and 12:35; Kirchschläger, 1992: 1113). "Have mercy on me" echoes the plea of the ten lepers (Lk 17:13) and, like that prior plea, evokes an image of cries of psalmists (Roth, 1997: 199; the verb *eleein* occurs only here and in Mk 5:19; Kirchschläger, 1992: 1113).

By way of anticipation, the reader might well hold the title "Son of David" in solution, for it is both true and prob-lematic for Jesus. In Lk 20:41-44, Jesus himself will raise the question, "How can they say that the Messiah is David's Son?" (Craddock, 1990: 217).

Verse 39:   Those who were in front ordered him to be quiet;
             but he shouted even more loudly,
             "Son of David, have mercy on me!"

This verse opposes the people "who were in front" (*hoi proagontes*, the verb occurs only here in Luke; C.F. Evans, 1990: 657) to the blind man (Meynet, 1981: 700). The opposition to the blind man from the very people who are following Jesus is rather surprising (Mattam, 1998: 21). The beggar seems to comprehend Jesus' orientation to the needy and makes his plea accordingly. Others, identified only as "those in front," see things differently. It may be that we are to think of "in front" spatially—that is, those in front of the others. A different, less benign reading is not only possible but perhaps preferable. "In front" may refer to those regarded as leaders—spatially first perhaps, but only because of their claims to being first in status (Johnson, 1991: 284). Whether these persons are disciples (cf. Lk 9:52; 18:15) or not is unclear. What is transparent is that "those in front" regard this blind beggar as outside the perimeters of Jesus' ministry, marginal to human society as normally configured, and outside the boundaries of God's grace. Indeed, they dismiss him in the same way that Jesus dismisses those who oppose the will of God (Green, 1997: 664).

The suggestion that the blind man's outburst would have struck those accompanying Jesus as impertinent (so C.F. Evans, 1990: 278) lacks support from the text. They do to the blind man what the disciples had done to those bringing children to Jesus (Lk 18:15; C.F. Evans, 1990: 659). The verb *epitiman* ("rebuke"; NRSV: "ordered") is used by Mark in the expulsion of demons (Mk 1:25; 3:12; 9:25) and the stilling of the storm (Mk 4:39). Besides, it is used as expression of sharp reprimand (Mk 8:30, 33; 10:13). It is in the latter sense that it is used in Mk 10:48 (Kirchschläger, 1992: 1114). In Luke, on the narrative level, the rebuke serves as the opportunity for the repetition of the messianic acclamation of Jesus. The blind man's persistent entreaty matches that of

the widow in Jesus' parable of the Persistent Widow and
the Unjust Judge (Lk 18:2-5; Stein, 1992: 463).

The central phrase of the episode is "Son of David, have
mercy on me!" The word-for-word repetition of "Son of David,
have mercy on me" as well as its place in the account
underscore the importance of what the blind man peristently
asserts (Meynet, 1981: 700). The episode is not just about
the blind man's faith. It is also about who Jesus is (Roth,
1997: 198, 200).

Verse 40:   Jesus stood still
            and ordered the man to be brought to him;
            and when he came near,
            he asked him,

Mark has the man throw off his cloak, a symbol of leaving his past behind. Luke omits this detail (Lk 18:40//Mk
10:50). Was this to symbolize that compared to following
Jesus, the past is of no significance (Twelftree, 1999: 163)?
The verb *keleuein* ("to order") occurs seventeen times in Acts,
but is found only here in the Gospel (C.F. Evans, 1990:
657). Instead of Jesus approaching the man, Jesus has the
man brought to him. With that movement, the man has
already left his old life as a beggar sitting by the side of the
road—everything that defined his identity and place in society—just as the other disciples have done (Lk 18:28; Ringe,
1995: 231).

Verse 41   "What do you want me to do for you?"
            He said, "Lord, let me see again."

The question is taken over word for word from Mk 10:51
(Fitzmyer, 1985: 1216). The outstanding feature in this part
of the story is the repeated *anablepō* ("see again"). The blind
man asks that he "see again" (Lk 18:41); Jesus gives the
command, "see again" (Lk 18:42); and the narrator reports
that immediately the blind man could "see again" (Lk 18:43).
This almost monotonous repetition (three times) of the term

anablepō ensures that the audience will recall Lk 4:18 and 7:22 and recognize this episode as further fulfillment of Jesus' messianic calling (Roth, 1997: 200; Schweizer, 1984: 289; Tiede, 1988: 318; Bock, 1996: 1510).

Verse 42:   Jesus said to him,
             "Receive your sight;
             your faith has saved you."

Instead of having Jesus respond to the blind man's request by saying, "Go; your faith has saved you" (Mk 10:52), Luke has Jesus say, "Receive your sight; your faith has saved you." This makes Jesus' power to heal the focus of attention rather than the man's faith, which is more closely related to his seeking Jesus in the face of the crowd's discouragement. Thus even though the word "power" does not appear here, this miracle is another instance of Jesus using Spirit-power to perform a miracle (cf. Lk 4:14)—a connection perhaps made even more obvious through the fulfillment of the eschatological expectation of sight being given to the blind (cf. Lk 4:18; 7:22; Isa 61:1; Twelftree, 1999: 163–164). There is no reason to take the story as a rebuke of the Twelve; rather, it is prophecy and promise of what Jesus will do for them (Craddock, 1990: 217). Jesus is the one who gives sight to the blind, and he will help the disciples to see (cf. Lk 24:16, 31, 44-45; Danker, 1988: 304). Still, Luke also retains the Markan emphasis placed upon the blind man's faith: "Receive your sight; your faith has saved you" (Beck, 1994: 108).

Verse 43:   Immediately he regained his sight
             and followed him,
             glorifying God;
             and the people when they saw it,
             praised God.

Luke's use of *euthus*, *eutheōs*, and *parachrēma*, all different ways of saying "immediately," can seem very puzzling when perceived apart from the characters in the story (see excursus below).

Luke underscores Jesus' competence to heal with the adverb "immediately" (Green, 1997: 665). When healed, the formerly blind man follows (*ēkolouthei*, Lk 18:43) Jesus. The term recalls Jesus' invitation to the rich ruler to follow (*akolouthei*, Lk 18:22) him (Roth, 1997: 198). Luke omits "along the road" (Mk 10:52). This omission is noteworthy since use of the phrase would have otherwise suited his concern about following Jesus on the road (Fitzmyer, 1985: 1217). Unlike the ruler who lacked the necessary faith and refused to follow Jesus (Lk 18:22-23), the blind man is like the disciples who forsook all (Lk 18:28). And like the Samaritan (Lk 17:15), he glorifies—that is, praises—God (Danker, 1988: 304). The final addition to the story of the healed man glorifying God and the people praising God is a common way for Luke to draw attention to the miracle being the work of God (Twelftree, 1999: 164; C.F. Evans, 1990: 658). For Luke, the conclusion is the key element: the healing has as its effect to elicit a particular response on the part of all present. They glorify God, who manifests his power through this Son of David, God's "Chosen One" (cf. Lk 9:35; Breck, 1994: 108).

The use of *laos* ("people") to describe the group of following disciples is very Lukan, since he often compares the people's positive response to the leaders' negative one (Ellis, 1966: 220). In fact, Luke will use *laos* eighteen more times before the end of the Gospel (Fitzmyer, 1985: 1217; Bock, 1996: 1511).

EXCURSUS
THE USE OF *PARACHREMA* AND *EUTHEOS* IN LUKE

Euthus appears more than forty times in Mark. Often *euthus* in Mark is joined with *kai* at the beginning of a clause, and stands apart from the verb. Given the repetitive and consecutive Hebraic use of the adverb in

Mark, it is not unexpected that Matthew has reduced its appearance in his text, and has taken it over only six (seven) times. It is somewhat unusual, however, that Luke has completely removed Mark's *euthus* from his text. In one place he modified it to *eutheōs* (Lk 5:13//Mk 1:42), and five times he changed it to *parachrēma* (Lk 5:25//Mk 2:12; Lk 8:44//Mk 5:29; Lk 8:55//Mk 5:42); Lk 18:43//Mk 10:52; Lk 22:60//Mk 14:72). But not one of the instances of *euthus* in Mark remains in Luke.

At this point it has been argued that the author of the Third Gospel held some stylistic or personal bias against the word and simply removed it from his source, often substituting his own favorite, *parachrēma* (so Grundmann, 1963: 183). This argument, however, is not convincing, because Luke does use *euthus* at Lk 6:49, either inserting it into or appropriating it from Q.

Here we should realize that the author never placed his favored *parachrēma* in the mouth of Jesus. Only the narrator in the story uses *parachrēma*. When Jesus speaks, he uses *euthus* (Lk 6:49) and *eutheōs* (Lk 12:36, 54; 14:5; 17:7; 21:9). Moreover, not one of these instances in Jesus' speech is traceable to a source, and Lk 21:9 shows in fact that the author purposefully inserted *eutheōs* into the Markan source (Lk 21:9// Mk 13:7//Mt 24:6).

Generally then, the author of the Gospel so redacted his sources as to have the narrator use *parachrēma* and Jesus use *eutheōs*. But why? What could have motivated such a narrational distinction? In his study of the two words, David Daube concluded that *parachrēma* has a definite place in Lukan theology. It always appears in a pregnant sense indicating the fulfillment that resulted from divine activity. It is, in the narration, the immediate compliance with a divine command or prediction. Very clearly *parachrēma* fits with the language of the worshiping community used by the narrator. *Eutheōs*, on the other hand, in the speech of Jesus seems to be a secular term. It never describes the immediate response to and fulfillment of a divine order (Daube, 1964: 65). Its meaning is non-theological—simply "at once" (Dawsey, 1986: 34-35).

But this insight can be carried a little further. It has already been noted that the author of the Third Gospel almost completely removed *euthus* from the speech of Jesus, replacing it with *eutheōs*. While both terms were commonly used in the first century, there is some indication that *eutheōs* was at that time considered somewhat less archaic than *euthus*. Thus the author's preference for *eutheōs* in the speech of Jesus might have been occasioned by a desire to make the language of Mark more contemporary. Nevertheless, it seems significant that while *euthus* appears often in the Septuagint, *eutheōs* does so rarely and certainly would not have had in Luke's community the "biblical" connotations of the former word. *Eutheōs* was a more secular term, and the contrast between *parachrēma* and *eutheōs* was perhaps greater than would have been the contrast between *parachrēma* and *euthus*. Thus the author might well have placed the more secular term into the speech of Jesus in order to heighten its contrast with *parachrēma*. The one *euthus* used by Jesus (Lk 6:49) could have been an oversight—but probably not, as it is dramatically fitting that in a sermon at the foot of the mountain (Lk 6:20-49) Jesus should speak in a way that would remind his hearers of the Old Sinai covenant, and so employ the language of Scripture. In addition to its contrast with *parachrēma*, Jesus' use of *eutheōs* is perhaps indicative of the popular style of his speech in Luke. Jesus speaks the language of the people (Dawsey, 1986: 35–36).

c. Dining with Zacchaeus *(Lk 19:1-10)*

Numerous connections secure the Zacchaeus episode within its immediate context, but by far the most impressive parallels are between the accounts of the rich ruler (Lk 18:18-30) and of Zacchaeus (Green, 1997: 666–667). Zacchaeus also is described as "rich" (Lk 19:2). Rather than being an honored *archōn* ("ruler," Lk 18:18) however, he is a shameless *archi-telōnēs* ("chief toll collector," Lk 19:2; Malina, 1981: 83). The shameless status of Zacchaeus in the community is further emphasized by his inability to get through the crowds to see Jesus. He is short of stature and must climb a tree and wait for Jesus to walk by in order to get a glimpse of him (Tannehill, 1986: 158–159 note 7). To his surprise, and the crowd's, Jesus stops, addresses him by name, and invites himself to Zacchaeus's house (Cosgrove, 1984: 175). The crowd's reaction is reminiscent of previous reactions to Jesus' association with toll collectors and sinners. They "grumble" (*diegogguzon*) because Jesus is the guest of a *hamartōlos* ("sinner"; cf. Lk 15:1-2).

Zacchaeus demonstrates his repentance by telling Jesus (*ton kurion*) that he will give half of his goods to the poor and restore fourfold whatever he has defrauded (verse 8; see York, 1991: 159 note 4). For Zacchaeus, giving up his wealth indeed signifies repentance. But it is a reflection of honor restored rather than honor lost. Jesus confirms this by telling him, "Today salvation has come to this house because he too is a son of Abraham" (Lk 19:9). The placement of "today" (*semeron*) in emphatic position demonstrates the present time quality of *sōtēria* ("salvation"), i.e., access to the kingdom (York, 1991: 159 note 5). The reference to Abraham is not so much an indicator of Zacchaeus's Jewishness as it is a sign of his worthiness (Marshall, 1978: 698; O'Hanlon, 1981: 25 note 62). He was a shameless outcast, no longer worthy of his Jewish heritage; now honor and heritage are restored. Jesus' final comment sums up not just the story of Zacchaeus but his earthly ministry: "For the Son of Man came to seek and save the lost."

The message of reversal is seen in the combination of the narratives in Lk 18:18-30 and 19:1-10. The story of Zacchaeus provides a second opposition to the rich *archōn*. The *archōn* seeks eternal life but is unable to gain it because he is unwilling to part with his wealth. Jesus implies, on the other hand, that the disciples who have left their possessions will have eternal life (Lk 18:30). Zacchaeus is then presented as a person of wealth who also receives salvation. The question of honor is a controlling factor in the different scenarios of the two individuals. The one without honor (Zacchaeus) and those who give up honor (the disciples) have access to eternal life. On the other hand, the one unable to humble himself (and those grumbling because Jesus associates with sinners?) implicitly are excluded from the kingdom (York, 1991: 160). The contrast between Zacchaeus's joyful abandon (Lk 19:6-9) and the ruler's sorrow (Lk 18:23) is instructive (Tiede, 1988: 312).

The strategic placement of this story at the conclusion of the journey to Jerusalem suggests that it is in some way definitive for Jesus' ministry on the pages of Luke (Matson, 1996: 70–71). The placement of the story at the end of Jesus' public ministry underlines its symbolic and summary

significance for Luke's presentation of Jesus' ministry (Pilgrim, 1981: 130).

A number of literary forms have been proposed for Lk
19:1-10. It has been viewed as a conversion story (Hamm,
1988: 436–437). But others classified it as a biographical apo-
phthegm (Bultmann, 1963: 55–57), a genuine personal leg-
end (Dibelius, 1970: 50–51), or a story about Jesus (Taylor,
1933: 75–76, 153). It has also been called a vindication story
(White, 1979a: 21) or a conflict story that has many similarities to the narrative of Levi in Lk 5:27-32 (Talbert, 1982:
176–177; compare Gérard, 1995: 98). Finally, it has also been
regarded as a quest story, which is a type of pronouncement
story (Tannehill, 1986: 111–112, 125; Bock, 1996: 1513 note
1 disagrees). Quest stories are structured around a person's
quest; they give the quester a prominent role alongside Jesus,
and do not end without reporting the success or failure of
the quest. Such quest stories are especially characteristic of
Luke (Tannehill, 1994: 205).

Some of the literary forms suggested for Lk 19:1-10 simply do not appear applicable, and others are really very similar
to one another (O'Toole, 1991: 108). Bultmann and Tannehill
basically agree on the general category of the literary form
of Lk 19:1-10. This general category needs to be specified
further, and so it is claimed that Lk 19:1-10 is a quest story,
a type of pronouncement story. Zacchaeus seeks to see who
Jesus is, and his quest and the answers he receives concern
not only him but Luke's readers as well. Luke ends with the
interesting twist that the quest really belongs to the Son of
Man (O'Toole, 1991: 109–110, 116; Green, 1997: 667). In
other words, two quests are taking place at the same time:
Zacchaeus, although he is rich, finds the salvation he seeks,
and Jesus finds the lost person he has come to seek. Both
perspectives on the story serve to defend Zacchaeus's right
to share in the salvation promised to the children of Abraham
(Tannehill, 1994: 201).

Verse 1:   He entered Jericho and was passing through it.

After the healing of the blind man at Jesus' entry into Jericho, the Zacchaeus story is introduced with a travel notice. The encounter with Zacchaeus occurs in Jericho or the very doorstep of Jerusalem. This is significant since, for Luke, Jerusalem serves as the goal of all Jesus' movements and is the city of his destiny (Neale, 1991: 180–181).

The verb *eiserchomai* ("to enter") is used more often in Luke than in the other Synoptics (Mt: 36 times; Mk: 30; Lk: 50; Acts: 32). It is used here as a travel notice together with *dierchomai* ("to pass through"). Luke employs *eiserchomai* as a travel notice in a number of key passages of the Travel Narrative because he presents Jesus' life as a "coming in" and "going out" of this world (Acts 1:21). In fact the first act of Jesus' public ministry is described with this verb. "He went to the synagogue (*eiselthen*) on the sabbath day, as was his custom" (Lk 4:16). Later, very often Jesus' entry into a town, synagogue, or house to preach, teach, heal and save is expressed by it. Especially noteworthy is Lk 24:29, where at the request of the disciples of Emmaus, "stay with us" (*meinon meth' hēmōn*), the risen Lord went in (*kai eiselthen*) to stay with them (*tou meinai sun autois*). We notice a similar use of *erchomai* and *meinai* in Lk 19:1, 6 ("He entered... I must stay in your house").

Parallel to Jesus' ministry, the disciples' ministry of preaching and healing is also introduced by *eiserchomai* already in the Gospel (Lk 9:4). It is all the more clear when we read through the Acts of the Apostles (Acts 1:13; 3:8; 5:21; 9:6, etc.). In Acts 16:15 Lydia beseeches the apostles, "If you have judged me to be faithful to the Lord, come and stay at my home" (*eiselthontes eis ton oikon mou menete*). Likewise, Acts 21:8 resembles Lk 19:1ff. very much. Here it is said that the apostles came to Caesarea and entered the house of Philip the evangelist (*kai eiselthontes eis ton oikon*) and stayed with him (*emeinamen par' autōi*). Especially in the

Lukan Travel Narrative one's entry into the kingdom is expressed by *eiserchomai*. In Lk 11:52 the verb is used in this sense twice and Lk 13:24 tells us that one has to enter (*agōnizesthe eiselthein*) by the narrow door to attain salvation. This verse occurs in close relationship with Jesus' journey to Jerusalem (Lk 13:22). In Lk 14:23; 17:27 and 18:17, 25 (twice) too *eiserchomai* is used to express the entry into the kingdom of God. Luke, therefore, gives much importance to this verb in his two-volume work, especially in connection with Jesus' and the disciples' journeys and one's entry into the kingdom (Kariamadam, 1985: 2–4).

The use of *dierchomai* is also more frequent in Luke than in the other Synoptics (Mt: once; Mk: twice; Lk: 10; Acts: 21; Schramm, 1971: 143–144; Miyoshi, 1974: 146 note 118). The verb is employed as a travel notice in Luke, especially to introduce Jesus' teaching and healing ministry. It is found with *eiserchomai* in Lk 19:1 and 4. At the end of the Nazareth pericope (Lk 4:30) *dierchomai* is found along with *poreuomai* to express Jesus' journey for evangelization (Lk 4:31). In Lk 17:11 *dierchomai* occurs along with *poreuomai* to express Jesus' journey to Jerusalem, immediately followed by the healing of the ten lepers (Lk 17:11-19). It is, then, abundantly clear that in Luke's Gospel *dierchomai* is often used as a travel notice to introduce the teaching and healing ministry of Jesus. This can be confirmed by Acts 10:38, where the ministry of Jesus is summarized by this verb.

This is also true of the ministry of the disciples. This may be seen especially from Acts (e.g., Acts 8:4-40; 11:19; 13:5-6). The last passage is strikingly similar to Lk 19:1f. One should note in particular the fact that in Acts *dierchomai* is found almost like a refrain in order to introduce the missionary journeys of Paul and his companions (Acts 14:24f.; 15:41; 16:6; 17:23). The last occurrence of *dierchomai* is in connection with Paul's preaching of the kingdom of God (Acts 20:25). Here, with *dierchomai* Paul's ministry is summarized as is done with Jesus' ministry in Acts 10:38. The above findings underline the importance of *dierchomai* in Luke-Acts, especially in connection with Jesus' ministry of preaching and healing, as well as that of the disciples (Kariamadam, 1985: 4–6).

Verse 2:   A man was there named Zacchaeus;
he was a chief tax collector and was rich.

The main figure of the story—next to Jesus—is introduced literally as "a man called by the name Zacchaeus," an expression found only here in Luke-Acts (Nolland, 1993: 904). He bears the name of the father of a famous rabbi from the end of the first century, Yohanan b. Zakkai. *Zakchaios* is the grecized form of the Hebrew name Zakkai or Zaccai (Neh 7:14; Ezra 2:9), found also in 2 Macc 10:19 as the name of an officer in the army of Judas Maccabee. Hebrew *zakkay* means "clean, innocent," a term often used in parallelism to *saddiq*, "righteous, upright" (Fitzmyer, 1985: 1223), but it is doubtful whether this etymology plays any role in the story (Nolland, 1993: 904).

Zacchaeus is qualified as a chief tax collector, more correctly chief toll collector (see comments under Lk 18:9-14), that is, an overseer in charge of collection of a variety of tolls (Danker, 1988: 304). This title (*architelōnēs*) is not found anywhere else in the New Testament, and is probably not attested in any Greek writing up to this period (Fitzmyer, 1985: 1223; Green, 1997: 668). That Zacchaeus was a "chief toll collector" implicates him more deeply in the corrupt tax system of the Roman government. In a corrupt system the loftier one's position, the greater one's complicity in that system. While nothing of the private life of Zacchaeus is revealed in the story, this much we know on principle: no one can be privately righteous while participating in and profiting from a program that robs and crushes other persons. Such dichotomous thinking has been a blight on the Church throughout its history, especially in those times and places in which individualism has dominated over community (Craddock, 1990: 218–219).

Luke's predilection for "toll collectors and sinners" is well known. *Telōnēs* occurs more frequently in Luke than in the other Synoptics (Mt: 8 times; Mk: 3; Lk: 10). In Lk 19:1-10 Luke ends his description of toll collectors in his Gospel. The toll collectors, by now a common feature in Luke's controversy stories, are represented by the chief toll collector Zacchaeus. Whereas the "sinner" material in the Gospel began with the toll collector Levi in Luke 5, the evangelist now climaxes Jesus' ministry with a similar encounter. But this time it is the chief toll collector and he represents, in a dramatic and cumulative sense, all of his kind who have gone before him in the gospel story (Lk 3:12; 5:27-28, 29; 7:29; 18:13-14). The call of the outcast is now symbolized and epitomized in the archetypal figure of Zacchaeus and his encounter with Jesus (O'Hanlon, 1981: 9).

Zacchaeus and the toll collector in Lk 18:9-14 are both called *hamartōloi* ("sinners"). Both display the characteristic behavior of Luke's paradigmatic "sinner," that is, they always produce the right response. The toll collector of the parable does so by his attitude of humility and contrition while Zacchaeus does so not only by his attitude but also, significantly, by his deeds. The events narrated in Lk 19:1-10 are a real-life demonstration of the attitudes set out in parable form in Lk 18:9-14 (Grundmann, 1963: 358). We cannot read the one incident without reflecting on the other and thus forming a fuller understanding of Luke's conception of what a "sinner" must do (Neale, 1991: 181).

One should also remember that *archōn* ("chief, ruler") plays an important role in Luke-Acts. *Archōn* is found frequently in Luke's two-volume work (Kariamadam, 1985: 9 note 40; Schürmann, 1969: 489). Often it is said that the rulers of the people rejected Jesus and his message (Lk 14:1; 18:9ff.; 23:13, 35; 24:20). The chief priest and the rulers delivered him up to be condemned to death. This point becomes even clearer if one reads Acts 3:17; 4:5 (the rulers and the elders and scribes gathered together in Jerusalem against the apostles); 4:8, 26; 13:27; 14:5; 16:19. On the one hand, the leaders of the people reject Jesus and the salvation brought by him, and on the other hand, a leader of the toll collectors receives Jesus and is thus saved (Lk 19:6ff.). This will again be more evident if we place the attitude of Zacchaeus over against that of the rich ruler (*archōn*) in Lk 18:18-30. In contrast to the behavior of the ruler who became sad for he was very rich (Lk 18:23), the chief of the toll collectors (Zacchaeus) receives Jesus joyfully, gives his goods to the poor, and is thus saved (Lk 19:8-9; Kariamadam, 1985: 8–9).

The second qualification of Zacchaeus is that he was rich. The close association of "toll collector" with "rich" suggests that Zacchaeus was rich precisely on account of his occupation (Matson, 1996: 71 and note 105). And yet, Luke does not say that he was a "rich chief toll collector" but that he was a "chief toll collector and rich," thereby emphasizing his wealth (Green, 1997: 668). Being a chief toll collector, Zacchaeus was in a position to make big profits. He was an exploiter and an oppressor (D'Sa 1996; 195). *Plousios* occurs often in Luke (Mt: thrice; Mk: twice; Lk: 11), especially in the Travel Narrative (9 out of 11 occurrences). The fact that Zacchaeus is rich is important to the plot, which deals with the question left dangling by Lk 18:18-27: whether and how a rich man can be saved (Tannehill, 1994: 202–203). At the close of the Travel Narrative, Luke introduces a rich man to show how he could be saved (Kariamadam, 1985: 9; Seccombe, 1982: 130–132).

Verse 3:   He was trying to see who Jesus was,
            but on account of the crowd he could not,
            because he was short in stature.

As in Lk 18:35-36, so in Lk 19:3a also, after the journey notice (Lk 19:1) and the introduction of the toll collector, the person's desire to "see" Jesus is expressed. "He sought to see who Jesus was" (RSV). *Zētein* ("to seek") with an infinitive is a Lukan expression. One may note especially the use of *zētein* with *idein* ("to see"). The two verbs are often used together and express in many cases the search of someone to understand the mystery of Jesus, the kingdom of God and one's salvation, as in the case of Zacchaeus (Kariamadam, 1985: 11, 12). It has been noted that the story begins with Zacchaeus seeking to see Jesus but that it ends with Jesus seeking out and saving the lost (Tannehill, 1986: 125; Matson, 1996: 71 note 107; Löning, 1971: 201; different: Nützel, 1980: 190).

Zacchaeus's search to see Jesus was motivated by more than curiosity (compare Raja, 1995: 141). Curiosity sometimes conceals an unconscious yearning to see God (Schweizer, 1984: 291). Perhaps we may talk of the "holy curiosity" of Zacchaeus, which prompted him to frenetic activity (Ahern, 1987: 348, 349). He wanted to see "who Jesus was." It is a search for the savior. The expression *tis estin* ("who he was"; literally, "who he is") occurs frequently in Luke, especially at the beginning of the Travel Narrative where it is used in connection with Jesus' identity: ". . . no one knows who the Son is (*tis estin ho huios*) except the Father, or who the Father is (*tis estin ho patēr*) except the Son. . ." (Lk 10:22). The last two occurrences of *tis estin* are found toward the end of the Travel Narrative (Lk 18:36; 19:3). The words "who Jesus was" are reminiscent of the central question poised over the Gospels concerning the identity of Jesus, with the understanding that the resolution of this identity becomes an attestation of faith (Hobbie, 1977: 287; Stein, 1992: 467; Green, 1997: 669).

In the first part of the story (verses 1-6), the first actor is always called "Jesus." This name is a human title; it refers to a Nazarene who was traveling through Palestine, preaching and healing—a kind of a prophet who drew large crowds. Subsequently, in the second part of the story (verses 7-10), the name "Jesus" disappears (except in verse 9) and is replaced by "Lord" and "Son of Man." These two designations clearly attribute a superior value to this man Jesus (Vogels, 1978: 488).

"On account of the crowd" does not just mean that Zacchaeus could not look over the crowd. The crowd constitutes an obstacle to Zacchaeus's seeing Jesus. They bar this man's way to Jesus just as they had done in the case of the blind man, preventing the latter from confessing Jesus as the "Son of David" (Lk 18:39). In both cases Jesus has to intervene to save the persons in question (Lk 18:40 and 19:5; Kariamadam, 1985: 14). Being short, he climbs a tree to get a better view. A sycamore tree should provide good cover and let him get away with his covert surveillance without jeopardizing his dignity (Ringe, 1995: 232).

Zacchaeus was "short in stature." Lk 19:3 is the only passage in the New Testament where the term *hēlikiai* is rendered as "stature"; everywhere else it means "age" or "term of life." If this were also the meaning here, we should translate, e.g., "because of his youth." This would account for his treatment as an insignificant person for whom the crowd would not make room (Green, 1997: 669). Some scholars see in the translation, "short in stature" only a detail that adds color to the story and, therefore, simply for the literary effect. But Luke's audience may have recalled that Jesus had spoken at Lk 12:25 about the futility of attempting to add a cubit to one's stature (Danker, 1988: 305; Hendrickx, 2000: 214–215).

One may even go beyond this perspective in order to understand the meaning of the expression in the Lukan context. It is to be remembered that one of the important requirements to enter into the kingdom and an essential quality for conversion is to be "small." Both in the "prologue" to the Travel Narrative and towards its end Luke insists on the fact that the "little ones" enter into the kingdom of God: ". . . the least among you is the greatest" (Lk 9:48b) and "Let the little children come to me, . . . for it is to such as these that the kingdom of God belongs" (Lk 18:16). In Lk 19:3 *mikros* ("little"; NRSV translates here "short") may be seen in a positive light with regard to the chief toll collector. The above considerations indicate that the stature of Zacchaeus concretely evokes those attitudes which Jesus has in mind for those who are to enter the kingdom (Kariamadam, 1985: 16–17).

Verse 4:   So he ran ahead and climbed a sycamore tree to see him, because he was going to pass that way.

The verb *protrechō* ("to run"; *prodramōn* is the aorist participle) found in the beginning of the verse is used only here by Luke. It is also used in Jn 20:4 (Peter and John running to the tomb) and nowhere else in the New Testament (Kariamadam, 1985: 17–18), but the simple *dramōn* is used in Lk 15:20 to describe the father running toward his returning son. The sycamore tree can be a very high tree, but its lower branches are near the ground. This explains how Zacchaeus could climb the tree (Vogels, 1978: 487; C.F. Evans, 1990: 662; Bock, 1996: 15–17).

Zacchaeus's effort is further explained by the fact that Jesus "was going to pass that way (*ēmellen dierchesthai*)." *Emellen* is found only in Luke among the Synoptics (Lk 7:2; 9:31; 10:1; see also Acts 12:6; 16:27; 27:33). All usages of *ēmellen* in Luke, except Lk 7:2, are in connection with a travel situation expressing Jesus' journey to Jerusalem (Kariamadam, 1985: 19).

Verse 5:   When Jesus came to the place,
            he looked up and said to him,
            "Zacchaeus, hurry and come down,
            for I must stay in your house today."

"When Jesus came to the place (*topon*). . . ." The word *topos* is found frequently in Luke in connection with Jesus' journey. Especially the similarities between Lk 19:4-5 and

19:1 (and 23:33) are striking. In all these texts Jesus' journey is indicated by the verb *erchomai* and it is related to *topos*. The travel notice in Lk 10:1 at the beginning of the Travel Narrative and the journey situation in Lk 19:4-5 at the end of the Travel Narrative are almost parallel.

Anablepsas ("looking up") connects this pericope with the preceding. The occurrence of the verb *anablepō* in Lk 18:41, 42, 43 and 19:5 indicates that we are dealing here with a hook word or link word. Among the Synoptics Luke uses the verb more often to indicate that Jesus looked up somewhere (Lk 9:16; 19:5; 21:1). It is interesting to observe that at first Zacchaeus wants to see Jesus (Lk 19:3) and as a consequence Jesus sees the need of Zacchaeus (Lk 19:5; Kariamadam, 1985: 20–21). The text does not indicate how Jesus knows Zacchaeus's name (Plummer, 1901/1977: 434; C.A. Evans, 1990: 283; Marshall, 1978: 696). It is the wrong question to ask since the text does not address the issue (Fitzmyer, 1985: 1224). Jesus not only spots Zacchaeus, but makes a spectacle of him by inviting himself to Zacchaeus's home. You have to chuckle, at least a little (unless you happen to be Mrs. Zacchaeus, left with the problem of rearranging household plans to provide dinner for the unexpected guest and his entourage; Ringe, 1995: 232).

"Today" (*sēmeron*) occurs more frequently in Luke than in the other Gospels. Out of forty-one occurrences of this term in the New Testament almost half are found in the Lukan writings (Luke: 11; Acts: 9). In Lk 19:9 it is emphasized by its place in the verse. In continuity with the Old Testament idea of "today" Luke alerts the reader to the present reality of salvation and all the blessings connected with it by this expression (Conzelmann, 1960: 36; Flender, 1967: 157; Tiede, 1988: 320). Jesus' birth and death are presented in Luke in connection with a salvific today (Lk 2:11; 23:43). The beginning of his public ministry is also characterized with this term (Lk 4:21). Lk 5:26 is particularly noteworthy. After the cure of the paralytic and the forgiveness of his sins

(Lk 5:17-26) people marvel, praise God and say, "We have seen strange things today." The adverb *sēmeron* is found at the end of the verse and thus the reader's attention is directed to it. Towards the end of the Travel Narrative too Jesus' mission is depicted in close connection with *sēmeron*. The parallelism between Lk 19:5 and 9 suggests the identity between the coming of Jesus and the coming of salvation (Kariamadam, 1985: 22–23; Hendrickx, 1996: 196). "Today" is one of Luke's favorite ways to express the presence of God's salvation in the presence and ministry of Jesus (Pilgrim, 1981: 131). The coming "today" of Jesus to the house of Zacchaeus is the coming of salvation "today" (Vogels, 1978: 49).

Dei ("must") is one of Luke's favorite expressions. Behind the "must" of Jesus' presence stands the will of God operative in the whole life and death of Jesus (Pilgrim, 1981: 131; Stein, 1992: 467). According to God's plan (*dei*; Miyoshi, 1974: 147), Jesus brings salvation to the house of Zacchaeus by staying with him. Luke uses *oikos* ("house, household") and *menō* ("to stay, to remain") more often than the other Synoptics (*oikos*: Mt: 10 times; Mk: 12; Lk: 33; Acts: 25; *oikia*: Mt: 25; Mk: 18; Lk: 25; Acts: 12; *menō*: Mt: 3; Mk: 2; Lk: 7; Acts: 13; Schürmann, 1953: 97–98). Luke is especially interested in *menō* (and compounds) to denote acts of hospitality (Moessner, 1989: 124). The guest motif in particular is typically Lukan (Grundmann, 1966: 28, 132). In many passages in Luke-Acts the terms *oikos* and *menō* are found together (e.g., Lk 1:56; 5:29; 8:27). Almost all of them, except Lk 8:27, express the idea of someone remaining in a house as a guest. Though *oikos* is not explicitly used with *menō*, the concept of remaining with someone as a guest is very clearly seen in Lk 24:29 (twice); Acts 9:43; 18:3; etc. (Gérard, 1995: 100). Salvation and peace are connected with the reception of Jesus as guest. Jesus' visit to someone brings with it salvation (Kariamadam, 1985: 24). To stay or remain in someone's house implies that a meal would be eaten (see Lk 10:7; Just, 1993: 188). In the Zacchaeus episode salvation is equated with Jesus (compare, "I must stay in your house today" [verse 5] and "salvation has come to this house" [verse 9]; D'Sa, 1996: 196).

Verse 6: So he hurried down and was happy to welcome him.

Jesus' instructions to Zacchaeus are met with immediate and exact obedience (*pseusas katabēthi. . . speusas katebē*, "hurry and come down. . . and he hurried down"; see Lk 2:16: *speusantes*, the shepherds "went with haste" and with joy (Neale, 1991: 182; Tannehill, 1994: 203; Green, 1997: 670). The language of welcome evokes that of the mission charges (see especially Lk 10:8-9), and its import is underlined by the language of joy (Nolland, 1993: 905). There is a progressive development of the narrative between the desire of Zacchaeus to see Jesus (Lk 19:4), Jesus' command to him (Lk 19:5), and Zacchaeus's response to this command (Lk 19:6). This pattern reminds us of the desire of the blind man to see (Lk 18:41), Jesus' command to him (Lk 18:42) and its consequence (Lk 18:43). The command and authority of Jesus the Lord are expressed in the central part of both passages (Lk 19:5 and 18:42). It is Jesus the Lord (*kurios*, Lk 18:41 and 19:8) who gives sight to the blind and the gift of conversion to sinners (Kariamadam, 1985: 25–26).

Out of four occurrences of the verb *hupodechomai* ("to welcome, to receive") in the New Testament three are found in Luke-Acts (Lk 10:38; 19:6; Acts 17:7; Hendrickx, 2000: 80). The two occurrences of *hupodechomai* in Luke are at the beginning and the end of the Travel Narrative (Lk 10:38 and 19:5). In both cases Jesus the Lord is received in the house of someone as he enters a village or town (Marshall, 1978: 697).

Zacchaeus receives Jesus with joy (*chairōn*). *Chairōn* is placed for emphasis at the end of the sentence, as at Lk 15:5; Acts 8:39 (C.F. Evans, 1990: 662). Joy is the response of faith (Tiede, 1988: 321). The verb *chairō* and the noun *chara* are more frequently used in Luke than in the other Synoptics (*chairō*: Mt: 6 times; Mk: 2; Lk: 12; Acts: 7; *chara*: Mt: 6; Mk: 1; Lk: 8; Acts: 4; Navone, 1970: 71–87). Luke repeatedly changes his Markan source by *chairō*. Here in Lk 19:6 *chairōn* functions as a graphic participle at the end of the sentence, which is typically Lukan. It indicates a joy due to the nearness of salvation (Jeremias, 1971: 183–184; Tiede, 1988: 319). This joy, rarely found in Mark (except Mk 4:16//Mt 13:20//Lk 8:13), and which Matthew mentions only occasionally, permeates the Gospel of Luke. It occurs at the birth of John the Baptist (Lk 1:14, 41, 58), at the annunciation to Mary (Lk 1:28), at the visitation (Lk 1:41, 44), and at the annunciation made to the shepherds (Lk 2:10). *Chara* describes the inner dimension of Luke's last beatitude (Lk 6:23: "leap for joy" [*skirtēsate*] is found only in Luke; Mt 5:12 has "be glad" [*agalliasthe*]; Dupont, 1969: 319–324). The plan for Christian joy presented in the beatitudes is continued in the Travel Narrative where there are twenty references of joy and ten pericopes in which this theme is basic (Kariamadam, 1985: 28 note 104).

We notice especially that in the beginning of the Travel Narrative Jesus rejoices over the Father's revelation to the *nēpioi* (NRSV: "infants"; Lk 10:21-22). Towards the end of the Travel Narrative Zacchaeus, a toll collector and a sinner, who belongs to the category of the "marginalized" is presented. Jesus takes the initiative to visit Zacchaeus and the latter is happy about it. His immediate reaction is one of joy because it is "good news of great joy" (Lk 2:10; D'Sa, 1996: 199). The privilege of the poor and marginalized is also found at the center of the Travel Narrative. The parable of the Great Banquet and the eschatological joy (Lk 14:16-24) illustrates this. Through the three parables of joy found in Luke 15, the joy experienced in finding the lost is very much emphasized. Zacchaeus is also a person who is "lost" (Lk 19:10), but he finds joy in the mercy of Jesus. The joy of the lost ones is also found in Lk 5:29. Here, in order to express his joy in the presence of Jesus, the toll collector Levi throws a great party (different in Mk 2:15 and Mt 9:10; Kariamadam, 1985: 27–28). One cannot but recall here the words of the psalmist as an undercurrent: ". . . let the hearts of those who seek the Lord rejoice. Seek the Lord and his strength; seek his presence continually" (Ps 105:3-4; Raja, 1995: 142).

Verse 7:   All who saw it began to grumble and said,
              "He has gone to be the guest of one who is a sinner."

The "crowd" of verse 3 become "all" at this stage of the story (Dupont, 1991: 267; Danker, 1988: 305; Tannehill, 1994: 206), meaning "all who saw it" (Green, 1997: 671). *Diagogguzō* ("to grumble") occurs only twice in the New Testament and both instances are found in Luke (Lk 15:2 and 19:7). We also find *gogguzō* and *goggusmos* in Luke-Acts, once each (Lk 5:30; Acts 5:1). *Diagogguzō* is found in Lk 15:2 in the introduction to the parables of mercy and joy (Lk 15:1-3; see Hendrickx, 2000a: 101–102). Jesus' association with toll collectors and sinners and the criticism of his adversaries are often found in the Gospel of Luke (Dupont, 1969: 230–232). The redactional character of Lk 19:7 may be grasped in particular from its similarity with Lk 5:30; 15:2 (see also the situation described in Acts 11:1-3). In all these passages in the Gospel "murmuring" (*diagogguzō* or *gogguzō*) followed by *legontes* ("saying") concerns Jesus' eating or lodging with sinners. In Lk 19:7 too the crowd uses the word "lodge" which implies the complete setting which in the Middle East always includes a meal (Hamm, 1991: 250; D'Sa, 1996: 199). The murmuring of the adversaries occurs in the context of feasting or joy (Lk 5:29; 7:36; 15:1-2; 15:6-7, 9-10, 22-24; 19:6), invitation to or act of repentance (Lk 5:32; 7:37; 15:7-24; 19:8, 10). Jesus' adversaries do not share in his eschatological joy, nor are they prepared for repentance. (The murmuring against Jesus may be compared with the murmuring of the people against Moses in the desert; Kariamadam, 1985: 31 and note 118). In Lk 19:37-40 the Pharisees criticize the disciples of Jesus for their messianic joy. When Luke writes about the Jewish criticism of Jesus in his Gospel, he may have in mind the situation of the Church, where Jewish Christians criticized the admission of Gentiles into the faith (Löning, 1971: 206–207).

Despite superficial appearances of popularity, Jesus, as the events revealed, was out of touch with the mainstream. Too far out. Many a creative thinker after him has discovered that the general populace ("all") is reluctant to embrace even ideas that in the long run may be to its interest (Danker, 1988: 305).

Verse 8:   Zacchaeus stood there and said to the Lord,
             "Look, half of my possessions, Lord,
             I will give to the poor;
             and if I have defrauded one of anything,
             I will pay back four times as much."

Verse 8 is widely considered as a Lukan insertion since it introduces a typically Lukan theme into the story: the effects of conversion, which Luke likes to present in the context of giving up one's possessions and which is addressed to the Christian community (Ernst, 1977: 513; Grundmann, 1963: 358; Dupont, 1973: 162; Nützel, 1980: 188; Schweizer, 1984: 290: hardly part of the story in its original form; but was it added by Luke?; somewhat different: Craddock, 1990: 219; different: Klein, 1987: 68–69: verses 7 and 10 are redactional, not verse 8).

The effect of Jesus on the life of Zacchaeus puts the murmurers to shame. It also places the idea of restitution within the framework of what God has done for him in the person of Jesus (Schweizer, 1984: 292). In past scenes of controversy we have come to expect at this point the introduction of a statement from Jesus to answer and justify the action just undertaken (Lk 5:31; 7:35, 40; 15:3-32; 18:14).

The story here differs in that Zacchaeus rises to speak and so, for the first time in Luke's Gospel, the "sinner" is able to articulate his own response directly to Jesus (Neale, 1991: 184). *Statheis* ("standing," "he stood," or "he stood his ground" [Ahern, 1987: 350]) carries the full weight one would expect it to carry in Luke's narrative, where that word in participial form nearly always signals a public pronouncement (e.g., Acts 2:14; 5:20; 17:22). To picture Zacchaeus rising to speak as the host of a meal, then, is not unreasonable (Hamm, 1988: 435), although we are not told if this took place after Zacchaeus came down from the tree, in Zacchaeus's home, or after dinner (Stein, 1992: 468).

According to the introduction of verse 9, it is to Zacchaeus that Jesus' answer is addressed. But verse 9b speaks of him in the third person; he too is a son of Abraham. This remark constitutes a good answer to the murmuring of verse 7, and therefore to Jesus' opponents (Nützel, 1980: 189–190), but it is hard to see the connection of verse 9b with verse 8. It would perhaps be easier to establish a rapport between verse 8 and the first part of Jesus' answer in verse 9a: "Today salvation has come to this house." The generalizing conclusion found in verse 10 can easily be attached to the first as well as to the second part of verse 9. The way verse 10 talks about Jesus' mission has no direct rapport with Zacchaeus's dispositions manifested in verse 8. These observations raise questions concerning the homogeneity of the story (see Dupont, 1991: 265–266).

Zacchaeus's *actions* undergo great transformations. At the beginning of the story, he is designated by his profession: toll collector. He is therefore somebody who *gathers up* (verse 2). Then a change takes place: he welcomes Jesus to his home (verse 6) and he gives half of his goods to the poor (verse 8). In other words, he *shares*. At the beginning he *grabs* things for himself; at the end he *gives* to others (Vogels, 1978: 489). By underscoring Zacchaeus's act of giving one-half to the poor, Luke forcefully informs his readers that the new way of discipleship goes beyond what any law can require, that it is much more than a token gift, that, in fact, it is a total commitment of one's wealth for the poor (Pilgrim, 1981: 133).

The *speech* of Zacchaeus is often interpreted as a vow for a reformed lifestyle in gratitude for Jesus' behavior towards him (e.g., Schlatter, 1960: 403; Tannehill, 1986: 123; Marshall, 1978: 697; Grundmann, 1963: 360; O'Hanlon, 1981: 16; Bock, 1996: 1520; Matson, 1996: 70-74; Pilgrim, 1981: 132). Jesus calls Zacchaeus; Zacchaeus responds with a promise of a change of behavior and restoration for past wrongs. Jesus then declares his salvation and inclusion among the sons of Abraham. Understood in this way, the story is a concrete example of "conversion" (Conzelmann, 1960: 228-230), and Zacchaeus is the ultimate penitent. Ultimately, this may be the correct interpretation, yet the reading of the Greek text suggests another possible interpretation.

The verbs are present tense (*didōmi, apodidōmi,* "to give," "pay back") and a more natural understanding of the statement would seem to be that the giving of his possessions and the restoration of fraudulently obtained income have already been the habit of Zacchaeus: "Look, half of my possessions, Lord, I give to the poor; and if I have defrauded anyone of anything, I pay back four times as much" (compare the NIV: "Lord, Lord, here and now I give half of my possessions..."). Taken this way, our chief toll collector is not repenting and vowing a changed life but defending himself against the charges of the crowd. This interpretation has been summed up in the following way: "The story tells of a man who is stereotyped by his job, resented and wrongly accused by his neighbors, who defended himself against the false charge, and whose good name was vindicated by Jesus" (White, 1979: 89; compare Fitzmyer, 1985: 1218–1222, summarized and criticized by Hamm, 1988: 433–435). White calls the passage a "vindication" story and his argumentation is quite convincing. Alan C. Mitchel has also argued that Jesus brings vindication, rather than conversion, to Zacchaeus (Mitchel, 1990: 153–176).

Despite White's argumentation there are two reasons why we believe the traditional interpretation to be, in the last analysis, the correct one. The first is based on considerations internal to Lk 19:8. The determinative factor lies in the second half of the verse, in the comment about the restoration of fraudulently taken goods. In order for White and Fitzmyer to say that the charity and restoration professed by Zacchaeus was his customary manner of business, they must say that the "fraud" was unintentional (White, 1979: 92; Fitzmyer, 1985: 1225). What Zacchaeus was saying, according to this view, was that he made fourfold restoration when it was discovered that people were inadvertently overtaxed. Obviously, no one (except perhaps a very poor business person!) would intentionally defraud and then make restoration at fourfold the price.

In response to White's position, it must be pointed out that the word used to describe Zacchaeus's activity (*sukophanteō*) is far too strong a word to be construed as unintentional wrongdoing (in Lk 3:14, the only other occurrence in the New Testament, it is used to refer to violent robbery by soldiers; Neale, 1991: 186 and note 2; Gérard, 1995: 99). For confessed fraud Roman law required fourfold restitution in cases of theft. And according to Jewish law fourfold restitution was neither required nor appropriate for a "mistake" but only for deliberate acts of theft (Neale, 1991: 185–186), e.g., the theft of sheep (Ex 22:1; C.F. Evans, 1990: 663; Bock, 1996: 1513, 1520).

On the other hand, neither can the whole of Lk 19:8b be understood as a promise or vow about his future actions, unless Zacchaeus is promising both to defraud *and* to restore in his future activities. Would a repentant sinner foresee his new lapses? (Fitzmyer, 1985: 1221). More pointedly, would he admit to the possibility in the flush of this moment? (Neale, 1991: 186 note 4). The statement, "and if I have defrauded anyone of anything. . . ," can only make sense as an admission of past crimes which have remained undiscovered to this point and for which no restitution has been made. The Greek does not express doubt, and should be rendered, "From whomever I have extorted. . ." (C.F. Evans, 1990: 663). The last half of the statement, *apodidōmi tetraploun* (NRSV: "I will pay back four times as much") must be a statement of resolve to finally set things aright. Zacchaeus is in fact "repenting." The verb *apodidōmi* is not so much a futuristic present (that is, "I will repay. . .") as a simple statement of present resolve (Creed, 1957: 231). The New International Version (NIV) may, after all, best capture the meaning of these present tenses: "here and now" Zacchaeus not only makes right his wrongs but goes beyond this to give half his goods to the poor. For Luke it is repentance in its most convincing form (Neale, 1991: 186–187).

In this story, then, the stress is not placed upon Zacchaeus's faith in Jesus, nor is the story a call to full discipleship. The emphasis lies rather upon the results of Zacchaeus's reception of salvation (Pilgrim, 1981: 132).

The criticism of the adversaries of Jesus is followed by the concrete act of conversion of Zacchaeus. The *de* at the beginning of verse 8 (not translated by NRSV) shows that Zacchaeus's action is contrasted with the conduct of the adversaries (Plummer, 1901/1977: 434). Verse 8 begins with the phrase *statheis de* ("stood"), a phrase used by Luke to introduce solemn acts. Here it indicates the solemnity of the declaration of Zacchaeus and gives it a religious and quasi liturgical character (Plummer, 1901/1977: 434). *Kurios* (*kurie*) to designate the earthly Jesus is also characteristic of the third evangelist.

Idou ("look") is rarely found in Mark (8 times) but is very frequent in Luke (56 times). By giving one half of his possessions to the poor, Zacchaeus practices what John the Baptist required in Lk 3:10-14: "Whoever has two coats must share with anyone who has none" (Lk 3:11), that is, one half. *Sukophanteō* ("to defraud") is found only in the Zacchaeus episode and in Lk 3:14. The redactional character of Lk 3:10-14 is noted by almost all commentators (e.g., Schürmann, 1969: 168–169). This passage is an advice to the crowds, and more particularly to toll collectors and soldiers to avoid injustice and practice sharing (Hendrickx, 1997: 27–37). In Lk 19:8 *sukophanteō* refers to deliberate injustice, and Zacchaeus promises to restore his extortions "fourfold." Almost all commentators say that Zacchaeus went beyond the usual Jewish regulations in his restoration (e.g., Grundmann, 1963: 360). Fourfold restitution is by almost any reckoning excessive (see Lev 6:5; Num 5:6-7; 2 Sam 12:6; Green, 1997: 671 note 208; but see above). But Duncan M. Derrett has tried to prove that the Jews used to think in terms of fourfold restitution (Derrett, 1970: 284 and note 5). The gesture of Zacchaeus may be contrasted with the behavior of the rich ruler in Lk 18:18-23. It shows the genuineness of the former's conversion (Kariamadam, 1985: 33–34, 35-36). Conversion is to receive Jesus in one's home with joy so that he may stay. Zacchaeus does not ask "What must I do to inherit eternal life?" (Lk 18:18). He knows that by receiving the Lord, and through him salvation, his life must change, his life *is* changed (Breydon, 1989: 58, 59).

Supporting the view that we are dealing here with a conversion story is a feature overlooked by most commentators, namely, the corporate character of Zacchaeus's conversion. Jesus responds to Zacchaeus's appeal by declaring that "today salvation has come to this household" (Lk 19:9). The story of Zacchaeus recounts not only a conversion but a particular kind of conversion—the bestowal of salvation to the personified *oikos* by the Lukan Jesus (Matson, 1996: 74 and note 121). The whole family of Zacchaeus turned to God in true repentance. This phenomenon becomes readily observable in Acts when entire households convert to the Christian faith on the basis of the faith of the householder, particularly in the story of the Roman jailer who rejoices

with all his household (*panoikei*) because he believed in God
(*pepisteukōs*: Acts 16:34; Matson, 1996: 74–75 and note 125).

There is a significant connection between the rich ruler
(Lk 18:23) and Zacchaeus (Lk 19:2). What the rich ruler
cannot bring himself to do, Zacchaeus does gladly by divest-
ing himself of his riches (O'Hanlon, 1981: 182). By means
of a reversal we find that the rich and hated toll collector
does the proper thing and wins God's approval, whereas the
essentially law-abiding rich ruler cannot enter the kingdom.

Verse 9:   Then Jesus said to him,
              "Today salvation has come to this house,
              because he too is a son of Abraham.

In verse 9 the redactor attempts to combine two answers (Lk 19:9a and 9b). Lk 19:9b may be considered as the
traditional answer to the objectors of verse 7. But Luke was
probably not satisfied with this answer alone. He wanted to
insist more on the theme of salvation and added Lk 19:9a
to Jesus' answer. In Luke's view salvation is not only for
Zacchaeus but also for the Christian community (compare
Dupont, 1991: 268) which, like him, calls Jesus "Lord." It
has been suggested that Luke intended this story as the paradigm *par excellence* for the wealthy Christians in his community (Pilgrim, 1981: 129).

The term *sōtēria* ("salvation") is found only in Luke and
Lk 19:9 is the last of four uses in the Third Gospel. Salvation of the house or household is typically Lukan. The presence of this theme in Lk 19:9a is already an anticipation of
the theme in Acts. Salvation of the household is found in
Acts 10:2; 11:14; 16:15, 31, 34; 18:8 (Kariamadam, 1985:
39–40; Danker, 1988: 306; Tiede, 1988: 321–322; Craddock,
1990: 220; Raja, 1995: 146–147). Luke's use of salvation
language (*sōtēria*, *sōzein*), especially in the Travel Narrative,
makes most sense when salvation is understood in terms of
inclusion in God's people. It serves to identify present social realities more than the future destiny of individuals. Sal-

vation means to belong to the remnant people God is creating out of Jews and Gentiles in the present season (Johnson, 1993: 525, 536; Hobbie, 1977: 288; Green, 1997: 673). *Sōtēria* means a new beginning for Zacchaeus and his household (Nützel, 1980: 192; Green, 1997: 673).

The response found in Lk 19:9b may have been the original ending of the story since it is a good reply to the objectors. If at the beginning of the story Zacchaeus is disqualified as chief of the toll collectors and rich with the phrase *kai autos*, (Lk 19:2), he is here qualified as a son of Abraham by the same expression. God's promise to the fathers from Abraham onward is a theme which runs through Luke-Acts (Dahl, 1966: 139–158; Hendrickx, 2000: 283–284). Luke has more references to Abraham than the other Gospels (Mt: 7 times; Mk: once; Lk: 15; Jn: 11; Acts: 7). He insists on the continuity of saving history. The salvific events of the New Testament are the fulfillment of the promises made in the Old Testament. Luke speaks of the children of Abraham in Lk 3:8; 13:16; 19:9; Acts 13:26, 33 (Acts 3:25). Mention of God's covenant, oath and promise to Abraham is made in Lk 1:55, 67-73; Acts 7:2-8, 17; 26:6. Abraham in the hereafter is depicted in Lk 13:28; 16:22-31; 20:37-38. Luke introduces the idea of the God of Abraham, Isaac and Jacob, the God of the fathers in Lk 20:37; Acts 3:13; 7:32. Lk 13:16 and 19:9 refer to a daughter of Abraham and a son of Abraham respectively after criticism by Jesus' opponents concerning the latter's merciful deed. The wording in both verses is also similar (Drury, 1977: 74). At the end of both pericopes (Lk 13:11-17 and 19:1-10) it is shown that Jesus' mission is to make all men and women the children of Abraham to make them all participate in the promise made to Abraham and his descendants. God's promise to Abraham is fulfilled to his children through the ministry of Jesus (Dahl, 1966: 150, 153; Kariamadam, 1985: 41–42; Dupont, 1991: 269–273; Kuschel, 1994: 97–103).

We are not explicitly told why Zacchaeus has won Jesus' approval, only that he too is a "son of Abraham." Luke leaves us to our own devices to derive the significance of Zacchaeus's actions. But this has been characteristic of Luke; he always leaves a certain vagueness about the penitential activities of his "sinners." We are given only glimpses of penitent attitudes and never advised of the full or long-term effect or behavior. Levi simply leaves his toll table and this seems to be enough (Lk 5:28); the "sinful woman" (Lk 7:36ff.) and the toll collector (Lk 18:9-14) grieve for their sin, but does a change of life ensue? Does the lost son finally become a productive member of the family (Lk 15:11-32)? Does Zacchaeus switch profession or make other significant changes in reponse to his encounter with Jesus? Such details are not given, neither are they necessary for the stories to have their persuasive effect. Luke gives us no detailed paradigm of repentance, no programme of deeds; it is more like an ethos of repentance which pervades these passages. Grief over the past, contrition, humility, deeds of restoration, these are all a part of Luke's view of repentance. But the effect is derived cumulatively from all his "sinner" material, it is never stated in explicit terms in one place (Neale, 1991: 187–188).

Verse 10:   For the Son of Man came to seek out and save the
             lost."

Some commentators see this verse as a Lukan addition to the story, while others argue for its pre-Lukan origin. Luke seems to have reworked a free-floating logion adapting it to his own purpose. Verse 10 has obvious links with Lk 5:32, but its imagery is inspired by Ez 34:16, "I will seek the lost, and I will bring back the strayed. . . ." The difference of Lk 19:10 from Ezekiel is the addition of sōsai ("save") in Luke (van Unnik, 1957: 192). Towards the end of the Travel Narrative he insists on the saving mission of Jesus (Kariamadam, 1985: 42-43, 45, 48).

Luke has capped the story with the familiar saying: "For the Son of Man came to seek out and save the lost." Herein lies the second reason why the story of Zacchaeus must ultimately be considered one of repentance and not of vindication. From the point of view of the Lukan narrative, verse 10 is determinative for the way in which Luke wishes the incident to be interpreted. Zacchaeus is the "lost" one. The "Son of Man" (Loewe, 1974: 326) has appeared to rescue this lost sheep of the house of Israel and set him back within the fold. It is the Ezekiel 34 theme revisited once again (Green, 1997: 673). We have found it throughout the Gospel and this event is clearly meant by Luke to be the ultimate example of the efficacy of Jesus' ministry as the shepherd who calls the "lost" back home. Zacchaeus repents and his deeds win him the shepherd's praise. Luke calls forth echoes of Lk 5:30; 15:4-7, 8-10 and especially Lk 5:32 into a single phrase which sums up his view of the purpose of Jesus' mission: "The Son of Man came to seek out and save the lost" (Neale, 1992: 188). The "Son of David" of Lk 18:35-43 gives way to the "Son of Man" in the present episode (but note the Davidic content of the allusion to Ezekiel 34). To the deliverance in Lk 18:35-43 of a man lost in blindness and poverty corresponds now the deliverance of a man lost in wealth and corruption (Nolland, 1993: 903), which is but another kind of blindness.

The popular use of the phrase "to save the lost" has been much more narrow than in Luke. One hears it almost exclusively in terms of a conversion and often in an even more restricted sense of "preserving a soul for heaven." Here in the case of Zacchaeus, his "being saved" refers to a conversion, to be sure, but not in any private sense. Not only is his household involved but also the poor who will be beneficiaries of his conversion as well as all those people whom he may have defrauded. His salvation, therefore, has personal, domestic, social, and economic dimensions (Craddock, 1990: 220).

There are thousands of Zacchaeuses in our days who are yearning for, searching after and seeking God. They want an experience. And many sincere seekers do hear the words addressed to them, "Hurry and come down; for I must stay at your house today" (Lk 19:5). Sincere and true seekers will always find rest in their seeking (cf. Mt 11:28-30) as Zacchaeus found joy as well as salvation as a result of his seeking.

The initiative of Jesus breaks through symbolically for all times the oppressive barriers of caste, creed, color, race, language, etc. It breaks through the limits of decorum by the fact that Jesus does not wait to be invited, but invites himself; it breaks through the distinction of sinners and the righteous since Jesus, the holy one of God, seeks to be in the company of the disreputed. The Lukan Jesus shows that, on the one hand, no social rank, however mean or low excludes salvation, and on the other, it is offered especially to the last, the least and the lost.

Lk 19:1-10 is not a story of an individual seeker after God. It is our story. It is the story of all the seekers of God and of all who seek for what is good and beautiful in the world and in human beings. It is a story that tells us that in seeking God we must encounter his image and likeness in every human being, especially the poor. It is a story that reminds us that it is in and through ordinary events that Jesus enters into our life. It is a story that instructs us that in the midst and the heart of the hustle and bustle of the world there is a God who is calling us to attention and service. It is a story that demands from everyone that we seek him in order to be sought by him (Raja, 1995: 143, 145, 148).

d. *The Parable of the Pounds* (Lk 19:11-27)

The parable of the Talents or of the Pounds, found in Mt 25:14-30 and Lk 19:11-27, is a curious parable. The differences in the parable found in Matthew from that found in Luke are significant enough to raise questions about whether they are different versions of a common source (Q; e.g., Weder, 1978: 193; C.F. Evans, 1990: 665: same parable, though certainly not taken directly from a common source) or distinctive variations on a common theme (Tiede, 1988: 323; see Lambrecht, 1978: 243–244). Do we have one parable redacted by two evangelists or two oral performances using similar themes? (Fitzmyer, 1985: 1228–1233; Blomberg, 1990: 214–221). The matter is further complicated by Luke (or the pre-Lukan tradition?), who has apparently interwoven vestiges of a second parable (the Throne Claimant; see Lk 19:12, 14, 15a, 17) to create a longer version of the parable of the Pounds (Herzog II, 1994: 150; McBride, 1999: 78; compare Weder, 1978: 194–195; Resenhofft, 1979–1980: 318; Lambrecht, 1985: 600; Puig i Tarrech, 1985: 171–172; Kim, 1998: 160–161; Weiser, 1971: 226, 269 calls it an *Erzähleinheit*, a "narrative unity"). The story of a nobleman traveling abroad to acquire for himself the title of king has an interesting historical parallel in Archelaus, the eldest son and successor of Herod the Great (Tiede, 1988: 323–324; McBride, 1999: 78–79). According to Eusebius of Caesarea the apocryphal *Gospel of the Nazoreans* contained also a version of the parable (Didier, 1967: 257).

Scholars commonly identify three stages in the tradition history of the parable, usually working backward from the canonical texts to their reconstructed earlier forms. These three stages are identified as follows: (1) the parable as eschatological warning; (2) the parable as parenetic instruction; and (3) the parable of Jesus (Didier, 1967: 251–271; de la Potterie, 1985: 615; compare Weder, 1978: 193–210).

In its *current settings in Matthew and Luke*, the parable has been interpreted eschatologically. Matthew places the parable in the midst of his discourse on the judgment (Mt 24–25). Lk 19:11-27 has fashioned the parable as a response to those who presumed that (now that Jesus was close to Jerusalem) the long-awaited parousia was approaching. This is clearly stated in Luke's framing (verse 11) and in his structuring of the action.

Each slave is given the same amount and the same charge (verse 13); what is true of one member of Luke's community is true of all without distinction. They exhibit their faith in the one who "reigns over them" by following his instructions. But others do not share their faith, and the introduction of the materials from the Throne-Claimant parable seems to turn the focus of the parable on those who question the Risen Lord's claim (Scott, 1989: 222). The third slave evidently represents a type of this group, which may explain why Luke portrays the third slave so negatively. In Luke's parable, this slave hides his pound in a cloth napkin (*soudarion*) rather than in the ground (Mt 25:18, *ōruxen gēn*), thereby indicating his irresponsibility, and Luke's master does not merely pronounce judgment but condemns the third slave "by your own words." Like the others for whom he is a stand-in, this slave is an enemy of the newly enthroned king because he objected to his reign. His action with regard to the pound is here interpreted eschatologically, and the judgment he receives reflects the attitudes he held and their subsequent effect on his "trading" (Herzog II, 1994: 150–151).

The parable constitutes Jesus' final teaching on the journey to Jerusalem (McBride, 1999: 78; J.T. Sanders, 1985: 665). The parable is particularly well suited to its narrative location, for it is in Jerusalem, where Jesus will be presented and rejected as king (Lk 19:38; 22:29; 23:2-3, 11, 37-38, 42). In this respect the parable looks forward to the subsequent rejection expressed by the religious leadership at the (triumphal) entry as well as the entire Jerusalem narrative (Cunningham, 1997: 119).

Luke places the parable in the last phase of the Travel Narrative in such a way that the parable interprets the ensuing Jerusalem narrative as the human rejection/divine confirmation of Jesus' kingship, and defines the relation of those

Jerusalem events to eschatology. In the Lukan form, the parable distinguishes the arrival of Jesus at Jerusalem from the end-time appearance of the kingdom, yet identifies the rejection of Jesus by the leaders of Israel (by "this generation": see Lk 17:25) as a repudiation of the kingship of Jesus—which is itself the decisive fact of the eschatological kingdom (Carroll, 1988: 97; Kim, 1998: 163).

There is little in the parable itself which demands considering it an allegorical tale about the ascension-parousia (*pace* S. Brown, 1969: 194; Kaestli, 1969: 40; Grundmann, 1966: 363; Mc Gaughy, 1975: 235–245; Marshall, 1978: 701; Lambrecht, 1985: 601; Stein, 1992: 473). In particular, there is nothing in Luke's version to indicate a temporal delay of the parousia. Matthew's parable of the Talents appears to have affected the reading of Luke's story (de la Potterie, 1985: 619–621). By the way he has clustered Mt 25:14-30 with the Ten Bridesmaids (Mt 25:1-13) and the Judgment of the Nations (Mt 25:31-46) within his eschatological discourse, Matthew has made his parable one of eschatological judgment. Matthew alone has any indication that the man was gone "a long time" (Mt 25:19). One cannot take Luke's "distant country" (Lk 19:12) as indicating a significant temporal delay (Johnson, 1982 and note 24; *pace* Creed, 1957: 232; Dupont, 1969: 382; Kaestli, 1969: 39–40). Luke has no significant delay in the nobleman's return as king. Everything gets carried out with dispatch. The "getting of the kingdom" is not an unrealized event of the future, but one already accomplished in the story (Lk 19:15; Tiede, 1980: 79). The reward to those who have handled their charge well does not consist in some future overseeing of possessions, but is present ("take charge"), and consists in power (*exousia*) over cities within the king's realm (Lk 19:17, 19). They play a present leadership role within the kingdom gained by the nobleman. This political reward for the faithful use of possessions integrates the two parts of the story, and indicates as well that the "political" aspect of the parable is not secondary but, in the present version, primary (Johnson, 1982: 143–144).

On the level of the parable as *parenetic instruction*, the addition of a free-floating proverb ("to all those who have, more will be given; but from those who have nothing, even what they have will be taken away"; Lk 19:26; Mt 25:29; see Mt 13:12; Mk 4:25; Lk 8:18) and some moralizing redactional touches have led many scholars to identify a second stage in the tradition history of the parable. In this stage, the church attempted to adapt a parable of Jesus told to a specific audience by generalizing its message (Dodd, 1961: 148; Jeremias, 1963: 62; etc.). In recent years, the parable has been read in the context of peasant values in early Mediterranean societies, especially the notion of limited good and preference for the "use value" over "exchange value" (Rohrbaugh, 1993: 33–36). This would certainly alter the parenetic meaning of the parable in a way that would differentiate it sharply from the canonical versions of the parable. If Rohrbaugh is right, the parable would resemble an exhortation to the village values of limited good and an exchange economy while reinforcing the typical peasant's antagonism toward the growing exchange economy, that is, an agrarian economy undergoing changes caused by commercialization (Herzog II, 1994: 151–152).

To judge from modern commentary on the parable, this second stage of the tradition continues to exercise a profound influence on twentieth-century readings. Dan Via, for instance, finds that the refusal to risk leads to repressed guilt, which, when projected onto another, leads to "the loss of opportunity for meaningful existence" (Via, 1967: 119). And John Donahue is convinced that "out of fear for failure, he refused even to try to succeed" (Donahue, 1988: 106–108). As these representative examples reveal, the parable's moral center of gravity is located in the nobleman's judgment of the third slave. Clearly, the parable has proven a fruitful text for developing moral commentary (Herzog II, 1994: 152–153).

Regarding *the parable of Jesus* (see Weiser, 1971: 259–262; Puig i Tarrech, 1985: 188–193; for a [hypothetical] reconstruction of the original parable, see Weder, 1978: 202–203), it has been argued that Jesus constructed a parable around a postexilic maxim found in Lk 19:20b-21 (parallel in Mt 25:24b-25) which deals with the "hardness" of the master and the subsequent fear engendered in the third slave (McGaughy, 1975: 241–245). The maxim reflected postexilic Judaism's understanding of God as stern and harsh (see, e.g., Job 23:13-17), as well as its belief in its mission to keep the Torah intact in a hostile world. Against this way of construing the mission of Judaism, Jesus told the parable of the Pounds/Talents, arguing that preserving the Torah by building a hedge around it was not enough. In this context, the parable was about neither eschatology nor ethics but contributed to an ongoing discussion about the mission of the house of Jacob in the world (see Isa 49:6).

Given the fact that upwards of ninety percent of agrarian populations were rural farmers, the original audience may have included Galilean peasants. If it did, the commonly perceived thrust of the parable becomes problematic (Rohrbaugh, 1993: 33). What are we to make of this parable in which we see a nobleman "laying out his money to money-lenders and agents," "pursuing and amassing new wealth," "wrangling and interrogating his slaves," "inspecting the ledgers" and "casting up accounts" with the slaves to whom he has entrusted his money? And what are we to make of the slaves who cooperate with the scheme, proudly announcing their success and, if not anticipating, at least receiving a handsome award? For whom could such a story possibly be seen as good news?

Such persons as this nobleman can be seen as honorable and such a story seen as good news only if the story is told from the vantage point and value system of the rich, that is, those who have and use power to extract the shares of others for themselves. Such are the very opposite of those praised by Sir 31:8-11.

And what of the servants? The "venturesome" and "industrious" pair could be heroes only to those who believed it is right to amass wealth by contriving to get a bigger share of the limited good. The third slave, the one who gained nothing, could be viewed as "wicked" only by persons with this same elitist mentality. He is widely condemned by interpreters as a failure.

To a peasant, however, who believes that there is nothing within his or anyone else's power that can be done to increase the limited good, who believes that rich people are thieves without mercy and that honorable men seek only what is already theirs, to such a peasant could this text have been anything but frightening? (Rohrbaugh, 1993: 35).

There is a third extant version of this story in the so-called *Gospel of the Nazoreans*, known to us only from quotations and allusions in the Church Fathers and a few later writings. Neither the Nazorean author nor Eusebius who comments on the pertinent passage, could imagine commending slaves who used a master's money for additional gain, which raises questions concerning the common interpretation (Rohrbaugh, 1993: 36–37).

Verse 11:   As they were listening to this,
             he went on to tell a parable,
             because he was near Jerusalem,
             and because they supposed
             that the kingdom of God was to appear immediately.

As in Lk 18:1, 9 the reason for the parable, and thus the key to its meaning, precedes the parable itself (Stein, 1992: 472; Green, 1997: 674, 677; Mattill, 1979: 121–130). Verse 11 is critical to an understanding of the function of the parable of Lk 19:11-27 in the narrative. Practically all interpreters agree that this verse makes Luke's understanding of the parable clear (Johnson, 1982: 140; J.T. Sanders, 1981: 665; de la Potterie, 1985: 622). The parable both helps to interpret and is interpreted by its surrounding context

(Green, 1997: 675–676). That Luke has composed Lk 19:11 is almost universally acknowledged, and for good reason. The vocabulary is Lukan, and so is the style (C.F. Evans, 1990: 670). As is his custom elsewhere, Luke employs a question or supposition to "set up" eschatological instruction (Lk 12:40; 17:20; 21:7; Acts 1:6—the parable may anticipate the corrective issued in Acts 1:6-8; Danker, 1988: 307), or, more generally, teaching in parables. Moreover, the inclusion of verses 11, 28—"near Jerusalem". . . "going up to Jerusalem"— points to Lukan composition of both verses (Carroll, 1988: 97; de la Potterie, 1985: 627–629 and Puig i Tarrech, 1985: 171 consider Lk 19:28 as the final verse of the episode).

With the introductory genitive absolute *akouontōn de autōn tauta* ("as they were listening to this"), Luke explicitly ties verses 11-27 to the preceding story of Zacchaeus (Kim, 1998: 165)—specifically, to the assertion of Lk 19:9-10. Jesus' words are spoken against a backdrop of the expectations of those who have just heard his words to Zacchaeus (Tiede, 1988: 324; Marshall, 1978: 700). The present participle *akouontōn* suggests that the preceding sayings are still ringing in their ears or being turned over in their minds (Marshall, 1978: 703). Luke envisions no change of scene at all (Green, 1997: 677).

Who are the *autoi* ("they")? The word is ambiguous (Craddock, 1990: 222). The strict grammatical antecedent would be the *pantes* ("all") of Lk 19:7, who grumbled because Jesus entered the house of Zacchaeus. They fit Luke's usual way of presenting the hostile leaders of the people, and the content of their complaints (see e.g., Lk 15:1-3; Johnson, 1977: 109–113). If the parable is told specifically to opponents, the harsh ending would surely be the point. It is possible, however, that the *autoi* refers generally to either the *ochlos* ("crowd") or *mathētai* ("disciples") who make up the other parts of Jesus' entourage as he goes toward Jerusalem. We last saw the *ochlos* in Lk 18:36 (designated as *laos* in Lk 18:43) at the healing of the blind man who proclaimed

Jesus as Son of David (Lk 18:37-39). The *mathētai* last appeared as represented by the Twelve in Lk 18:31, the audience for the third passion prediction (Lk 18:31-34). There are, then, three possible audiences for the parable: the crowd, the disciples, or the opponents (Fitzmyer, 1985: 1233–1234). In the journey narrative, Luke is generally careful to specify Jesus' audiences, and purposefully (Mosely, 1963: 139–149). To the disciples, he has Jesus address teachings on discipleship; to the crowd, calls for repentance, and warnings; to the opponents, sayings of rejection and judgment (Johnson, 1977: 107–108). His failure to make this audience clearer to his readers leads one to think that the group to whom the parable was spoken was meant to consist of all those with Jesus on the way to Jerusalem, with the parable addressing each segment in diverse ways, and Luke's readers most of all (Johnson, 1982: 145; Craddock, 1990: 222).

Is the story told to confute the audience's expectations, or confirm them? This is the critical issue posed by Lk 19:11, and one not easily resolved. The usual understanding is, of course, that the parable is told to refute the expectation (see e.g., Conzelmann, 1960: 113; Dodd, 1961: 153; Jeremias, 1963: 59). But is there anything in the introduction itself which leads to this conclusion? Luke says that the parable was told because of two circumstances: he was near Jerusalem, and "they supposed that the kingdom of God was to appear immediately." That he was near Jerusalem is not in doubt (Lk 18:31). If Luke wanted the parable to serve as a rebuttal, then it must have been addressed to their expectation.

A look at the Gospel as a whole leads to the following conclusions. Luke's way of introducing parables is various. Only once does he explicitly refute the outlook of his listeners. Sometimes he uses the parable to confirm the viewpoint of the audience. Other times still he uses the introduction and the parable as a way of illustrating something about the progress of his larger story. This is clearest in the parable of the Great Banquet (Lk 14:16-24) and the parables of the Lost (Luke 15:1-32). It may well be the function of the parable of the Pounds, as well. In any case, there is nothing in Luke's language or other usage to demand our seeing the parable as a refutation of the expectation expressed in Lk 19:11 (Johnson, 1982: 146–148).

Regarding the content of Lk 19:11—what is being confirmed or confuted—there are at least three possibilities here. Usually the emphasis is placed on *parachrēma* ("immediately"; see e.g., Plummer, 1901/1977: 439; de la Potterie, 1985: 625–626; see, excursus under Lk 18:43), and the place in the sentence would justify this stress. It is a distinctively Lukan word which always refers to a palpable, physical event. Here *parachrēma* is combined with the verb *mellō* ("be about to") often used to indicate an immediate hope (Mattill, 1979: 123). Lk 19:11 is the only place where reference of *parachrēma* might be to an event of larger or more indeterminate proportions. If the parable confirms the introduction, Jesus' entrance as king and the events of the passion are proximate enough to be called *parachrēma*. But if this word is the target of disconfirmation, it is by no means necessary to conclude that the author is justifying a parousia delayed for generations. The confutation of *parachrēma* could be taken care of within the temporal range of Luke's narrative (anytime past the *sēmeron* of Lk 19:9), with not an eye to a distant return of the Lord (Johnson, 1982: 148–149), but, for instance, on the royal inthronization of Jesus on the Mount of Olives (which happens "near Jerusalem") and the following events (Lk 19:29-40; de la Potterie, 1985: 633–634).

The verb *anaphainō* is in a position of greater emphasis even than *parachrēma*. It is usually taken to mean, simply, "appear." Does it point to a full-scale, visible realization of the kingdom, or specifically to the return of the Son of Man for judgment? Or can an "appearance" be accomplished by some sort of symbolic manifestation of the kingdom, such as the proclamation of a king by his followers? Again, the issue of confirmation or disconfirmation is important. It is necessary, in any case, to emphatically deny the assumption that *anaphainō* is part of the technical language connected to the parousia (see Johnson, 1982: 149; de la Potterie, 1985: 622–624). Neither can we assume that *anaphainō* always means the same as *phainō*, although it sometimes does. In the light of its usage in contemporary literature (see Johnson, 1982: 150), it is not at all impossible that Luke intended *mellei hē basileia tou theou anaphainesthai* to mean that "the kingdom of God was going to be declared." This would find immediate confirmation in the proclamation of Jesus as king in Lk 19:38. But what point does Luke want to make about the kingdom of God? If the function of the parable is to confirm the expectation of Lk 19:11, then Luke illustrates something about the kingdom, and those who reject it. And by having Jesus proclaimed as king in Lk 19:38, he says something about the relation of Jesus to this kingdom. This is straightforward. But if the point of the parable is to refute Lk 19:11, several other possibilities present themselves.

Already in Lk 1:33 we were told that Jesus would rule over Israel forever. The question of the restoration of the kingdom to Israel is raised explicitly in Acts 1:6, and only obliquely answered. Three aspects of "kingdom" must therefore be considered: the kingship of Jesus, rule over Israel, and the kingdom of God. Do they mutually impinge? If the point of the parable is to clarify a misconception contained in Lk 19:11, how does it do this? Does it assert that messianic rule over Israel is not the same thing as the kingdom of God, although Jesus is proclaimed as king in the entry into Jerusalem (Dupont, 1969: 381)? Does it assert that the rule of Jesus over God's people is not yet the full realization of God's rule and kingdom (Conzelmann, 1960: 198)? The kingdom is an ongoing reality, but it will appear in a climactic phase at the end of history (Danker, 1988: 308). Luke has a two-stage view of the kingdom: it arrives now but comes in fullness later (Nolland, 1993: 913; Bock, 1996: 1531).

Much weight rests on a less than clear construction. A simplistic view of Lk 19:11 which, without qualification, identifies *basileia tou theou* with the return of Jesus at the parousia misses that complexity altogether and begs the question of the passage's meaning (Johnson, 1982: 150–151).

Verse 12:   So he said,
           "A nobleman went to a distant country
           to get royal power for himself and then return.

Luke's "so" emphasizes what the "because" of verse 11 had already made clear—namely, that Jesus' parable takes its meaning from its immediate context (Green, 1997: 678).

Interpreters have been troubled at all stages of the tradition history of the parable with the portrayal of the "nobleman" (*eugenēs*; Lk 19:12, only here in the Gospels; Acts 17:11; 1 Cor 1:26). Luke makes explicit what Matthew implies. The "man" (*anthrōpos*) embarking on a journey away from his household ("a distant country"; compare Lk 15:13) is a noble or aristocrat (Herzog II, 1994: 158). Because he has always been assumed to be a God figure, the third slave's character description of him has posed a problem. Some have taken the description as being nothing more than part of the "dramatic environment" of the parable, which could not be translated into moral terms. The more common approach is to discredit the third slave's words. They are an expression of repressed guilt projected into the nobleman as a way of blaming him for his own failure (Via, 1967: 119), or a fearful misreading of the "considerable magnanimity" of the one who entrusted to him an amount equal to fifteen years of wages (Donahue, 1988: 108).

Scott turns the anomaly into a hermeneutical clue for reading the parable (Scott, 1989: 226–234). The hearer is forced to choose between the third slave's image of the nobleman and the image that emerges from his actions in the parable. Stated otherwise, these competing images are the explicit image put forward in aphorism by the third slave, and the image implied in the actions of the first two slaves (Scott, 1989: 234). But in the course of developing his reading, Scott did acknowledge that the third slave's characterization of the nobleman appeals to a conventional type, the "absentee landlord who bleeds the land dry" (Scott, 1989: 230).

Unlike Mt 25:14-30, the Lukan form of the parable focuses on kingship, not stewardship. Luke achieves this transposition through insertion of the motif of the throne claimant in verses 12, 14, 15a, 27:

> "A nobleman went to a distant country to get royal power for himself and then return... But the citizens of his country hated him and sent a delegation after him, saying, 'We do not want this man to rule over us.' When he returned, having received royal power, he ordered... But as for these enemies of mine who did not want me to be king over them—bring them here and slaughter them in my presence.'"

This plot sandwiches the parable dealing with the slaves' accountability for their performance during the absence of the nobleman. The central section of the parable (Lk 19:13, 15b-26), in a manner consistent with Lk 12:35-48, envisages the delay of the parousia and urges faithful, energetic obedience in the interim.

Most interpreters have seen in this emphasis upon delay a correction of the supposition in verse 11. That is, in this parable Jesus dampens the expectation of some that his approach to Jerusalem signals an imminent appearance of the kingdom; rather, they must anticipate a protracted delay (see *eis chōran makran* ["to a distant country"] in Lk 19:12; Noack, 1948: 28-29; Conzelmann, 1960: 113; Bartsch, 1963: 109; Kaestli, 1969: 39; Schneider, 1975: 41-42; Weinert, 1977: 506; Fitzmyer, 1985: 1232).

Obviously, the author was not interested in identifying the slaves with the disciples—or the nobleman with Jesus, for that matter. As is well known, the story resembles that of Archelaus, who on the death of Herod went to Rome to receive his kingdom, but was followed by a deputation of Jews who did not want him to rule. The slaughter at the end of the parable, while out of character for Jesus, is quite appropriate for Archelaus. There are some other elements in the parable that also seem to typecast it with the Herodians. Thus the desire for revenge; the demand for profit and wealth; the fear of the third slave, etc. Many of the parables' characteristics are also reminiscent of taxation practices. Given these elements, it seems likely that the Lukan Jesus does not identify himself with the nobleman, but rather intends to play the old kingdom to which Zacchaeus belonged off against the new kingdom to which Zacchaeus now belongs. Jesus told the parable to emphasize the contrast between two kingdoms: God's kingdom that brings salvation, but means giving, and the worldly kingdom that is unjust, built upon taking, and leads to death (Dawsey, 1986: 97–98).

Verse 13:   He summoned ten of his slaves
            and gave them ten pounds,
            and said to them,
            'Do business with these until I come back.'

As a result of the influence of the Throne-Claimant allegory, Luke has increased the initial number of slaves from three to ten (a round number), although in line with the number of the parable of the Talents, only three appear in the reckoning scene (compare Lk 19:13 with Mt 25:15; McGaughy, 1975: 238; Ernst, 1977: 519; compare Resenhofft, 1979-1980: 321; Danker, 1988: 308), following the standard storyteller's pattern of three cycles of action (see also, e.g., Lk 10:29-37; Ringe, 1995: 235; Craddock, 1990: 223). The nobleman gives one *mna* (pound, mina) to each slave. One mina was worth about four months' wages (Bock, 1996: 1533).

"To do business" may be too weak a translation for the practices assumed by the text; "turning a profit" refers to exploitation in the service of managing profitably the capital at one's disposal (Green, 1997: 678).

Many commentators have attempted to interpret the parable without attending to its setting or scene. Because that scene is the household of an urban elite, it is helpful to sketch that scene in more detail. Many a scholar is inclined to give the parable a spiritual application, regarding the pounds as spiritual gifts or talents of some kind, rather than as a token of a financial reality. Against the allegorical application of this parable it has been stated that in Lk 19:13 the work demanded of the slaves (disciples) could easily be equated with missionary service. But it means primarily action in the world. Luke wishes to emphasize the importance of secular activity (Flender, 1967: 77). Placing the characters in their social role may provide information that can help to evaluate the different judgments expressed about the nobleman and his slaves.

The ancient world was organized on three levels, the household, the city, and the imperium or kingdom. The most basic, social, economic, political and cultural unit was the household (*oikos*); not the peasant household of the village but the great household of the elite families. The household was a microcosm of the next level of organization, the city (*polis*). The city was more than an isolated island; it was the hub of an extensive economic and political network that controlled the lands radiating out of it. The final level of organization was the imperium or kingdom. Just as a *polis* was a collection of significant households, so a kingdom was a collection of significant cities, along with the land controlled by them (Herzog II, 1994: 156).

Because the entire system was fundamentally built upon the households of the elites, the aristocrats who headed these powerful families (the *paterfamilias* or the *oikodespotēs*) required the assistance of internal bureaucracies. The staff of household retainers included stewards/managers, scribal accountants, tutors, and other related figures. The household bureaucracy, in imitation of the imperial bureaucracy, was organized hierarchically, the most competent and trusted retainers rising to the highest level. Indeed, the greater the wealth of an aristocrat, the more elaborate his household bureaucracy needs to be. A large household staff was a sign of status and power (Kautsky, 1982: 190–192).

The head of the household could not stay home if he intended to protect his interests and expand his influence. Not only would he travel to his estates but he would travel abroad in hopes of increasing his investments, building patron-client networks, and currying favor with imperial overlords. For the accumulation of his wealth, the basis of his power and prestige, to continue in his absence, he needed to entrust important portions of it to his household retainers. This briefly sketched background serves as a framework for interpreting the parable of the Pounds (Herzog II, 1994: 157).

In Matthew, the phrase "to each according to his ability" (*kata tēn idian dunamin*; Mt 25:15) could easily well be translated "to each according to his power," where power indicates rank or status. In the matters of the household economy (*oikonomia*), a retainer would gain power according to his ability and capacity to manage the wealth for which he was responsible, so the more literal translation of *dunamis* is not as strange as it may seem at first glance.

One "talent" (or pound in Luke) is no mean amount of money to place in another's hand. Therefore, it is unlikely that the aristocrat is testing his staff, as so many of the moralizing readings of the parable imply; the retainers who appear in the opening scene are his most trusted inner circle.

Verse 14:   But the citizens of his country hated him
            and sent a delegation after him, saying,
            'We do not want this man to rule over us.'

The elements about "kingship" in verses 12, 14 and 15a stand out largely by comparison with Mt 25:14-30. The words *politai* ("citizens"; Lk 15:14; 19:14; Acts 21:39 and Heb 8:11) and *presbeia* ("delegation"; Lk 14:32; 19:14) are used almost exclusively by Luke in the New Testament (Didier, 1967: 260–261). The imperfect *emisoun* ("hated") indicates an on-going attitude (Schweizer, 1984: 295).

Luke has nothing to correspond to the description of the slaves' activity in Mt 25:16-18; on the other hand, it is possible that Lk 19:13b is an equivalent for this description. In any case the theme of the kingdom is taken up again at this point (Marshall, 1978: 704–705).

Verse 15:   When he returned, having received royal power,
            he ordered these slaves to whom he had given the money,
            to be summoned
            so that he might find out what they had gained by trading.

Unlike in Matthew, in Luke the nobleman on his return has to settle a double account: he calls his slaves to find out how much each one has earned with the money entrusted to him and gives orders that his fellow-countrymen who had opposed him be put to death in front of him (verse 27; Lambrecht, 1978: 250).

The first words of the second part of the parable are parallel to the introductory verse of the first: "A noble man went to a distant country *to get royal power* for himself and then *return*" (verse 12b); "When he *returned, having received royal power*" (verse 15a; de la Potterie, 1985: 636; Puig i Tarrech, 1985: 171).

The difference between the Lukan and Matthean versions of the parable culminates in the reckoning scene. By introducing the fragments of the throne-claimant parable, Luke transformed the reckoning into a court scene. The aristocrat departs a "nobleman" but returns a king, "having received royal power." His royal return sets up a reckoning with two sets of servants, loyal subjects (*douloi*, "slaves"; Lk 19:15) and disgruntled citizens (*politai*, Lk 19:14). The third slave is revealed as a spokesman for the citizens who opposed the ruler, and in his speech (Lk 19:20-21) he articulates their discontent and shares their fate (verse 27; Herzog II, 1994: 162).

The expression "what they had gained by trading" (*diepragmateusanto*) indicates more the effort exerted than the result obtained (Didier, 1967: 261 quoting Lagrange).

Verses 16-17:   (16) The first came forward and said,
        'Lord, your pound has made ten more pounds.'
  (17) He said to him, 'Well done, good slave!
        Because you have been trustworthy
        in a very small thing,
        take charge of ten cities.'

A 1,000 percent return was not impossible in the first century C.E. (Stein, 1992: 473). The praise offered by the oppressive aristocrat mystifies the ugly realities suppressed beneath the profit margin: "Well done, good slave!" The first two retainers are good in terms of the nobleman's values because they have proven to be effective exploiters of the peasants, and they have been trustworthy because they have produced a level of increased wealth in line with the aristocrat's expectations (McBride, 1999: 85).

The sheer extent of the aristocrat's wealth comes through his follow-up: "you have been trustworthy in a very small thing." A very small thing! Those who are faithful in "a very little" are entrusted with much (a deliberate echo of Lk 16:10; Green, 1997: 679), here spelled out as "authority over ten cities" (Danker, 1988: 308). It is hard to grasp the steep curve of wealth concentration in agrarian societies. Those in the ruling class, roughly the top 2 percent of the population, controlled the vast majority of the wealth. In this lofty circle of power, wealth was reckoned in pounds/ talents (Mt 25:15, etc.), which were but a "few things" (Mt 25:21). Even allowing for some conspicuous exaggeration on the part of the aristocrat to impress the slaves by alluding to the vastness of his wealth, his comments are accurate.

The promise follows his praise: "I will put you in charge of many things" (Mt 25:21) // "take charge of ten cities." Such a political reward heightens the encounter (Tiede, 1988: 325). Each slave has gained a more powerful position in the elite's household bureaucracy, but their dependency as clients has also been reinforced. The clients are never allowed to forget who is the source of their patronage.

Unspoken in this exchange but very much on the retainers' minds is the continued opportunity for "honest graft" while in the master's service. Little wonder the satisfied aristocrat mystifies the whole cycle of oppression by inviting them to "enter into the joy of your master" (Mt 25:21). He is inviting his clients into a celebration of their plenty in the midst of others' deprivation and want (Herzog II, 1994: 163).

Verses 18-19: (18) Then the second came, saying,
                    'Lord, your pound has made five pounds.'
              (19) He said to him,
                    'And you, rule over five cities.'

The second slave illustrates that there is no fixed goal to be achieved by all. There are gradations, but they have more to do with the talents given each individual than with reward. In any case he is not reproached for being less successful but praised for his faithfulness even in lesser success (Schweizer, 1984: 295). The recompense of the "good slaves" is historical, not eschatological: they will exercise authority over cities (Lk 19:17, 19).

Verses 20-21: (20) Then the other came, saying,
                    'Lord, here is your pound.
                    I wrapped it up in a piece of cloth,
              (21) for I was afraid of you,
                    because you are a harsh man;
                    you take what you did not deposit,
                    and reap what you did not sow.'

The third slave is clearly the focus of the parable. It is strange that he should be called "the other" (*ho heteros*). Some scholars take the expression to mean "the next" (see Lk 4:43; Blomberg, 1990: 219; Marshall, 1978: 478). The use of "the other" implies that the story originally contained only three slaves (Marshall, 1978: 706). He receives as much attention as the first two slaves combined (McBride, 1999: 85). Aside from the fact that this servant belongs to the inner circle and enjoys the nobleman's trust, the hearer knows nothing about him and expects him to follow the lead of the other retainers.

There is, no doubt, a repertoire of scenarios available to the narrator. In Matthew, he has buried the talent in the ground. By doing so, he takes the best available precaution against theft and liability (Jeremias, 1963: 61 note 51). Though the Lukan slave ties the money in a piece of cloth—*soudarion*, literally, "a cloth for perspiration"; probably referring to a scarf worn around one's face or neck for protection from the sun (Acts 19:12; Stein, 1992: 473; Nolland, 1993: 915)—, thus taking what the Mishnah specifies as the riskier course (Bock, 1996: 1538), he nonetheless preserves the pound as any honorable person would do. He does not participate in the scheme to double the nobleman's money, but honorably refrains from taking anything that belongs to the share of another. Worth noting in this connection is Lev 6:2 which forbids defrauding a neighbor in a matter of deposit. Josephus takes this to mean taking back more than one has deposited with a trustee (Josephus, *Against Apion*, 2.208; Rohrbaugh, 1993: 36; see also C.F. Evans, 1990: 671–672).

When called before his aristocrat patron, the third slave's speech would have astonished the hearers. He cuts through the mystifying rhetoric that has dominated the exchange between the elite and his first two retainers, and he identifies the aristocrat for what he is, strict, cruel, harsh, and merciless. In effect, he shames his master through his unexpected attack. More to the point, the third retainer describes the nobleman as an exploiter who lives off the productive labor of others (McBride, 1999: 88). He takes the lion's share of the harvest that others have sown, and he gathers (*sunagōn*) in what others have winnowed (*dieskorpisas*; Mt 25:24). In Lk 15:13 the same two verbs appear together, where they carry metaphoric meanings important to this speech. In Luke, the verb "gather in" suggests the conversion of goods to cash, a meaning that is appropriate here. The nobleman monetizes the wheat that others have winnowed. The prodigal son's scattering of his monetized inheritance is translated as "squandering" or "wasting." The secondary meaning is apt. What does the nobleman do with the wealth he has "gathered in" or monetized? He squanders it in riotous living, in socially approved forms of conspicuous consumption and status display. Indeed, excess and wasteful consumption is a value to be pursued because it displays a wealth so great that waste does not threaten it (Kautsky, 1982: 187–197).

In the "limited good" world of the peasant, seeking "more" was morally wrong. Because the pie was "limited" and already distributed, an increase in the share of one person automatically meant a loss for someone else. Honorable people, therefore, did not try to get more, and those who did were automatically considered thieves. Thus the two servants who increased their master's wealth would have been viewed by any peasant hearers of this story as simple robbers who cooperated with the evil master in his extortionist schemes. From the peasant point of view, then, it was the third slave who acted honorably, especially since he refused to participate in the rapacious schemes of his master (Malina-Rohrbaugh, 1992: 390). In contrast to Mt 25:30, the third slave is not punished. He remains just a slave as he was before verse 13 (Schweizer, 1984: 295).

Verse 22:   He said to him,
              'I will judge you by your own words,
              you wicked slave!

> You knew, did you, that I was a harsh man,
> taking what I did not deposit
> and reaping what I did not sow?

The judgment is immediate. Having spoken the truth, the slave must be vilified, shamed, and humiliated so that his words will carry no weight. It comes in the form of an address, "you wicked [and lazy, Mt 25:26] slave!" An oppressive elite labels the slave "wicked" and "lazy" for the purpose of stigmatizing him and dismissing his implied criticism. His address is an attack on the whistle-blower. The slave has unmasked the "joy of the master" (see Mt 25:21) for what it is, the profits of exploitation squandered in wasteful excess, and he has demystified "good" and "trustworthy" by exposing the merciless oppression they expose (Herzog II, 1994: 165).

Verses 23-24: (23) Why then did you not put my money into the bank?
Then when I returned,
I could have collected it with interest.'
(24) He said to the bystanders,
'Take the pound from him
and give it to the one who has ten pounds.'

The word for "bank" is literally "table." The usage is related to that in Mk 11:15 of the tables of the moneychangers (C.F. Evans, 1990: 672). The consequence of the judgment is obvious: the nobleman deprives the third slave of the pound and gives it to the most productive retainer. The nobleman condemns the third slave. But did Jesus? How do we know that? And did Jesus commend the nobleman? Most modern readers assume that he did. But pruned of its later Lukan and Matthean additions, where does the text say that? It is just as possible that Jesus did not, that he is in fact condemning the nobleman's viewpoint in the same way his peasant hearers would have done. After all, we have the statement of Jesus in the *Gospel of Thomas* # 95, judged to be authentic by recent scholarship: "If you have money, do not lend it at interest, but give it to one from whom you will not get it back." Similar statements are made in the Synoptics (e.g., Lk 6:35; Rohrbaugh, 1993: 38).

Verse 25:   And they said to him, 'Lord, he has ten pounds!'

Some manuscripts and ancient versions omit the whole verse, but it is found in the best Greek manuscripts. The majority of editors and commentators accept the verse, since it is difficult to explain its entry to the text (e.g., as a marginal comment), and easier to explain its omission in view of its absence from Matthew and the difficult transition to verse 26 (Bock, 1996: 1544–1545). But this still leaves the possibility that it is a secondary addition to the parable. It belongs probably to the pre-Lukan stream of tradition rather than to the original form of the parable (Marshall, 1978: 708).

Those who "stood by" (verse 24) are quite surprised at the nobleman's order. The identity of the bystanders is not clear (Marshall, 1978: 707). The rejoinder of the bystanders serves to introduce the principle expressed in the next verse (Danker, 1988: 309).

Verse 26:   'I tell you,
            to all those who have, more will be given;
            but from those who have nothing,
            even what they have will be taken away.

A reply from the nobleman is expected. Instead Jesus himself answers (Grundmann, 1966: 365; Marshall, 1978: 708; Schweizer, 1984: 295). The statement should be seen as functioning in the Lukan text as an aside by Jesus, rather than as part of the narrative progress of the parable. It is unlikely that this verse has been an original element of the parable: that it is also found in a quite different context (Lk 8:18) raises the possibility that it is a "floating saying" (Nolland,

1993: 916, 917). In its present context, it has been regarded as a "sentence of holy law" in which the proverbial sense has been replaced by an eschatological meaning (Käsemann, 1969: 98–99).

Verse 27:   But as for these enemies of mine
             who did not want me to be king over them —
             bring them here and slaughter them in my presence.'"

Luke again escalates the traditional parable to the political level (Tiede, 1988: 325). The other characters are described in political and military terms: they are described first of all as co-citizens of the throne claimant (Lk 19:14); nevertheless they "hate" him and do not want him to exercise royal power over them (Lk 19:14, 27); therefore they are called the "enemies" of the king (Lk 19:27a); the punishment imposed on them is terrible: the king orders that they be slaughtered in his presence (Lk 19:27b). These various themes—the exercise of royal power, the participation in this power by the slaves, the hate of the citizens for the king, their slaughter—are not related to eschatology. We cannot see what these elements of the story could mean if the parable intended to respond to the problem of the parousia. The application of the parabolic features should rather be achieved on the plane of history and the life of the Christian community (de la Potterie, 1985: 621–622).

e. The Entry and Fate of Jerusalem (Lk 19:28-44)

The evangelist no doubt intends Lk 19:28-44 (Jesus' arrival at Jerusalem) to be taken as a unit. Preceding Jesus' entry into the temple (Lk 19:45), Luke announces for the last time (Lk 19:28) Jesus' ascent to Jerusalem. He follows this announcement with a three-stage description of Jesus' drawing near (*eggizein*, verses 29, 37, 41): preparation and procession (Lk 19:29-34, 35-36); acclamation of the disciples as well as the reaction of the Pharisees (Lk 19:37-38, 39-40);

and Jesus' woe over the city (Lk 19:41-44). For the first two stages of Jesus' approach, Luke employs Mark, although he makes a number of important changes, particularly regarding the identity of those who acclaimed Jesus and the scope of their acclamation. As to the last portion of the second stage (verses 39-40) and the whole of the third stage (verses 41-44) it is difficult to decide whether Luke composed these verses (opinion preferred by Giblin, 1985: 48) or made use of a preexisting block of material (Grundmann, 1966: 367; see Lambrecht, 1985: 592; Giblin, 1985: 47).

After the theme of Jesus' journey is reiterated in the central section (Lk 9:51; 13:22; 17:11; 18:31; 19:11), his coming to Jerusalem must be viewed as climactic. While some maintain that Jesus' coming to the city at Lk 19:28-44 is aptly described as "triumphal" (e.g., Flender, 1967: 92; Ernst, 1977: 526), others recognize that it is not (e.g., Ellis, 1966: 223). But what is not explained is the explicit linkage of Jesus' pronouncement of judgment on the city and the events of the entry as depicted by Luke. Jesus laments, "If you, even you, had only recognized on this day the things that make for peace" (Lk 19:42); later he adds, "they will not leave within you one stone upon another; because you did not recognize the time of your visitation from God" (Lk 19:44). Luke alone among the evangelists makes explicit the connection between the entry and God's judgment on the city (see Mark 11).

Indeed, this connection might strike the modern reader as perplexing and a little out of character, for after Jesus is greeted outside Jerusalem the tenor of the episode turns quickly from joy to lament. What could account for Jesus' unanticipated response to the situation and the tone of finality that characterized it? Even if the Pharisees in Lk 19:39-40 are seen as opposing Jesus, their comments are almost trivial compared to opposition he has faced elsewhere (e.g., Lk 11:15, "He casts out demons by Beelzebul"). Jesus' remarks in Lk 19:41-44 seem all out of proportion to the offense.

The key to the understanding of Jesus' comments in Luke is the background of celebratory welcomes in the ancient world (*parousiai*). When seen in the light of this background, it is clear that Jerusalem's response to Jesus should be characterized as an appalling insult, which, in turn, explains his remarks about the coming destruction of the city (Kinman, 1999: 279–280).

Several features of the *parousiai* were normal or typical. First, the welcome was commonly bestowed on kings or other ruling figures. Second, the welcome was normally extended as the dignitary approached his city, that is, before the city was entered. Third, the religious and political elite from the city, along with other bands of "welcomers" would meet the guest and escort him into the city. Fourth, the large body of citizens in attendance would mark the occasion by wearing ornamental clothing such as white robes and wreaths. Finally, the dignitary would be lauded in speeches presented on behalf of the city, expressing its sense of privilege at the visitation. The magnitude of the greeting could indicate the gratitude of the city for past benefactions as well as lay the groundwork for favors the city might hope to receive from its guest in the future; a failure to provide a customary welcome could have grave consequences (Kinman, 1999: 284).

For Luke the kingship of Jesus is revealed at his entry by (1) the acceptance of the label "son of David" (Lk 18:35-43); (2) his implied identification with the nobleman in the parable of Lk 19:11-27; (3) his commandeering of the animal in accordance with *aggareia* (impressment for public service) conventions; (4) the special animal he rides; (5) the garments from the onlookers used to saddle the animal and pave the path beneath Jesus; and (6) the acclamation of the disciples and, in particular, their address to him as "king." From other comments in the Gospel, one has inferred that those in Jerusalem, including its citizens and leaders, could hardly have been aware of the reports about Jesus or his approach to the city (Kinman, 1999: 288–289).

Luke's audience would have been familiar with customs associated with celebratory welcomes, particularly those involving rulers. Luke has molded his narrative to depict Jesus as a royal figure whose followers herald his arrival in Jerusalem. The climactic point of the Gospel has now arrived. But the question remains: What sort of greeting will Jerusalem give to him? And how might this greeting be related to his subsequent comments in Lk 19:41-44? (Kinman, 1999: 289).

The present episode needs to be read closely with Lk 19:11-28: Luke has gone to some pains to present them in parallel. The present royal arrival in Jerusalem is no bid for immediate enthronement there. The narrative here is built upon a basis of biblical allusions and quotations that point to the royal dignity of this arriving figure, but also to the gulf that separates him from the normal understanding of the exercise of the prerogative of royal power (Nolland, 1993: 927–928).

(1) Preparation and Procession (Lk 19:28-36)

In the course of the Gospel, Jesus has journeyed throughout Palestine preaching. In a break with his custom of walking everywhere, Jesus approaches Jerusalem on the back of a colt. As far as Lk 19:28-34 is concerned, there are few appreciable differences between Mark and Luke; in each, one of the most striking features of the story is the sheer amount of space used to tell it. The fact that Jesus rides rather than walks together with the amount of narrative material dedicated to the acquisition of the animal mark the event as noteworthy (Kinman, 1995: 91).

In both Mark and Luke, the preparations for Jesus' entry mark it as regal. The royal connotations of the event are suggested by several features. First of all, in terms of Old Testament precedents, the Lukan concern with *how* Jesus comes to the city is shared by only two stories; namely, the coming of Solomon (1 Kgs 1) and the arrival of the ark (2 Sam 6). Each of these is a kind of royal welcome.

Verse 28:   After he had said this,
             he went on ahead, going up to Jerusalem.

The term *emprosthen* can mean "he went on *before* [his disciples]" (Plummer, 1901/1977: 444; Marshall, 1978: 711) or "he went *forward*" (Fitzmyer, 1985: 1247). Either sense is possible, but the absence of any mention of the disciples and the journey context favor the latter sense, even though it is a little redundant (Bock, 1996: 1552).

Some scholars hold that Luke rounds off the parable of the Pounds with the present words that created with verse 11 an inclusion around the parable. The verse then constitutes the conclusion of the parable rather than the beginning of the following. The links between verses 27 and 28 have been extensively emphasized (de la Potterie, 1985: 627–629). The forward journey to Jerusalem is now to be seen in the light of the parable (Nolland, 1993: 917). But the majority of interpreters consider verse 28 the beginning of the following section (e.g., Giblin, 1985: 48).

Verse 29:   When he had come near Bethphage and Bethany,
             at the place called the Mount of Olives,
             he sent two of his disciples,

Altering the Markan plural (Mk 11:1) to the singular, in line with his sharper focus on Jesus' own determination in moving towards the city, Luke proceeds to the first stage of Jesus' approach by way of the Mount of Olives. To early Christian auditors the reference to the Mount of Olives would have been especially significant, for this was the locale of the end-time events (see Zech 14; Danker, 1988: 311). Bethphage may well be a district marking the proximate limits of Jerusalem, not just a village. In any event, Bethany, the place of Jesus' eventual departure (Lk 24:50-51), which is certainly a village, stands out as the more important place in Luke's narrative as a whole, and may be the town to which the disciples were sent (Lk 19:30; Giblin, 1985: 48).

Two disciples are sent ahead, as has been the case, apparently, during most of the journey to Jerusalem (Lk 9:52; 10:1), and as Jesus does again to prepare the supper with his disciples on the night of his arrest (Lk 22:8; Ringe, 1995: 240; Craddock, 1990: 226).

Verses 30-33:   (30) saying, "Go into the village ahead of you,
and as you enter it
you will find tied there a colt
that has never been ridden.
Untie it and bring it here.
(31) If anyone asks you,
'Why are you untying it?'
just say this, 'The Lord needs it.'"
(32) So those who were sent departed
and found it as he had told them.
(33) As they were untying the colt,
its owners asked them,
"Why are you untying the colt?"
(34) They said, "The Lord needs it."

The instructions are explicit, complete with identifying questions and replies (Lk 19:30-31). The same words convey both the instructions and the report of how they are carried out (Lk 19:32-35a; Ringe, 1995: 240).

As to 1 Kgs 1, Luke's record of the specific instructions given by Jesus to the disciples together with the fulfillment of the instructions may be reminiscent of the account of the plans made to prepare for Solomon's entry. Just as 1 Kings first has David giving orders as to how Solomon's entry was to occur and then narrates the fulfillment of his instructions, so the Markan and Lukan narratives record Jesus' words and their fulfillment. If, as is likely, the ark narrative stood behind the accounts of the entry of Solomon and Zion's king, it is possible to view it as also lying behind the account of Jesus' entry. The concern for the transport of Jesus, the king, could be seen as analogous to the preparations made for the coming of Yahweh, the king, symbolically in the ark. To view Jesus' coming as in some fashion like those of the king and the ark would be to stress the sense in which his entry should be seen as the coming of God via his agent (Kinman, 1995: 91–92).

Jesus' use of a colt (*polos*, Lk 19:30) and its description also points to him as king. Firstly, it is similar to the animal ridden by Zion's king and Solomon (Zech 9:9 uses the specific term *polos*; 1 Kgs 1 does not). Secondly, the fact that the animal has not been ridden before (Lk 19:30) could have suggested to Luke and his readers that it was preserved for royal use. For sacred purposes animals were used that had not previously been employed in other service (1 Sam 6:7; Craddock, 1990: 226). Thirdly, certain features of the colt's description may be linked to the "Oracle of Judah" in Gen 49:10-12, a passage which, in the view of some, has messianic connotations (Giblin, 1985: 49 and note 8). It has been argued that the oracle of Gen 49:10-12 was increasingly interpreted as messianic in the New Testament era and that Zech 9 was probably based on the oracle (Blenkinsopp, 1961: 55–64; Nolland, 1993: 924). The figure of Gen 49:10-12 is a coming ruler from the line of Judah (Gen 49:10), the expectation of the nations (Gen 49:10) who binds his colt to the vine (Gen 49:11). By comparison Jesus is from the line of Judah (Lk 3:23, 33), a light for revelation to the nations (Lk 2:32) who has "his" colt bound (Lk 19:30). On the whole, the presence of a special mount for the entry highlights the royal nature of the event (Kinman, 1995: 92–93).

The evangelist does not envision a demonstration of welcome which simply arose spontaneously as Jesus approached. Even the repetition of what people would say and what the owners did expresses the conviction that Jesus was staging this entrance (Tiede, 1988: 329).

One should observe that, in the context of the relationship

between *hoi kurioi autou* ("its owners"; verse 33) and *ho kurios autou* ("the Lord"; literally "its Lord"; verses 31, 34), Jesus acts quite unostentatiously, albeit with a clear indication that he is the animal's owner more than "its owners." While the impressment of animals might be made by soldiers, magistrates or rabbis (Derrett, 1971: 248–253), it was above all else a royal prerogative (Tiede, 1988: 329). For those familiar with the Old Testament, it may call to mind Samuel's comment in 1 Sam 8:16, that a king would "take your donkeys, and put them to his work." Luke centers on the Lord's prerogative. The Markan note about the animal's return is omitted by Luke, so that Jesus' absolute right to the animal is emphasized by Luke. The requisition formula and Luke's omission of the pledge to return the animal may underline the royal aspect of the story (Kinman, 1995: 93–94).

Verses 35-36: (35) Then they brought it to Jesus,
                         and after throwing their cloaks on the colt,
                         they set Jesus on it.
                    (36) As he rode along,
                         people kept spreading their cloaks on the road.

The concluding, second portion of the first stage depicts a kind of processional enthronement on the part of Jesus' disciples. They place their garments on the colt, an allusion to the enthronement procession of Solomon (1 Kgs 1:33), and have Jesus mount the animal (1 Kgs 1:33), again recalling the coronation procession of Solomon (Tiede, 1988: 329). After this gesture of Jesus' disciples' acknowledgment of their king, Luke once again draws attention to Jesus' own ongoing journey ("as he rode on"), omitting reference to the crowds (*polloi*, Mk 11:8). The disciples, who constitute the logical subject of *hupestrōnnuon* ("they kept spreading") are also said to have placed their garments on his way. Luke restricts the reader's attention to Jesus and to his disciples (Giblin, 1985: 50).

While Luke has followed Mark for the most part in describing the preparations for the entry, in his account of the procession he stresses the royal imagery in a way that Mark does not. The use of the verb *epibibazō* to describe the disciples' placing of Jesus on the colt draws attention to Jesus/ Solomon (and thus *royal*) connections in Luke (Grundmann, 1966: 366–367; Marshall, 1978: 714). The verb is found in the entry story of Solomon in 1 Kgs 1. In contrast to Luke, Mark does not use it. Elsewhere in Luke the verb is found at Lk 10:34, where the Samaritan puts the wounded man on his mount and Acts 23:24, where the centurions provide a mount for Paul to take him to the governor. Since other features of the story are royal and the verb is employed in 1 Kgs 1 (and not, for example, in Zech 9:9), scholars may be right to see Solomonic connections here. The more important point, however, is that it marks Jesus' entry as royal according to an Old Testament precedent.

As in Mark's account, in Lk 19:35 the disciples heap their garments upon the colt before Jesus sits astride it. In verse 36 garments are used to pave the path. A similar detail is present in the Old Testament account of Jehu's accession to power—there, after he is recognized as king, each bystander hurries to place a garment on the steps under his feet (2 Kgs 9:13). It is clearly an act of homage; more than that, its Old Testament background marks it as a gesture made to a king.

Mk 11:8 records that in addition to placing their garments on Jesus' path the multitude fetched leafy branches from the fields and scattered them on the road in front of him. Luke does not preserve this detail (Lk 19:36). Commentators have offered various explanations for the omission.

Firstly, it has been suggested that Luke had no interest in the detail. But it is improbable that Luke or his readers would have found the mention of the branches incomprehensible or irrelevant. In the first place, the employment of foliage was a feature of certain Roman entries. Second, the Old Testament refers to occasions on which foliage played a role in processions or other rituals (Lev 23:40; Neh 8:13-15; 1 Macc 13:51; 2 Macc 10:7). It seems unlikely, therefore, that the Lukan omission of this detail is best explained on the basis of his lack of interest in it or on account of his readers' inability to understand it (Kinman, 1995: 115–116).

A second explanation for the omission has to do with the timing of the entry. Luke gives the impression that the entry takes place near the Passover (Lk 22:1; cf. Mk 14:1). However, in Lev 23:40 and 1 Macc 13:51, the display of foliage at a procession is connected with the Feast of Tabernacles and the celebration of Hanukkah. Luke may, therefore, have considered the mention of foliage as anachronistic and confusing to his readers.

A third theory about the omission relates to a Lukan political apologetic and the precedent set by the mention of foliage with Maccabean history and Graeco-Roman processions. Two episodes in Maccabean history are germane to the discussion of "foliage": at the cleansing of the temple by Judas Maccabaeus after the battle of Lysia (see 1 Macc 4:36; 2 Macc 10:7), and during the procession at the re-dedication of the temple by Simon Maccabaeus (1 Macc 13:51). In Jesus' time these branches were distinctive nationalist symbols. Luke may have felt that the omission of this potentially troublesome detail was advisable (Kinman, 1995: 116–117; Ford, 1984: 109).

Nowhere else in the gospel stories has Jesus ridden, and this riding seems to go against the tradition of pilgrims walking into the holy city together at feast time. Thus, Jesus is deliberately distinguishing himself from those with whom he was traveling. That he intended this to be a symbolic act, one might call it a prophetic sign (Borg, 1987: 174), seems likely. That the sign was meant to say something about Jesus' intentions and self-revelation seems certain (Witherington III, 1990: 106).

(2) Disciples' Acclamation and Pharisees' Reaction
(Lk 19:37-40)

Verses 37-38: (37) As he was now approaching the path
down from the mount of Olives,
the whole multitude of the disciples
began to praise God joyfully with a loud voice
for all the deeds of power that they had seen,
(38) saying,"Blessed is the king
who comes in the name of the Lord!
Peace in heaven and glory in the highest
heaven!"

In the second stage (verses 37-40) Luke introduces a larger group, but speaks even of this multitude (*plēthos*) as made up of disciples. He now devotes attention to what is *said*, whereas in the preceding stage, except for the brief inter-changes between Jesus and his disciples and between the latter and the colt's owners, he concentrated on what was *done* (Giblin, 1985: 50).

Luke introduces the new stage by noting Jesus' own movement ("as he was now approaching"). Acclamation by Jesus' disciples conveys the note of anticipation of what might follow on a still larger scale (Giblin, 1985: 51). But, strictly speaking, the disciples direct their praises to God, not in anticipation of a victory still ahead, but for the "deeds of power" that they have already witnessed (Lk 19:37; Ringe, 1995: 240; Malina and Rohrbaugh, 1992: 392). The phras-ing echoes Lk 7:22, "Go and tell John the Baptist what you have seen and heard," and points back to Lk 4:18, for it is the fulfillment of the anointed one's role which has been "seen and heard" by those who believe (Tiede, 1988: 329–330; Danker, 1988: 312–313). Luke specifies where the gath-ered multitude began its acclamations: "at the descent of the Mount of Olives" (verse 37). The Mount of Olives is mentioned only once in the Old Testament, at Zech 14:4, where it is said that on "that day" "his [the Lord's] feet will stand on the Mount of Olives....." It is hard to say why

Luke has mentioned it here. It may simply be attributed to his interest in details of the life of Jesus (Lk 1:1-4); he does not seem to make much of the eschatological implications found in Zechariah, unless one sees it as providing a background for the eschatological expectations held by the disciples to which Jesus replies in Lk 19:11-27. On the one hand, the mention of the specific location outside the city ("down from the Mount of Olives") may have relevance for Luke's depiction of the entry as a *parousia* gone bad, since one characteristic of the *parousia* was that it began outside the city. Luke (and only Luke) explains that the procession, such as it was, began as any *parousia* would—outside the city. The mention of the Mount of Olives as such does not seem to enhance the royal motif of the account (Marshall, 1978: 714–715; Fitzmyer, 1985: 1250; but see Bock, 1987: 125).

Psalm 118 points to the mode of entry of kings in antiquity, providing particulars on what was said and recited by the king, priests, and people when the royal procession approached the eastern gates of the city, passed through them, and went into the temple precincts. Luke (like the other Gospels) cites expressions from Ps 118:26 (Lk 19:38), but a full understanding of the psalm's function in the Gospel tradition depends on the reader's knowledge of the whole psalm (J.A. Sanders, 1993: 143–153) to grasp the complete significance of the entry as a symbolic act. In the time of Jesus Psalm 118 was recited at the Festival of Tabernacles or Booths in the fall, at Passover in the spring, and also at Hanukkah. In pre-exilic times, however, that is, before 587 B.C.E., Psalm 118 was a royal psalm that would have been recited at the annual enthronement of the king during the fall equinoctial celebration of the New Year (Dahood, 1970: 155; Ellis, 1966: 191; for a presentation of Psalm 118 indicating which parts were said by the king, the people, and the priests, see J.A. Sanders, 1993: 146–147). Luke has not previously used "king" of Jesus, though in this section Jesus is consistently a royal figure. The term becomes important in Luke 23. Jesus is now on his way to royal rule, but only in the terms that Lk 19:11-38 has defined this (Nolland, 1993: 927).

Luke attributes the acclamation to "the whole multitude of the disciples." This phrase has been regarded as a "Lukan hyperbole" (Fitzmyer, 1985: 1250) and it has been suggested that Luke expressly mentions a large crowd in order to stress that Jesus had many followers (Ernst, 1977: 526). But by identifying the group as Jesus' *disciples*, Luke's text conceivably reduces rather than enlarges the size of the crowd (C.F. Evans, 1990: 680). For Luke only disciples are in a position to discern the significance of this entry. Besides, a general crowd response here would create confusion about the reference of Lk 13:35b, by making it possible to think that what was anticipated there had now already arrived (Nolland, 1993: 926). There is no ovation by the general crowds that are in the city for the festival; Jesus is honored and praised by his followers. This is not the group which turns cold and later calls for Jesus' crucifixion. The portrait of such a fickle crowd must come from some account other than Luke's (Craddock, 1990: 227). Thus, one need not imagine that the crowd accompanying Jesus was so large as to have commanded the soldiers' attention.

The background of Pilate's entry into Jerusalem assists our understanding why Roman soldiers would have been unperturbed by the sort of "triumphal entry" given to Jesus according to the gospel narratives. Accompanied by soldiers, Pilate entered Jerusalem seated upon a horse or riding a chariot a short time before Jesus' "triumphal entry." Pilate had come to maintain order and to conduct trials; he was greeted by city officials, however reluctantly, with at least an outward show of respect. Jesus, on the other hand, was seated upon a young donkey, met by the cheers of his followers, and rebuked by the authorities. Small wonder, then, that Jesus' coming would have been unlikely to attract the interest of Pilate's soldiers: it was, by their standards, a rather "atriumphal" entry (Kinman, 1994a: 448). Skepticism about the possibility

of such an occurrence, based on the supposition that the
authorities would have acted against Jesus, is grounded on
the assumption that this event was of much greater magnitude than it likely was. Furthermore, if this event happened
outside the city and in the press of the festival crowd, then
it may well have gone unnoticed by the authorities, unless it
was later reported to them. One must not envision an authority under every bush watching Jesus' every move (Marshall,
1978: 710; Witherington III, 1990: 106–107).

The significance of the act for Jesus is suggested by the
triangular intersection of Jesus' saying on Caesar (Lk 20:25),
Jewish donkeys (beasts of burden as royal animals), and the
Roman entrance processions (Tatum, 1998: 129–143).

The welcome-cry of the disciples (verse 38) consists of
the citation from Psalm 118 (taken over from Mark) into
which Luke inserted *ho basileus* ("the king"). The overall
effect of the Lukan presentation is two-fold. First, the greeting of verse 38 ("the king") is, perhaps, the clearest example
of Luke's desire to draw the reader's attention to the fact
that Jesus is king. This probably replaces the Markan mention of the "kingdom of David" and draws attention to the
person in view. Looking to the Old Testament, the acclamation of Jesus as king in verse 38 may find a parallel in
the cries which on occasion greeted Solomon and other kings
(1 Sam 10:24; 1 Kgs 1:34, 39; 2 Kgs 11:12). As to Luke's
citation of Psalm 118, the royal element of the song which
may have originally been present re-emerges in Luke with
the specific mention of "the king" (Marshall, 1978: 715).
The ease with which Luke's original audience would have
made these connections with Psalm 118 is unknown, although
the task would doubtless have been facilitated once they
had been directed to the psalm by the phrase *ho erchomenos*
("he who comes"). The fact that Jesus comes "in the name
of the Lord" (verse 38) means that he comes as God's agent
or representative. If he is king, he is king on behalf of God.
The implications of this are obvious: To the extent that the

city welcomes Jesus, it welcomes the Lord; if it rejects Jesus, it in effect also rejects God and invites the consequences of such an act (Kinman, 1995: 96).

The second and perhaps even more important point: Jesus' identification as "the one who comes in the name of the Lord" clearly marks the event as messianic (this is also the Markan perspective). A messianic understanding of the figure from Ps 118:26 would have been well known to Luke and his readers. Significantly, already in Luke Jesus has been identified as "the coming one" (Lk 3:16; 7:19) in connection with messianic deeds (Marshall, 1970: 126 and note 5). The use of the phrase by the disciples (and with Jesus' approval) at the entry is striking in that it constitutes a pointed messianic acclaim from the disciples and a messianic acknowledgment by Jesus in a very open and public setting. On its own, the fact that it occurred just outside Jerusalem would have been provocative enough; the fact that it took place near a festival Passover (Lk 22:1) when large crowds of pilgrims would have been making their way to the city (see Acts 2:5-11), adds to the public nature of the event (Kinman, 1995: 96–97).

The Lukan Jesus' planning of the event suggests his awareness and promotion of its messianic connotations; furthermore, his response to the Pharisees in Lk 19:39-40 implies his approval of the messianic acclaim. By refusing to take the Pharisees' advice to rebuke his disciples (found only in Luke), Jesus gives tacit support to the disciples (Kinman, 1995: 97).

The entry, a messianic act, raises the question of whether or not the acclaim given to Jesus here should be viewed as fulfillment of Lk 13:35, where Jesus tells Jerusalem that it will not see him "until the time comes when you say, 'Blessed is the one who comes in the name of the Lord.'" Does Jerusalem greet him? It is unlikely that Luke intends the reader to view the acclamation at the entry as fulfillment of Lk 13:35. Why? According to Luke it is not the more general Markan "many" (*polloi*) who welcome Jesus, but rather "the whole multitude of the *disciples*" (*hapan to plēthos tōn mathētōn*, verse 37). The Lukan account appears to narrow the scope of those who participate in Jesus' acclaim. Jesus has been welcomed by his followers, but not by the Jerusalem leaders (Marshall, 1978: 715; *pace* Fitzmyer, 1985: 1242). This point may be underscored if the broader context of Psalm 118, from which Luke draws one clear quotation, is kept in mind. According to the psalm those inside the city were to welcome the king with the cry "Blessed is the one who comes in the name of the Lord" (Ps 118:26a) and those inside the temple were meant to say "We bless you from the house of the Lord" (verse 26b). The temple authorities, i.e., the chief priests and the rulers that appear later in the passion narrative to oppose Jesus, who might be viewed as analogous to those in the psalm who were to welcome the coming king, are absent from the scene. There is no one to welcome Jesus to the city/temple and the sense in which Lk 13:35 is not fulfilled is made clear. If the Pharisees, whose comments in Lk 19:39 are to be understood as criticism of Jesus (Kinman, 1995: 98 note 26), can be viewed in some way as analogous to the religious leaders of the psalm, the implication again is that Jerusalem (or, at least, certain religious leaders) has not met its king in an appropriate way. As a result, the entry does not fulfill Lk 13:35 (Kinman, 1995: 97–98).

It has often been held that Luke's omission of the phrase "coming kingdom of our father David" is rooted in his political apologetic (compare Lk 19:38 and Mk 11:10; C.F. Evans, 1990: 681; Fitzmyer, 1985: 12:51; Conzelman, 1960: 75, 139). But Luke plainly identifies Jesus as king. Would this have been less problematic for his political apologetic than Mark's mention of David's kingdom? (Kinman, 1995: 117–118).

Lk 19:38 diverges from Mark by ascribing to the disciples a comment reminiscent of one made earlier in Luke by the heavenly host (Lk 2:14; for a comparison of Lk 2:14 and 19:38, see Kariamadam, 1997: 256–258). It has been observed that the phrase is part of an "enigmatic couplet" (Marshall, 1978: 715).

Many attempts have been made to explain the peace in heaven found in Lk 19:38b and there is not yet a fully satisfactory explanation of this important verse in Luke (Kariamadam, 1997: 258; for various opinions, see Ibidem, 258–261). One interpretation of the passage takes the disciples' acclamation as an anticipation of the salvation which Jesus is about to realize (Foerster, TDNT 2: 431 thinks that *eirēnē* ["peace"] refers to salvation). Another interpretation of the passage suggests that what is significant about "peace" in the context is that it is no longer on earth. According to this view, the most striking feature of the phrase is its correspondance to the angelic acclamation (Lk 2:14). At Lk 2:14, Jesus' birth results in praise to God and peace on earth, in particular, among people to whom God is gracious (Fitzmyer, 1981: 410–412). The different locales for *eirēnē* (i.e., on earth and in heaven) form a contrast between Lk 2:14 and 19:38 which is difficult to overlook (Baarlink, 1985: 175; Nolland, 1993: 927). "Heaven" is the sphere into which Jesus will bring his *pax* in Lk 19:38 (Kinman, 1995: 118).

The expression "peace in heaven" means, first of all, that the consummation of peace and salvation brought by Jesus, the king of peace, is achieved only in heaven as his final glorification takes place in heaven (see Ellis, 1966: 227; Ernst, 1977: 527). This meaning is possible in the context in which the author writes Lk 19:38b. It may be noted that the political aspirations of Jesus' followers were set aside by him in the parable of the Pounds (Lk 19:11-27). Furthermore, the author shows clearly in Lk 19:38a that Jesus is not a king of this world, but the king who comes in the name of the Lord. Surely the messianic peace had its beginning upon earth with Jesus' birth (Lk 2:14) and it continued to manifest itself in his public ministry. And the mission of the Church is indeed to preach peace and salvation to the whole world. Jesus' suffering, death, resurrection and ascension are conditions of the final achievement of the messianic peace. In other words, his going up into heaven as the bearer of peace is a condition of the final achievement of peace and salvation in heaven. We may notice in this connection that the risen Lord imparts peace to his disciples (Lk 24:36). Hence the evangelist brings the theme of peace in heaven in the context of Jesus' ascent (*anabainōn*) to Jerusalem for his ascension (*analēmpsis* (see Lk 9:51; 19:28; Kariamadam, 1997: 264).

Verses 39-40: (39) Some of the Pharisees in the crowd said to him,
                   "Teacher, order your disciples to stop."
              (40) He answered, "I tell you,
                   if these were silent,
                   the stones would shout out."

The response of the Pharisees to the disciples' acclamation of Jesus and his subsequent rebuke of the Pharisees are found only in Lk 19:39-40. This is the final mention of the Pharisees in Luke's Gospel. These "some of the Pharisees" who object remind the reader of the "some Pharisees" who tried to counsel Jesus to avoid Herod's wrath in Lk 13:31-35 (Tiede, 1988: 330; Cunningham, 1997: 120; Schweizer, 1984: 299–300). Illustrative of the king's rejection, of which Jesus has spoken in the parable of the Pounds, some Pharisees reject the identification of Jesus as king (Lk 19:39) and thus identify themselves as the "ones who do not want the king to rule over them" (Lk 19:14, 27; Cunningham, 1997: 120). But refusing to take the Pharisees' advice to rebuke his disciples, Jesus gives tacit support to the disciples.

Jesus phrases his refusal unusually. He answers the Pharisees, "I tell you, if these [people] were silent, the stones would shout out." No unanimity of interpretation exists concerning this seemingly enigmatic response. How would Luke's first readers have understood it?

There are several possible explanations of Jesus' comment. One, it is a proverbial expression derived from Hab 2:11 where inanimate objects are called to witness God's judgment (Plummer, 1901/1977: 448; Schneider, 1977: 387; Schmithals, 1980: 189; Fitzmyer, 1985: 1252). The verse appears in the midst of a litany of charges against the Chaldeans and foresees their eventual destruction. The Septuagint states, "The stone will cry out from the wall, and the knot will speak out of the wood." If a comparison with the Chaldeans is present, it would be another instance of Jesus regarding Israel's failure to welcome him (or his representatives) appropriately as more heinous than the sins of certain cities or peoples in the Old Testament (see Lk 10:12-14; Kinman, 1995: 98–99).

A second explanation, related to but not identical with the first, is that Jesus refers to the stones of the city "crying out" as witnesses against the religious authorities in anticipation of Jerusalem's destruction in C.E. 70 (Danker, 1972: 198; Ernst, 1977: 528). According to this interpretation a veiled reference to the past (i.e., Hab 2:11) is not primarily in view but rather the future destruction of the city. "If the disciples do not speak, if they do not proclaim Jesus as the redeemer of Israel and the bringer of peace, then the eloquent message of the tumbled stones of a destroyed city will cry out to the survivors that Jerusalem should have repented" (Gaston, 1970: 359). This interpretive option may include the prophetic use of Hab 2:11, which, according to the Qumran covenanters, speaks of the Kittim, i.e., the Romans who will destroy either the wicked high priest or the temple (Gaston, 1970: 126–127). Like the first option, this one interprets Jesus' comment as a pronouncement of judgment. Bolstering the view that the "stones crying out" is related to judgment is the fact that in the section to follow, Lk 19:41-44, Jesus employs the term "stone" in his destruction of Jerusalem as complete: "they will not leave within you one stone upon another" (Lk 19:44). A similar comment is made in Lk 21:6, "the days will come when not one stone will be left upon another."

In spite of its recent popularity there are sound reasons

to reject the view that the crying out of the stones has to do with judgment. The phrasing of Jesus' response seems to indicate that the hypothetical cry of the stones would re-place the concrete expression of the disciples. In other words, it is possible to understand Jesus' remarks to indicate that the responses of the disciples and the stones are equivalent. If this is the case, then the "judgment" motif is ruled out, inasmuch as the disciples' cry is clearly a royal acclamation, not a threat of judgment (Kinman, 1997: 99).

Rather than a veiled reference to impending judgment, Jesus' reply to the Pharisees is probably a straightforward metaphor, the meaning of which is something like "This moment is of such importance that it must find a response —if not a human one, then another; some things simply must be said" (Craddock, 1990: 227–228). On occasion the Old Testament speaks of creation responding with joy (and without hints of judgment) to the coming of God (e.g., Ps 96:11-13; Isa 55:12), although this is not always the case. In the biblical tradition there is a strong sense that nature participates in the witness and celebration of what God is doing (the verbally closest parallel is Hab 2:11; Nolland, 1993: 927). While it is often thought that the remark about "stones crying out" is Semitic (Marshall, 1978: 717; Jeremias, 1980: 281), it is by no means only Semitic. There is also a precedent for the metaphor in Cicero's description of his welcome at Rome (*Pis.* 52).

To understand the "stones crying out" as a reference to joyous acclaim avoids the pitfalls of assuming a judgment motif (as mentioned above) and is in keeping with the kind of metaphor employed in the Old Testament and other an-cient literature (Kinman, 1995: 100–101).

Jesus has neared his final destination, Jerusalem, and the Pharisees make their final appearance in the Gospel. As Jesus approaches the city riding upon a colt the whole multitude of his *disciples* rejoice and praise God, saying, "Blessed is the King who comes in the name of the Lord! Peace in heaven and glory in the highest!" (Lk 19:38; see Ps 118:26). The direct definition of "king" ascribed to Jesus by the multitude of disciples is ironic, because Jerusalem does not recognize the true significance of Jesus' presence (Lk 19:41-44). The multitude's adulation of Jesus not only involves ascribing to him a high amount of honor (*doxa en hupsistois*, Lk 19:38), it also involves his status as broker of God's kingdom. Jesus is called King, but he is a King who comes in the name of the *Lord*. The response of *some* of the Pharisees to the acclamation of the multitude poses similar questions about the Pharisees' attitude to Jesus as the warning given by them to Jesus concerning Herod (Lk 13:31-35). The parallel is even more striking because the shout of the disciples echoes Jesus' words in Lk 13:35: "Blessed is he who comes in the name of the Lord!" Is the Pharisees' statement a friendly word of warning or are they still opposing Jesus at every opportunity? (see Gowler, 1991: 272). The use of the term *some* leaves open the possibility that the statement is a word of warning, and that they are actually concerned about Jesus' safety. Nowhere does the narrative give the impression that the Pharisees are out to kill Jesus; they also will be completely absent from the passion narrative (Petzke, 1990: 173). Both of these absences are significant acts of omission. The narrator, though, does not assist the reader as to the Pharisees' inward motivations, and their speech lends little help as well. The only clue may be found in their own title for Jesus: "Teacher" (Lk 19:38). The term "teacher" is a title that is used in the narrative by those who have an indefinite opinion of Jesus. A certain amount of respect is engendered, but not nearly as much as the title "king" used by the multitude of disciples. Jesus' pronouncement serves as a rebuke to the Pharisees (Lk 19:40). Even if the Pharisees' warning were a friendly one, they still misunderstand Jesus' person and mission. They, as a group, bear no direct responsibility for the death of Jesus, but their opposition to the disciples' temerity leaves them outside of Jesus' circle.

Their resistance—or caution—creates a contrast with the disciples' homage of Jesus. On the other hand, the contrast between the disciples and the Pharisees could be seen as evidence that the Pharisees were completely in opposition to Jesus, not merely offering a friendly warning. There is a pattern of acceptance and rejection of Jesus in the narrative that is based upon a prophet's relationship with the people. Such a pattern of contrast between outside and inside (i.e., disciples and Pharisees) had been drawn from Lk 9:51 to 18:14 (Johnson, 1977: 198). If the reader perceives such a contrast, this pericope may fall into that pattern of acceptance or rejection of Jesus, the prophet and king.

One other nuance may be added. The reader may also perceive in Lk 19:40 an intertextual reference to Hab 2:11: "For the stone will cry out from the wall. . ." The context in Habakkuk involves a threat against a nation that gains material possessions by violence (Fitzmyer, 1985: 1252). The penalty for that nation consists of a reversal from glory to shame and final destruction (e.g., Hab 2:17; Ellis, 1966: 226). If Jesus' words are an allusion to Hab 2:11, then the negative remonstrance against the Pharisees and Jerusalem is made even stronger. Unfortunately, however, the narrator does not provide guidance, and readers are left to make their own decisions based upon the clues that have been supplied thus far in the narrative.

To sum up, this pronouncement story involving the Pharisees remains enigmatic. At the very least they misunderstand Jesus; at the very most they sympathize—but do not join—with the leaders of Jerusalem who accuse Jesus before Pilate. The Gospel of Luke, then, creates a picture of the Pharisees as the opponents of Jesus. They stand condemned, but a few ambiguous signs are allowed to be seen (Gowler, 1991: 272–274).

For Luke the kingship of Jesus is revealed at his entry by (1) the acceptance of the label "son of David" (Lk 18:35-43); (2) his implied identification with the noble man in the parable of Lk 19:11-27; (3) the orchestration of his entry, so reminiscent of Solomon; (4) his commandeering of the animal in accordance with *aggareia* conventions; (5) the special animal he rides; (6) the garments of the onlookers used to saddle the animal and pave the path beneath Jesus; and (7) the acclamation of the disciples and, in particular, their address to him as "king" (Lk 19:38). Over and above Mark, the kingship of Jesus has been stressed in Luke in the following ways: (a) by the context of the account where "son of David" perhaps has clearer political overtones than in Mark (by virtue of Lk 1:32-33 together with the implied identification of Jesus with the nobleman in the parable of Lk 19:11-27); (b) by the clear designation of Jesus as "king" (Lk 19:38). There is a concentration of royal and messianic motifs in the Lukan entry narrative. The parallels with the coming of Solomon and Zion's king are obvious and immediate. There may also be allusions to the coming of Yahweh (in the ark) to the city (see 2 Sam 6; Kinman, 1995: 101–102).

(3) *Jesus' Lament over the City* (Lk 19:41-44)

These verses are unique to Luke, and they fill the transition from the entry of the king to his cleansing of the temple with profound pathos. Luke's depiction of Jesus as prophet-Messiah reaches its peak in this episode. The oracle is filled with scriptural allusions drawn largely from Jer 6:6-21; 8:18-21; 15:5; and 23:38-40; as well as Ps 137 (136 LXX):9; Isa 29:3-10, and 2 Kgs 8:11-12. The phrases are heaped up from the old prophetic oracles of judgment against Israel, Jerusalem, and the temple, the words which were uttered in connection with her first destruction at the hands of the neo-Babylonian Empire.

The lament is structured into (1) a declaration of what is not the case ("If you had... But now"; verse 42), (2) a series of phrases stating the dire consequences ("Indeed, the

days will come upon you"; verses 43-44a), and (3) a final
reason or indictment ("because you did not recognize...";
verse 44b; Tiede, 1988: 331–333).

At this point we can note that in Mark's Gospel Jesus
curses a fig tree just before he arrives in Jerusalem (Mk 11:12-
14, 20-26). Not so in Luke, even though he is following the
general arrangement of Mark. The omission of the story of
the cursing of the fig tree has been variously explained
(Telford, 1980: 229–233; for six suggestions considered, see
Kinman, 1994a: 672–678).

Some, for example, have suggested that the story was
not in the version of Mark that Luke had before him. However, modern scholarship has widely tested and generally
accepted the view that Luke knew the Gospel of Mark as
we have it (probably except for Mk 16:9-20). Others have
advocated that the miracle in Mark has been omitted because it conveyed the same message as the parable that replaces it (Lk 13:6-9).

According to others, Luke has exchanged the fig-tree
miracle for a parable of a fig tree (Lk 13:6-9), most probably because of the clear, yet different message inherent in
each. On the one hand, no grace is offered in the Markan
miracle story. The tree is barren, it is cursed, and on in-
spection the next morning, Jesus and the disciples see the
tree withered from its roots (Mk 11:20). The message or
implication is that Jerusalem and its temple have come under the judgment of Jesus (Mk 11:15-17). But it is considered unlikely that Luke changed a miracle story into a parable. There are no other instances where what appears as a
miracle story in Mark is a parable or similar phenomenon
in Luke (Kinman, 1994a: 673 and note 14).

On the other hand, for Luke, Jesus is less an instrument
of judgment (cf. Lk 9:52-56) and more one who pleads for
and offers grace (Lk 13:1-9). Indeed, at the point where Mark
has the miracle of the cursing of the fig tree (Mk 11:12-14),
Luke has Jesus weep over the city (Lk 19:41-44). It is prob-

able that Luke understood the Markan account, and in particular the mention of the fig tree, as a reference to Israel. Mark says that the fig tree (Israel) will never again bear fruit. This is at odds with Lukan eschatology with regard to the fate and future of Israel, for other passages in Luke-Acts intimate a future role for the nation in the plan of God. Consequently, Luke omitted it (Kinman, 1994a: 675–676; see also Twelftree, 1999: 164–165; Hendrickx, 2000: 269–272).

From the Lukan narrative perspective, the destruction of Jerusalem has already occurred and thus cannot be part of the events of the end time (see Lk 21:20-24b; Conzelmann, 1960: 134–135; Braumann, 1963: 120–127). Lk 19:41-44 understands this destruction as punishment that has already been visited upon Jerusalem within history for having rejected Jesus. According to Lk 21:24c, however, this punishment is temporary: "until the times of the Gentiles are fulfilled." Whatever else this might mean (Wolter, 1992: 309 note 16), together with Lk 19:41-44 this prospect suggests that Luke did reckon with the eschatological restoration of Jerusalem after its punishment was carried out. In this sense J. Bradley Chance understood this reference as proof that according to Luke, Jerusalem would be restored after the conclusion of the "times of the Gentiles" in "its eschatological destiny as the city of salvation" (Chance, 1988: 138). This interpretation receives additional support from Lk 2:38, where the prophetess Anna, articulating the author's own views, identifies Jesus as the one from whom the deliverance of Jerusalem is to be expected (Tannehill, 1986: 70; Wolter, 1992: 309–310).

The vocabulary of the account points the reader back to the Old Testament prophets as does the subject and the remark that Jesus wept as he approached the city (Fitzmyer, 1985: 1258; Ernst, 1977: 528–529; Kinman, 1995: 138).

At this stage of Luke's Gospel, that is, just after Jesus' entry, the mingling of royal and prophetic traditions becomes increasingly complex (Marshall, 1990: 51-54). Prior to the entry, in which regal elements are highlighted by Luke, the Lukan Jesus is repeatedly portrayed as a prophet (Lk 4:24; 13:32-33; 7:16, etc.). And within the whole of Luke-Acts there are many examples of Jesus' prophetic words being fulfilled in his life or the lives of the disciples (Frein, 1994: 28-33). In the light of Lk 13:32-34a it is not surprising if Luke returns tó a prophetic motif (from a royal one) as Jesus approaches the city at the end of the Travel Narrative in Luke 19 (Kinman, 1995: 133-134).

Prophetic figures in the first century may be divided into two groups. There were, on the one hand, those who seem to have carried a message which, in tone and substance, was consonant with that of the ancient prophets. On the other hand, a second group consisting of anti-Roman figures sounded triumphalist notes.

The subject of Lk 19:41-44—warnings about judgment on the city (Jerusalem) and the nation—is a familiar one in the ancient prophets (see Kinman, 1995: 115-116).

Verses-41-44: (41) As he came near and saw the city,
                      he wept over it,
           (42) saying, "If you, even you,
                      had only recognized on this day
                      the things that make for peace!
                      But now they are hidden from your eyes.
           (43) Indeed, the days will come upon you,
                      when your enemies will set up ramparts around
                        you
                      and surround you,
                      and hem you in on every side.
           (44) They will crush you to the ground,
                      you and your children within you,
                      and they will not leave one stone upon
                        another;
                      because you did not recognize
                      the time of your visitation from God."

The stage is set for Jesus' prophetic lament and judgment in two ways. There is, first, his drawing near to the
city of Jerusalem. Luke has employed the verb "to come near"
(*eggizō*; cf. Lk 18:35,40; 19:29,37,41) like a litany, using it
repeatedly to slow the pace of the narrative and to dramatize the long-awaited arrival of Jesus (Bock, 1996: 1560),
Israel's regal prophet, at the center of the Jewish world. Second,
and even more crucial, is the failure of Jerusalem to receive
its king with praise and blessing, registered in Lk 19:28-40.
This failure attracts not only the retort from Jesus recorded
in verse 40, however, but leads to a prophetic threat oracle.
The oracular form has three components: the address or summons, the indictment, and the threat or announcement of a
verdict (Borg, 1992: 104–105). The address or summons is
implicit in the combination of Luke's note that Jesus "saw
the city" and the repetition of the personal pronoun "you."
Clearly, Jesus' oracle is delivered against Jerusalem. The power
and pathos of the oracle are served by its structure in the
Greek text, with verbs of warfare and violence appearing at
the beginning and the pronoun "you" at the close of each
clause (Green, 1997: 689).

Jesus' weeping stands in stark contrast with the rejoycing
of his disciples (Lk 19:37; Petzke, 1990: 172) and corresponds
to his earlier lament (Lk 13:34; but there is no mention of
weeping) as well as to that of the women on the way to the
cross (Lk 23:27-28; Kremer, 1988: 188). Only in Lk 19:41
and John 11:35 do we read of Jesus' weeping in the Gospels.
Jesus wept, however, not for himself and his fate but rather
for the fate of Jerusalem and the people of Israel (Lk 23:28-
31). Compare the weeping of the Old Terstament prophets:
2 Kgs 8:11; Jer 8:18-21; 9:1; 14:17. The experience of Psalm
137 after the destruction of Jerusalem in 587 B.C. will soon
be relived (Stein, 1992: 483–484).

Jesus' lamentation is especially reminiscent of that of
Jeremiah (Jer 9:2 [9:1 MT]; 13:17; 14:17), but the wider
canvas is finally the sympathy of the suffering prophet, of

Deuteronomy's Moses, of Jeremiah, Isaiah, and Hosea, caught up in the rage, anguish, frustration, and sorrow of God for Israel that constitutes the pathos of the story (Tiede, 1980: 78; Nolland, 1993: 931).

Jesus' lament is introduced by the hypothetical "If you had. . . had only recognized on this day" (Lk 19:41). This aposiopesis (the breaking off of a sentence in the middle), in which the apodosis (which must have been something like "but you do not") is omitted, draws attention to the statement (Tiede, 1980: 79; Kinman, 1995: 138 note 24). What is it that Jerusalem has failed to discern? It did not recognize "the things that make for peace" (verse 42); nor, as verse 44 indicates "the time of your visitation." What are "the things that make for peace," with whom is peace made, and how is "the time of visitation" to be understood?

Many commentators think that the "peace" to which Jesus refers (verse 42) is peace with God or peace in heaven (mentioned previously in Lk 19:38; Fitzmyer, 1985: 1258; Marshall, 1978: 718; Ernst, 1977: 529). For Luke, Jesus is instrumental in bringing that peace. Lk 2:14 indicates that peace with God for "people whom he favors" was achieved in some way by the birth of Jesus, God's son. The idea of peace with God through Jesus is implied in other passages in Luke (2:11; 7:50; 8:48). In these contexts "peace" seems practically equivalent to "salvation." At the least we see the association of "peace" with "salvation" in each passage in which peace is mentioned. If the peace mentioned in verse 41 has to do with peace with God, Jesus indicates that Jerusalem is somehow unaware of the condition for peace with God. In the context of Luke, this condition refers to an acceptance of Jesus as the Messiah, God's agent of salvation (Kinman, 1995: 138–139). "Peace" in Luke does not refer to subjective or individualistic tranquility ("peace of mind"). It is rather a soteriological term—*shalom*, peace and justice, the gift of God that embraces salvation for all in all of its social, material, and spiritual realities (Green, 1997: 690).

It has, however, also been suggested that with regard to this particular context another interpretation is to be preferred. For C.F. Evans the "peace" envisaged here may be mundane in character, that is, it concerns Jerusalem's relations with Rome rather than its "peace" with or salvation from God (C.F. Evans, 1990: 684; different, Green, 1997: 690). In context the destruction mentioned in Lk 19:41-44 is brought by Rome, so perhaps Jerusalem has failed to recognize how to get peace with Rome. The phrase *ta pros eirēnēn* ("the things that make for peace") may be a "semitechnical term for peace conditions proposed by combatants in war" (Evans, 1990: 684). The identical phrase appears in Lk 14:32 where one king sends an embassy to another to seek terms of peace prior to the outbreak of hostilities. The immediate context of Lk 19:41-42 (Lk 19:43-44), with its description of a military assault, lends credence to this theory. It has the advantage of assigning the phrase a consistent meaning within Luke and with its use in writings from roughly the same time period. If the proponents of this opinion are right, Luke is saying that the avenue of peace with Rome is open to Jerusalem and dependent upon the latter's response to him (Jesus). This understanding reinforces the connection between the fate of Jerusalem at the hands of the Romans and its rejection of Jesus.

"They will crush you to the ground, you and your children within you" is a traditional feature in the description of sieges (Ps 137:9; Hos 10:14; 13:16; Nah 3:10; 2 Kgs 8:12). It describes the slaughter in war that often befell the defeated in a most literal way and to which Lk 23:28-31 refers (Stein, 1992: 484). The Lukan Jesus strings together five images of military conquest and destruction (verses 43-44a; three in verse 43 and two in 44; Bock, 1996: 1562–1563) each of which is introduced by "and" (Schweizer, 1984: 300).

The Lukan Jesus predicts that Jerusalem will become the object of a fierce siege in the "days that will come," a phrase used by the Old Testament prophets to indicate coming events of great significance (seventeen times in the Septuagint, including 1 Sam 2:31; 2 Kgs 20:17; Jer 7:32-34; 31:38; 33:14; 49:2; Isa 39:6; Zech 14:1; Schweizer, 1984: 300).

Jerusalem's failure to discern and to act results in divine chastisement in a form of a further, imposed spiritual darkness. This shift is introduced by *nun de ekrubē* ("now they are hidden"; Lk 19:42b). The passive voice of *ekrubē* probably indicates the presence of God's hidden yet decisive intervention and introduces an ominous note into the proceedings—what began as spiritual myopia has led to the imposition of spiritual darkness. What the blind beggar saw (Lk 18:35-43) was not seen by the leaders of Jerusalem (Stein, 1992: 484). Ironically, in Lk 13:35 Jesus remarked that Jerusalem would not "see" him until it welcomed him "in the name of the Lord." Jerusalem, in fact, does not welcome Jesus and, in a sense, does not "recognize" or "see" him properly; as a result the things that make for peace have been "hidden" from them (Kinman, 1995: 139–140). One can perhaps hear in the background the words of Lk 19:14: "We do not want this man to rule over us" (Green, 1997: 688).

The explanation for Jesus' tears and the coming destruction in verse 42 is paralleled by the last phrase of verse 44 (Petzke, 1990: 173). The basis for the disaster is explained by Jesus in verse 44b: "because you did not recognize the time of your visitation from God." Two phrases in this clause reflect Old Testament concepts which illumine Jesus' remarks.

The first has to do with the recognition of the "time of visitation" (see Grundmann, 1966: 369). In the Septuagint, an "hour" (*hōra*), "day" (*hēmera*) or "time" (*kairos*) of "visitation" (*episkopē*) is found five times (Wis 3:7; Sir 18:20; Isa 10:3; Jer 6:15; 10:15). In each case, a time of evaluation is in view, but in the prophetic passages the note of rejection and condemnation associated with the visit is especially severe (different, Bock, 1996: 1563). The time of God's visitation brings punishment for those who pervert justice (Isa 10:1-3; in the Hebrew, Isa 10:3 speaks of "oversight" in the sense of "reckoning"), for the greedy (Jer 6:13-15) and for idolaters (Jer 10:1-15). In Isa 10:1-3 and Jer 6:13-15 the leaders are singled out for condemnation. When a specific time of visitation is mentioned in the prophets, it normally refers to the time of judgment on a spiritually obdurate nation which, it should be noted, comes as the penultimate divine act (i.e., the nation's restoration typically follows in prophetic texts). What is striking about Lk 19:44 is that "the time of visitation" is said to be overlooked by Jerusalem. This is all the more noteworthy when it is remembered that at two other places in Luke a "visitation" seems to have been recognized (Lk 1:68; 7:16). With respect to the context of the entry, Jesus' ministry has supplied a clear testimony to the nation and its leaders that he is the agent of God and the one who brings the kingdom; nevertheless, they have not recognized him.

The second phrase to be considered is *anth' hōn* ("because," "in view of the fact that"). It has been pointed out that the combination *anth' hōn* is reminiscent of the language employed by Jeremiah; in particular, in all eight cases where the Septuagint text of Jeremiah used *anth' hōn* to speak of judgment, it was in reference to the dire fate of the city, the temple, and the exile from the land (Tiede, 1980: 82). If the Greek "because" (*anth' hōn*) in Lk 19:44b is given its more literal sense of "in return for which," Jesus' words reflect an almost talionic (and therefore prophetic) sense of justice: the destruction of verses 43-44, which in the Septuagint would probably be associated with "the time of visitation," is "in return for" Jerusalem's failure to recognize the "time of visitation" (Jesus' coming). In effect, Jesus' statement means "Because you have missed the day of visitation, you will get a day of visitation that you cannot miss" (Kinman, 1995: 140–141).

In Lk 19:41-44 the earlier motif of joy and celebration is replaced with Jesus' anguish and prophetic lament (Kinman, 1995: 133). These verses also supply a rationale of the city's fate. The insertion of this material into the entry narrative is unique to Luke and makes the connection between the rejection of Jesus and the fate of Jerusalem explicit (Kinman, 1994: 669–678). The connection is made in two comments: in verse 42 Jesus laments that Jerusalem does not recognize "on this day" (*en tēi hēmerai tautēi*) what makes for peace; similarly, in verse 44 Jesus explains that destruction will come because Jerusalem did not recognize the "time of visitation" (*ton kairon tēs episkopēs*). This second comment may have in mind the whole of Jesus' ministry, if we take the phrase to refer to an extended period of time. Concerning *episkopē*, Luke has employed the related verb *episkeptomai* in three places: in the prayer of Zechariah in Lk 1:68 and 78, and in the acclaim of the people of Nain in Lk 7:16. In the first two, the word may refer to the anticipated ministry of the "horn of salvation" from the "house of David," whom God will raise up (Lk 1:69); but in the last it clearly points to the raising of the widow's dead son on the day of Jesus' visit (Lk 7:11-16). Even if we understand the "visitation" to refer to the whole of Jesus' ministry, Jerusalem's failure to discern it as a divine visitation culminates in the events that transpire "on this day," the day on which he at last appears at Jerusalem (according to Luke, Jesus has not been there since as a young boy he amazed the teachers [Lk 2:46]; Tiede, 1988: 331–333).

But rather than connecting God's judgment to events on the day of his entry, perhaps the pronouncement of judgment on the city is in response to repeated rejections of Jesus by the nation, of which the Pharisees' comment at the entry (Lk 19:39-40) is but the culmination. One has argued that Luke's central section may be summarized as a "conflict with Israel," and if that is so, perhaps the Pharisees' critical comments are the straw that breaks the camel's back (Matera, 1993: 57–77). Against this understanding, however, is the fact that in two episodes prior to the entry, Jesus gets a positive response (the blind man with faith [Lk 18:35-43] and Zacchaeus [Lk 19:1-10]). In addition to that, Jesus explicitly links his pronouncement of doom to the failure of the city that occurs "on this day" (Lk 19:42). In other words, Jesus links the judgment of the city not to what might have occurred prior to his coming to Jerusalem but rather to events on the particular day of his advent.

Jesus' remarks in Lk 19:41-44 constitute a rich mixture of Old Testament language and imagery. Many scholars have explored the Old Testament background of Jesus' remarks and their fulfillment in the events of 70 C.E. (e.g., Tiede, 1980: 82). In Luke alone Jesus explicitly links the events of his arrival to God's coming judgment on the city. How did the events of that day provoke Jesus' comments (Kinman, 1999: 289–290)?

Set against the background of celebratory greeting in the ancient world, Jerusalem's response to Jesus must be regarded as an appalling insult. The *parousia* of emperors, Hellenistic kings, and other distinguished figures featured a splendid welcome in which virtually all segments of society participated. Compared with that, Jesus' entry is not triumphal. In three ways Jesus' reception is seen to be small and insulting.

First, more than in Mark, the failure of Jerusalem is stressed by Luke, who seems to narrow the scope of the multitude who met Jesus (see Kinman, 1999: 290–291).

Second, the comments of certain Pharisees in Lk 19:39-40, who were apparently bystanders to the event (they speak up "in the crowd"), were intended to suppress the acclamation of the disciples. They demand, "Teacher, order (*epitimēson*) your disciples to stop." Luke's choice of the verb *epitimaō* is particularly telling, for it indicates that these Pharisees thought a severe reprimand was called for (see Kinman, 1999: 291).

Finally, although the crowds of Jerusalem have not met Jesus in the customary way, and at least some Pharisees have tried to suppress those disciples who welcome him, for Luke it is another set of characters—a set not mentioned until later in chapter 19—whose absence constitutes a major insult to Jesus and failure on the part of Jerusalem. Jerusalem's religious and social elite, whom Luke mentions later in the chapter, are absent at Jesus' entry (Braumann, 1963: 120–127; Kinman, 1999: 291–293).

BIBLIOGRAPHY

(Books and articles listed in the bibliographies of the previous volumes are not repeated here).

Ahern, Barnabas M. "The Zacchaeus Incident," *The Bible Today* 25 (1987), 348–351.

Aletti, Jean-Noël. "Parabole des mines et/ou parabole du roi. Lk 19:11-28. Remarques sur l'écriture parabolique de Luc," in Delorme, Jean. ed. *Les paraboles évangeliques: Perspectives nouvelles.* Lectio Divina 135. Paris: Editions du Cerf, 1989. 309–332.

Baarlink, H. "Friede im Himmel: die lukanische Redaktion von Lk 19:38 und ihre Deutung," *Zeitschrift für die neutestamentliche Wissenschaft* 76 (1985), 170–186.

Bailey, James H. *The Miracles of Jesus for Today.* Nashville: Abingdon Press, 1977.

Bartsch, Hans Werner. *Wachet aber zur jeder Zeit! Entwurf einer Auslegung des Lukasevangeliums.* Hamburg-Bergstedt: Herbert Reich, 1963.

Benjamin, Don C. "The Persistent Widow," *The Bible Today* 28 (4, 1990), 213–219.

Betz, Hans Dieter. "The Cleansing of the Ten Lepers (Luke 17:11-19)," *Journal of Biblical Literature* 90 (1971), 314–328.

Binder, Hermann. *Das Gleichnis von dem Richter und der Witwe (Lukas 18,1-8).* Neukirchen-Vluyn: Neukirchener Verlag, 1988.

Blenkinsopp, Joseph. "The Oracle of Judah and the Messianic Entry," *Journal of Biblical Literature* 80 (1961), 55–64.

Borg, Marcus. *Jesus: A New Vision Spirit: Culture, and the Life of Discipleship.* San Francisco: Harper & Row, 1987.

_____. "Luke 19:42-44 and Jesus as Prophet?" *Forum* 8 (1992), 99–112.

Bossuyt, Philippe and Jean Radermakers. *Jésus Parole de Grâce selon saint Luc.* Volume 2: *Lecture continue.* Brussels: Institut d'Etudes Théologiques, 1981.

Bovon, François, "Apocalyptic Traditions in the Lukan Special Material: Reading Luke 18:1-8," *Harvard Theological Review* 90 (1997), 383–393.

Braumann, Georg. "Die lukanische Interpretation der Zerstörung Jerusalems," *Novum Testamentum* 6 (1963), 120–127.

Breck, John. *The Shape of Biblical Language: Chiasmus in the Scriptures and Beyond.* Crestwood, New York: St. Vladimir's Seminary Press, 1994.

Breydon, France. *En danger de richesse. Le chrétien et les biens de ce monde selon Luc.* Aubonne: Editions du Moulin 1989.

Cantrell, Richard A. "The Cursed Fig Tree," *The Bible Today* 29 (1991), 105–108.

Catchpole, David R. "The Son of Man's Search for Faith (Luke XVIII,8b)," *Novum Testamentum* 19 (1977), 81–104.

Chance, J. Bradley. *Jerusalem, the Temple, and the New Age in Luke-Acts.* Macon, GA: Mercer University Press, 1988.

Crossan, John Dominic. *The Dark Interval: Towards a Theology of Story.* Niles, Illinois: Argus Communications, 1975.

Dahood, Michael. *Psalms III.* Anchor Bible 17A. Garden City: Doubleday, 1970.

Daube, David. *The Sudden in the Scriptures.* Leiden: E.J. Brill, 1964.

De la Potterie, Ignace. "La parabole du prétendant à la royauté (Lc 19,11-28)," in *A cause de l'Evangile: Etudes sur les Synoptiques et les Actes.* Mélanges offerts à Dom Jacques Dupont. Paris: Editions du Cerf, 1985. 613–641.

Delsuc, Jean. *Zachée, le Christ et l'Argent.* Paris: Editions S.O.S., 1976.

Derrett, J. Duncan M. *Law in the New Testament.* London: Darton, 1970.

_____. "Law in the New Testament: The Parable of the Unjust Judge," *New Testament Studies* 18 (1971–1972), 178–191.

_____. "Law in the New Testament: The Palm Sunday Colt," *Novum Testamentum* 13 (1971), 241–258.

_____. "Why Jesus Blessed the Children (Mk 10:13-16 par.)," *Novum Testamentum* 25 (1983), 1–18.

Didier, M. "La parabole des talents et des mines," in de la Potterie, Ignace. ed. *De Jésus aux Evangiles. Tradition et Rédaction dans les Evangiles synoptiques.* BETL XXV. Gembloux: Editions J. Duculot, 1967. 248–271.

Donahue, John R. "Tax Collectors and Sinners: An Attempt at Identification," *Catholic Biblical Quarterly* 33 (1971), 39–61.

Downing, F. Gerald. "The Ambiguity of 'The Pharisee and the Toll Collector' (Luke 18:9-14) in the Greco-Roman World of Late Antiquity," *Catholic Biblical Quarterly* 54 (1992), 80–99.

D'Sa, Thomas. "Exploiter Evangelized. Reflections Based on the Episode of Zacchaeus and Pastoral Practice," *Vidyajyoti* 60 (1996), 194–206.

Dupont, Jacques. *Les Béatitudes.* Volume II: *La Bonne Nouvelle.* Paris: J. Gabalda, 1969.

_____. "La parabole des Talents (Matt. 25,14-30) ou des Mines (Luc 19,12-27)," *Revue de Théologie et de Philosophie.* Serie 3. 19 (1969), 376–391.

_____. "Le riche publicain Zachée est aussi un fils d'Abraham (Luc 19,1-10)," in Bussmann, Claus and Walter Radl. eds. *Der Treue Gottes trauen. Beiträge zum Werk des Lukas.* Für Gerhard Schneider. Freiburg: Herder, 1991. 265–276.

Farrell, H. *The Eschatological Perspective in Luke-Acts.* Boston: Boston University Ph.D. Dissertation, 1972.

Flender, Helmut. *St. Luke: Theologian of Redemptive History.* Philadelphia: Fortress Press, 1967.

Ford, J. Massyngbaerde. "The Lost Sheep of the House of Israel," in Cassidy, Richard J. and Philip J. Sharper. eds. *Political Issues in Luke-Acts*. Maryknoll, NY: Orbis Books, 1983. 80–98.

Fowl, Steven E. "Receiving the Kingdom of God as a Child: Children and Riches in Luke 18:15ff.," *New Testament Studies* 39 (1993), 153-158.

Freed, Edwin D. "The Parable of the Judge and the Widow (Luke 18:1-8)," *New Testament Studies* 33 (1987), 38–60.

Frein, Brigid C. "Narrative Predictions. Old Testament Prophecies and Luke's Sense of Fulfillment," *New Testament Studies* 40 (1994), 22–37.

Fusco, Vittorio. "'Point of View' and 'Implicit Reader' in Two Eschatological Texts (Lk 19:11-28; Acts 1:6-8)," in Van Segbroeck, Frans et al. eds. *The Four Gospels 1992: Festschrift Frans Neirynck*. Louvain: Leuven University Press, 1992. vol. 2, 1677–1696.

Gaston, Loyd. *No Stone on Another. Studies in the Significance of the Fall of Jerusalem in the Synoptic Gospels*. Leiden: Brill, 1970.

Geiger, Georg. "Der Weg als roter Faden durch Lk-Apg," in Verheyden, Joseph. ed. *The Unity of Luke-Acts*. Louvain: Leuven University Press, 1999. 663–673.

Geiger, Ruthild. *Die Lukanische Endzeitreden. Studien zur Eschatologie des Lukas-Evangeliums*. Europäische Hochschulschriften 23/16. Frankfurt am Main/Bern: Peter Lang/Herbert Lang, 1976.

Gérard, Jean-Pierre. "Les riches dans la communauté lucanienne," *Ephemerides Theologicae Lovanienses* 71 (1995) 71–106.

Glöckner, Richard. *Neutestamentliche Wundergeschichten und das Lob der Wundertaten Gottes in den Psalmen*. Mainz: Matthias-Grünewald Verlag, 1983.

Glombitza, O. "Der dankbare Samariter. Luke XVII,11-19," *Novum Testamentum* 11 (1969), 241–246.

Grässer, Erich. *Das Problem der Parusieverzögerung in den*

synoptischen Evangelien und in der Apostelgeschichte. Berlin: Töpelmann, 1957.

Gueuret, Agnes. "Le Pharisien et le publicain (Lc 18,9-14)," in Delorme, Jean. ed. *Les paraboles évangeliques: Perspectives nouvelles.* Lectio Divina 135. Paris: Editions du Cerf, 1989. 289–307.

Hamm, Dennis. "Luke 19:8 Once Again: Does Zacchaeus Defend or Resolve," *Journal of Biblical Literature* 107 (1988), 431–437.

_____. "Zacchaeus Revisited Once More: A Story of Vindication or Conversion?" *Biblica* 72 (1991), 249–252.

_____. "What the Samaritan Leper Sees: The Narrative Christology of Luke 17:11-19," *Catholic Biblical Quarterly* 56 (1994), 273–287.

Heutger, Nicolaus. "Die lukanischen Samaritanererzählungen in religionsgeschichtlicher Sicht," in Haubeck, Wilfrid and Michael Bachmann, eds. *Wort in der Zeit,* Neutestamentliche Studien. Festgabe für Karl Heinrich Rengstorf zum 75. Geburtstag. Leiden: E.J. Brill, 1980. 275–287.

Hicks, John Mark. "The Parable of the Persistent Widow (Luke 18:1-8)," *Restoration Quarterly* 33 (1991), 209–223.

Hobbie, F. Wellford. "Expository Articles: Luke 19:1-10," *Interpretation* 31 (1977), 285–290.

Holmgren, Frederick C. "The Pharisee and the Tax Collector: Luke 18:9-14 and Deuteronomy 26:1-16," *Interpretation* 48 (1994), 252–261.

Johnson, Luke Timothy. "The Social Dimension of *sōtēria* in Luke-Acts and Paul," in Lovering , Eugene H. Jr. ed. *Society of Biblical Literature 1993 Seminar Papers.* Atlanta: Scholars Press, 1993. 520–536.

Joji, Kunduru. "From Brokenness to Wholeness—the Jesus Way," *Vidyajyoti* 61 (1997), 469–479.

Kaestli, Jean-Daniel. *L'Eschatologie dans l'oeuvre de Luc.* Geneva: Labor at Fides, 1969.

Kariamadam, Paul. The Zacchaeus Story (Lk 19:1-10): A Redaction-Critical Investigation. Alwaye, Kerala: Pontifical Institute of Theology and Philosophy, 1985.

_____. "'Peace in Heaven...' (Lk 19:38b)—An Explanation," Bible Bhashyam 23 (1997), 256–268.

Käsemann, Ernst. New Testament Questions for Today. London: SCM Press, 1969.

Kautsky, John. The Politics of Aristocratic Empires. Chapel Hill: University of North Carolina Press, 1982.

Kilgallen, John J. "The Importance of the Redactor in Luke 18,9-14," Biblica 79 (1998), 69–75.

Kinman, Brent R. "'The Stones Will Cry Out' (Luke 19:40): Joy or Judgment?," Biblica 75 (1994), 232–235.

_____. "Jesus' Triumphal Entry in the Light of Pilate's," New Testament Studies 40 (1994a), 442–448.

_____. "Lucan Eschatology and the Missing Fig Tree," Journal of Biblical Literature 113 (1994b), 669–678.

_____. Jesus' Entry into Jerusalem in the Context of Lukan Theology and the Politics of His Day. Leiden: E.J. Brill, 1995.

_____. "Parousia, Jesus' A-Triumphal Entry, and the Fate of Jerusalem (Luke 19:28-44)," Journal of Biblical Literature 118 (1999), 279–294.

Kirchschläger, Walter. "Bartimaeus—Paradigma einer Wundererzählung (Mk 10,46-52 par)," in Van Segbroeck, Frans et al. eds. The Four Gospels 1992. Festschrift Frans Neirynck. Louvain: Leuven University Press, 1992. 1105–1123.

Kodell, Jerome. "Luke and the Children: The Beginning and the End of the Great Interpolation (Luke 9:46-54; 18:9-23)," Catholic Biblical Quarterly 49 (1987), 415–430.

Kuschel, Karl Josef. Abraham: A Symbol of Hope for Jews, Christians and Muslims. London: SCM Press, 1994.

Lambrecht, Jan. Parables of Jesus. Insight and Challenge. Bangalore: Theological Publications in India, 1978.

_____. "Reading and Rereading Lk 18:31–22:6," in A cause de l'Evangile: Etudes sur les Synoptiques et les Actes.

Mélanges offerts à Dom Jaques Dupont. Paris: Editions du Cerf, 1985. 585–612.

Lenski, R.C.H., *The Interpretation of Luke*. Minneapolis, Minnesota: Augsburg Publishing House, 1964.

Ljungvik, Herman. "Zur Erklärung einer Lukas-Stelle (Luk. xviii.7)," *New Testament Studies* 10 (1963–1964), 289-294.

Loewe, William P. "Towards an Interpretation of Lk 19:1-10," *Catholic Biblical Quarterly* 36 (1974), 321–331.

Löning, K. "Ein Platz für die Verlorenen. Zur Formkritik zweier neutestamentliche Legenden (Lk 7:36-50; 19:1-10)," *Bibel und Leben* 12 (1971), 198–208.

Marshall, I. Howard. *The Origins of New Testament Christology*. Updated edition. Downers Grove: InterVarsity Press, 1990.

Matera, Frank. "Jesus' Journey to Jerusalem (Luke 9:51–19:46): A Conflict with Israel," *Journal for the Study of the New Testament* n. 51 (1993), 57–77.

Mattam, Zacharias. "The Cure of the Blind Man of Jericho (Lk 18:35-43): A Kerygmatic, Patristic and Theological Study," *Bible Bhashyam* 24 (1998), 17–26.

McCown, C.C. "Gospel Geography: Fiction, Fact and Truth, IV. Geography in the Third Gospel," *Journal of Biblical Literature* 69 (1941), 14–19.

McGaughy, Lane C. "The Fear of Yahweh and the Mission of Judaism: A Postexilic Maxim and Its Early Christian Expansion in the Parable of the Talents," *Journal of Biblical Literature* 94 (1975), 235–245.

Meynet, Roland. "Au coeur du texte. Analyse rhétorique de l'aveugle de Jéricho selon saint Luc," *Nouvelle Revue Théologique* 103 (1981), 696–710.

Mirro, Joseph A. "Bartimaeus: The Miraculous Cure," *The Bible Today* 20 (4, 1982), 221–225.

Mitchel, Alan C. "Zacchaeus Revisited: Luke 19,8 as a Defense," *Biblica* 71 (1990), 153–176.

_____. "The Use of *sukophantein* in Luke 19,8: Further Evidence for Zacchaeus' Defense," *Biblica* 72 (1991), 546–547.

Mosely, A. W. "Jesus' Audiences in the Gospels of St. Mark and St. Luke," *New Testament Studies* 10 (1963), 139–149.

Mussner, Franz. "Wann kommt das Reich Gottes," *Biblische Zeitschrift* N.F. 5 (1961), 107–111.

Noack, Bent. *Das Gottesreich bei Lukas: Eine Studie zu Luk. 20–24.* Uppsala: C.W.K. Gleerup, Lund, 1948.

O'Hanlon, John. "The Story of Zacchaeus and the Lukan Ethic," *Journal for the Study of the New Testament* n. 12 (1981), 2–26.

O'Toole, Robert F. "The Literary Form of Luke 19:1-10," *Journal of Biblical Literature* 110 (1991), 107–116.

Panier, Louis. "La parabole des mines: lecture sémiotique. Lc 19,11-27." in Delorme, Jean. ed. *Les paraboles évangéliques: Perspectives nouvelles.* Lectio Divina 135. Paris: Editions du Cerf, 1989. 333–347.

Perry, John M. "The Three Days in the Synoptic Passion Predictions," *Catholic Biblical Quarterly* 48 (1986), 637–654.

Phan, Peter C. "Kingdom of God: A Theological Symbol for Asians?," *Gregorianum* 79 (1998), 295–322.

_____. "Kingdom of God: A Symbol for Asians?," *Theology Digest* 47 (2000), 21–28.

Porcile, Maria Teresa and Angelica Ferreira. "The Parable of the Importunate Widow," in Amirtham, Sam. Compiler. *Stories Make People. Examples of Theological Work in Community.* Geneva: WCC Publications, 1989. 75–82.

Porter, S.E. "'In the Vicinity of Jericho': Luke 18:35 in the Light of Its Synoptic Parallels," *Bulletin of Biblical Research* 2 (1992), 91–104.

Puig i Tarrech, Armand. "La parabole des talents (Mt 25,14-30) ou des mines (Lc 19,11-28)," in *A cause de l'Evangile: Etudes sur les Synoptiques et les Actes.* Mélanges offerts à Dom Jacques Dupont. Paris: Editions du Cerf, 1985. 165–193.

Raja, R. J. "Seeking God, Sought by God. A Dvani-Reading of the Episode of Zacchaeus (Luke 19:10)," *Jeevadhara* 25 (n. 146, 1995), 139–148.

Rayan, Samuel. "Outside the Gate, Sharing the Insult," *Jeevadhara* 11 (1981), 203–231.

Reid, Barbara E. "The Ethics of Luke," *The Bible Today* 31 (5, 1993), 283–287 (a).

_____. "Luke's Mixed Message for Women," *Chicago Studies* 38 (1999), 283–297.

Resenhöfft, Wilhelm. "Jesu Gleichnis von Talenten, ergänzt durch die Lukas-Fassung," *New Testament Studies* 26 (1980), 318–331.

Rohrbaugh, Richard L. "A Peasant Reading of the Parable of the Talents/Pounds: A Text of Terror?," *Biblical Theology Bulletin* 23 (1993), 32–39.

Ryan, Rosalie. "Assertive Women in the Gospels," *The Bible Today* 25 (6, 1987), 352–357.

Sanders, Ed Parish. *Jesus and Judaism*. Philadelphia: Fortress Press, 1985.

Sanders, Jack T. "The Parable of the Pounds and Lucan Anti-Semitism," *Theological Studies* 42 (1981), 660–668.

Sanders, James A. "A Hermeneutic Fabric: Psalm 118 in Luke's Entrance Narrative," in Evans, Craig A. and James A. Sanders. *Luke and Scripture*. Minneapolis: Fortress Press, 1993. 140–153.

Schlosser, Jacques. "Les jours de Noé et de Lot. A propos de Luc xvii,26-30," *Revue Biblique* 80 (1973), 13–36.

_____. "Le pharisien et le publicain (Lc 18,9-14), in Delorme, Jean. ed. *Les paraboles évangeliques: Perspectives nouvelles*. Lectio Divina 135. Paris: Editions du Cerf, 1989. 271–307.

Schneider, Gerhard. *Parusiegleichnisse im Lukas-Evangelium*, Stuttgarter Bibelstudien 74. Stuttgart: KBW Verlag, 1975.

Schnider, Franz. "Ausschliessen und ausgeschlossen werden. Beobachtungen zur Struktur des Gleichnisses vom Pharisäer und Zöllner, Lk 18,10-14a," *Biblische Zeitschrift* 24 (1980), 42–56.

Schottroff, Luise. "Die Erzählung vom Pharisäer und Zöllner als Beispiel für die theologische Kunst des Überredens," in Betz, Hans Dieter and Luise Schottroff. eds. *Neues Testament und Christliche Existenz: Festschrift für Herbert Braun*. Tübingen: J.C.B. Mohr (Paul Siebeck), 1973. 439–461.

Schürmann, Heinz. *Der Paschamahlbericht Lk 22:(7-14) 15-18*. Münster: Aschendorff, 1953.

Sellin, Gerhard. "Komposition, Quellen und Funktion des lukanischen Reiseberichtes (Lk IX:51-XIX:28)," *Novum Testamentum* 20 (1978), 100–135.

Spencer, William David and Aida Besançon Spencer. *The Prayer Life of Jesus: Shout of Agony, Revelation of Love, a Commentary*. Lanham/New York/London: University Press of America, 1990.

Strobel, A. "In dieser Nacht (Luk 17,34)," *Zeitschrift für Theologie und Kirche* 58 (1961), 16–29.

Swezey, Ch. M. "Luke 18:18-30," *Interpretation* 37 (1983), 68–73.

Tan, Betty O.S. "The Parable of the Pharisee and the Tax Collector in Luke 18:9-14: A Study on the Practice of Prayer," *Asia Journal of Theology* 14 (2, 2000), 286–303.

Tannehill, Robert C. "The Story of Zacchaeus: Luke 19:1-10," *Semeia* n. 64 (1994), 201-211.

Tatum, W.B. "Jesus' So-Called Triumphal Entry. On Making an Ass of the Romans," *Forum* 1 (1998), 129–143.

Taylor, Vincent. *The Formation of the Gospel Tradition*. London: Macmillan, 1933.

Telford, William R. *The Barren Temple and the Withered Tree*. Sheffield: JSOT Press, 1980.

Trilling, Wolfgang. "Besitzversicht und Nachfolge (Lk 18,18-30)," in Christusverkündigung in den synoptischen Evangelien. Leipzig: St. Benno-Verlag, 1969. 123–145.

Twelftree, Graham H. *Jesus the Miracle Worker: A Historical and Theological Study*. Downers Grove, Illinois: InterVarsity Press, 1999.

van Unnik, Willem C. "L'usage de *sōzein* sauver et ses dérivés dans les évangiles synoptiques," in La formation des évangiles. Brugge: Desclée, 1957. 178–194.

Via, Dan O. "The Parable of the Unjust Judge: A Metaphor of the Unrealized Self," in Patte, Daniel. ed. *Semiology and Parables. An Exploration of the Possibilities Offered by Structuralism for Exegesis.* Pittsburgh, Pennsylvania: The Pickwick Press, 1976. 1–32.

Vogels, Walter. "Structural Analysis and Pastoral Work. The Story of Zacchaeus (Luke 19,1-10)," *Lumen Vitae* 33 (1978), 482-492.

Weinert, Francis. "The Parable of the Throne Claimant (Luke 19:12, 14-15a, 27) Reconsidered," *Catholic Biblical Quarterly* 39 (1977), 505–514.

Wenham, J.W. "Why Do You Ask Me about the Good? A Study of the Relation between Text and Source Criticism," *New Testament Studies* 28 (1982), 116–125.

White, Richard C. "A Good Word for Zacchaeus? Exegetical Comment on Luke 19:1-10," *Lexington Theological Quarterly* 14 (1979), 89–96.

_____. "Vindication for Zacchaeus?" *Expository Times* 91 (1979a), 21.

Wolter, Michael. "Israel's Future and the Delay of the Parousia, According to Luke," in Moessner, David P. ed. *Jesus and the Heritage of Israel. Luke's Narrative Claim upon Israel's Legacy.* Harrisburg, PA: Trinity Press International, 1999. 307–324.

Zimmermann, Heinrich. Das Gleichnis vom Richter und der Witwe (Lk 18,1-8)," in Schnackenburg, Rudolf, Josef Ernst and Joachim Wanke. eds. *Die Kirche des Anfangs. Festschrift für Heinz Schürmann zum 65. Geburtstag.* Leipzig: St. Benno-Verlag, 1977. 79–95.

Zmijewski, Josef. *Die Eschatologiereden des Lukas-evangeliums. Eine traditions- und redaktionsgeschichtliche Untersuchung zu Lk 21, 5-36 und Lk 17, 20-37.* Bonner Biblische Beiträge 40. Bonn: Peter Hanstein Verlag, 1972.